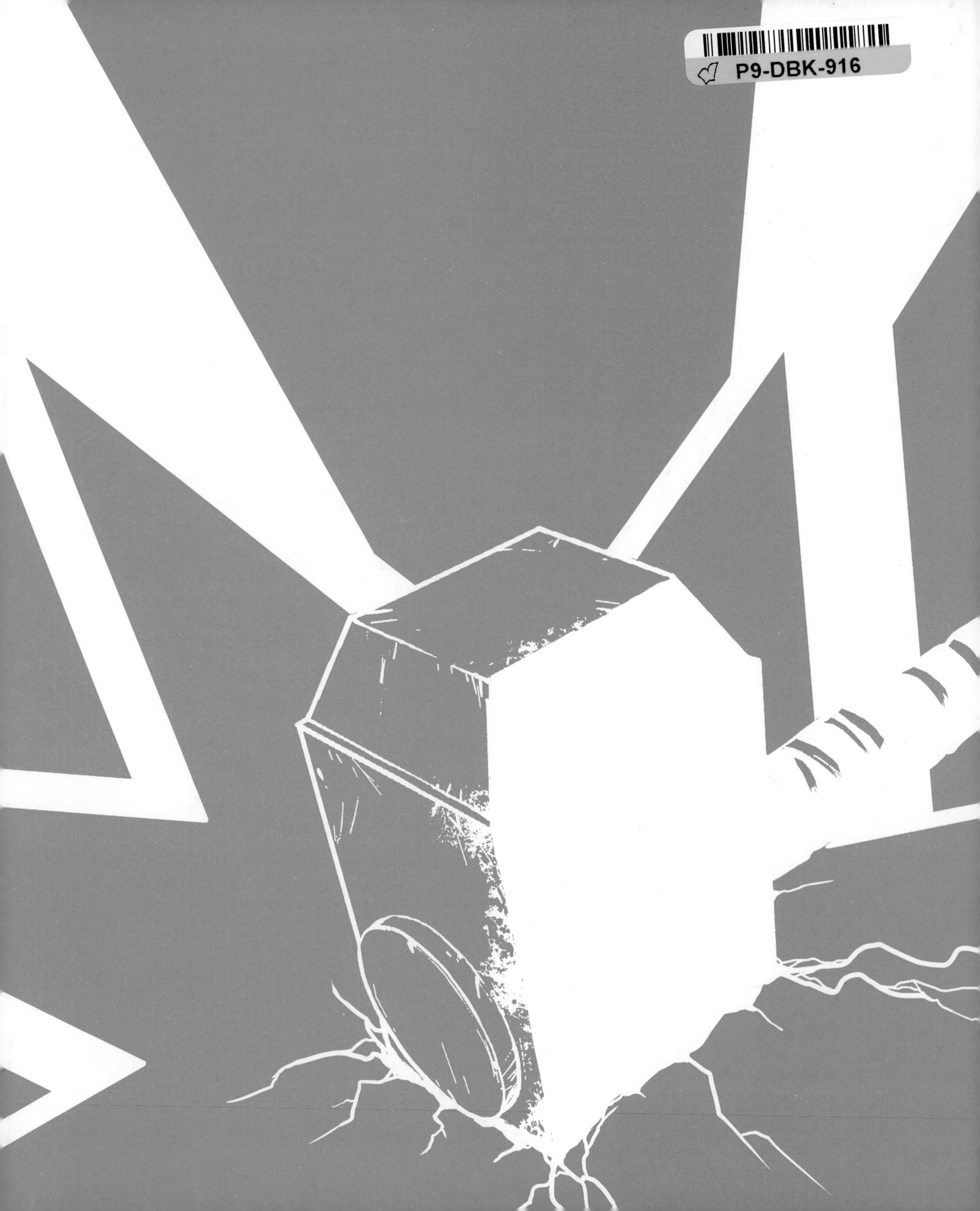

MARVEL

ABSOLUTELY EVERYTHING YOU NEED TO KNOW...

Written by

ADAM BRAY
LORRAINE CINK
JOHN SAZAKLIS
SVEN WILSON

CHAPTER ONE
CHARACTERS

CHAPTER TWO
TEAMS

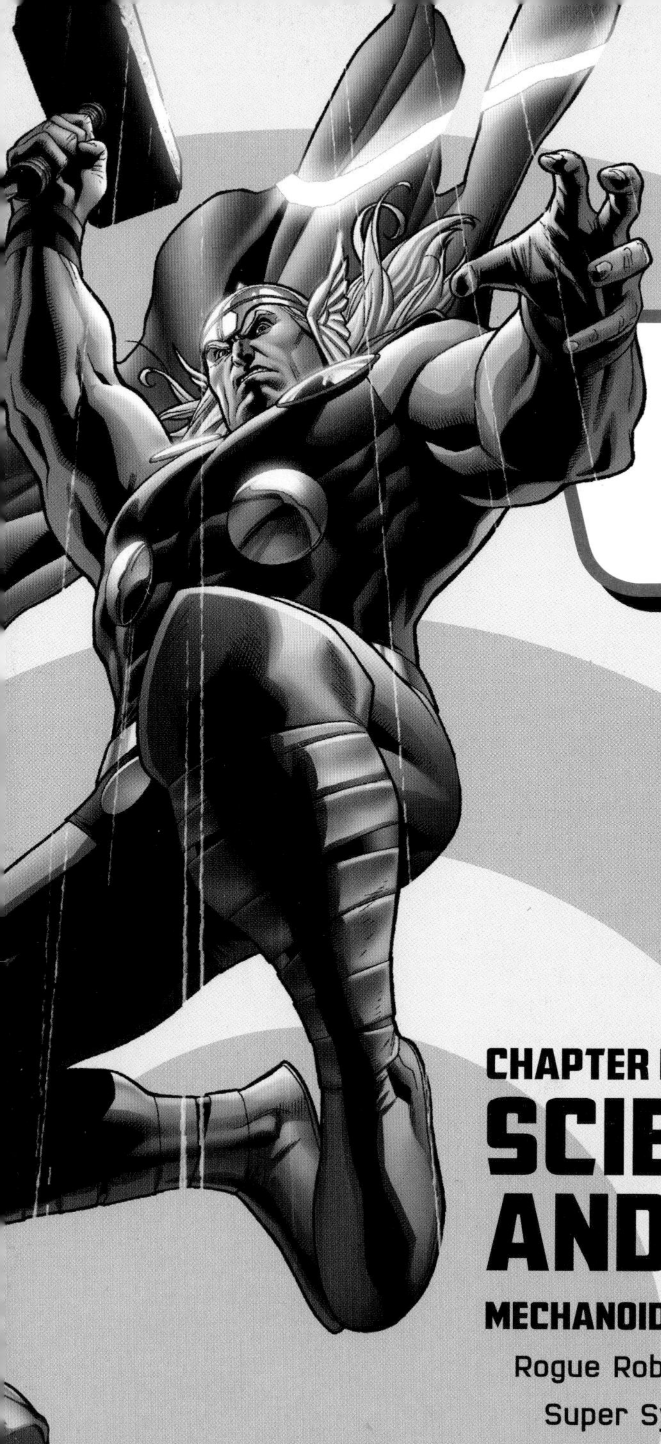
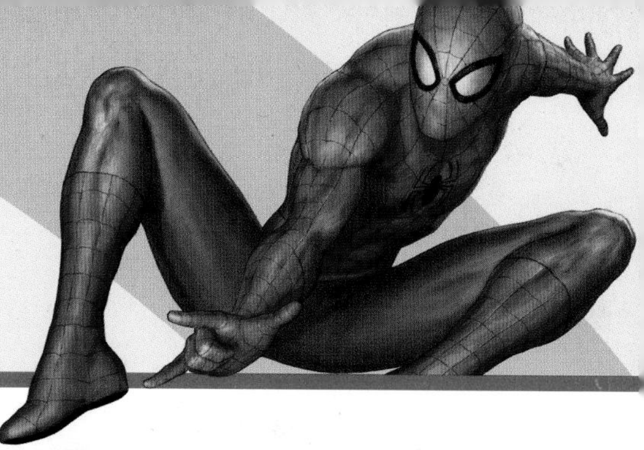

CONTENTS

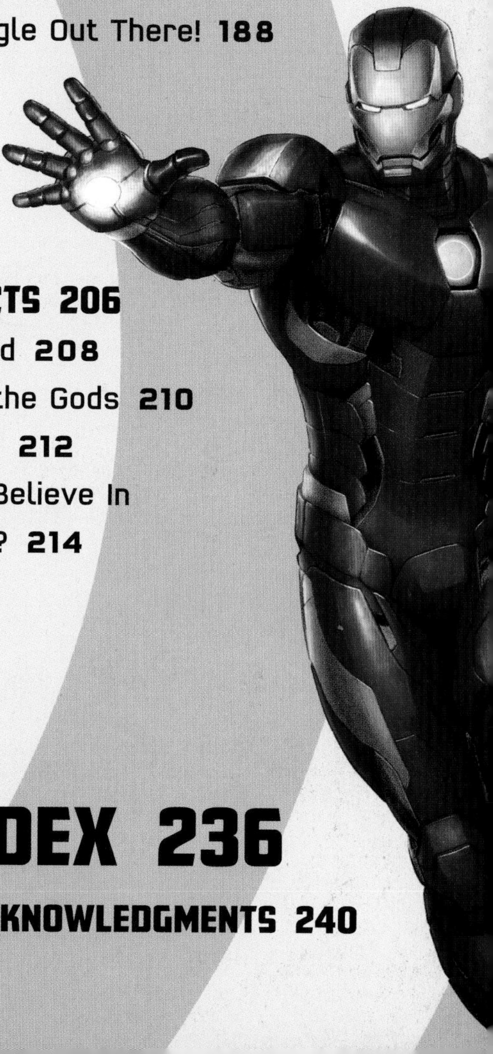

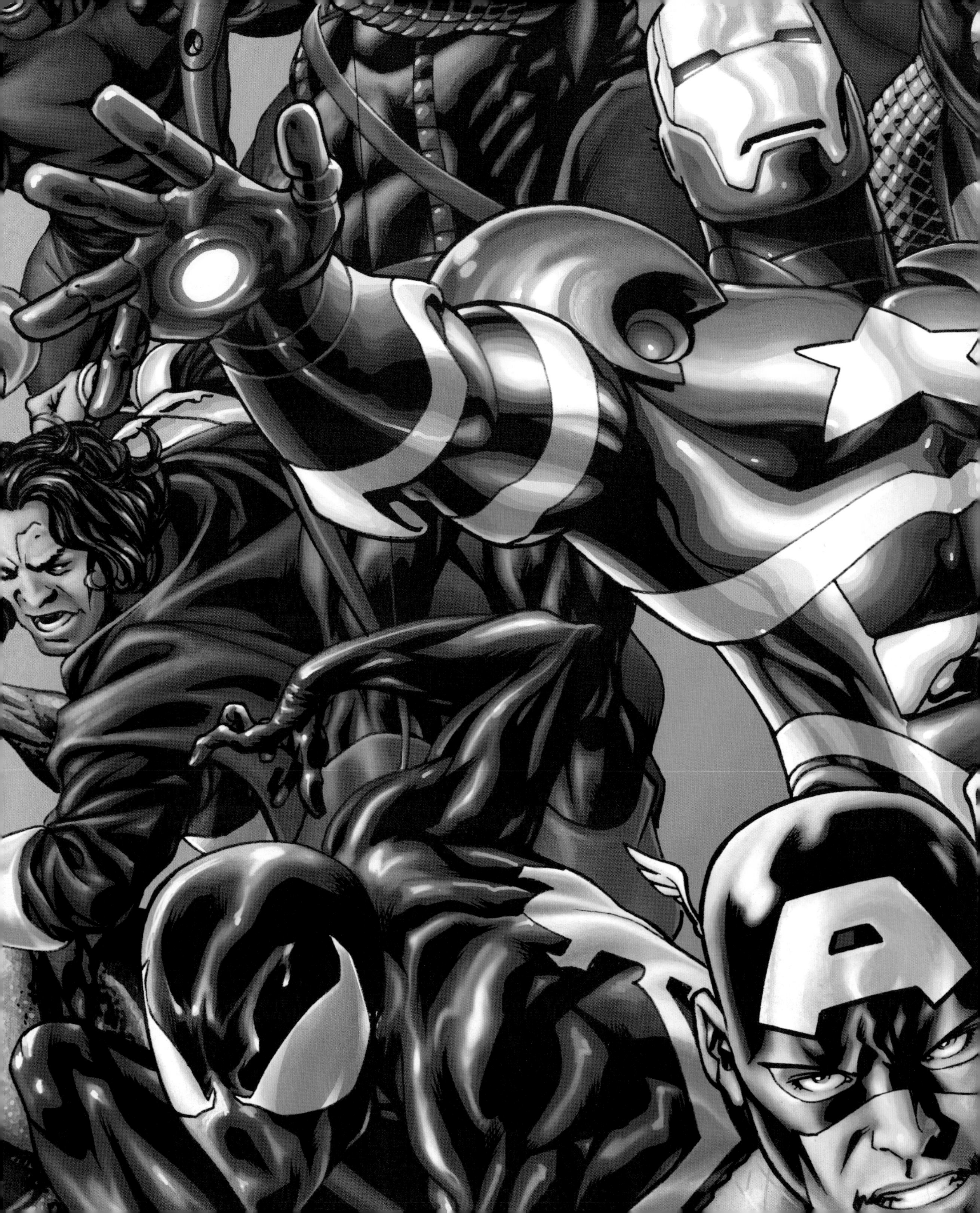

CHAPTER ONE
CHARACTERS

Which villain gives everyone in Manhattan the **POWERS OF SPIDER-MAN**?

What does Green Goblin **RIDE ON** to attack Spider-Man before he invents his **GOBLIN-GLIDER**?

How does Hulk **FLOOR FOES** without even touching them?

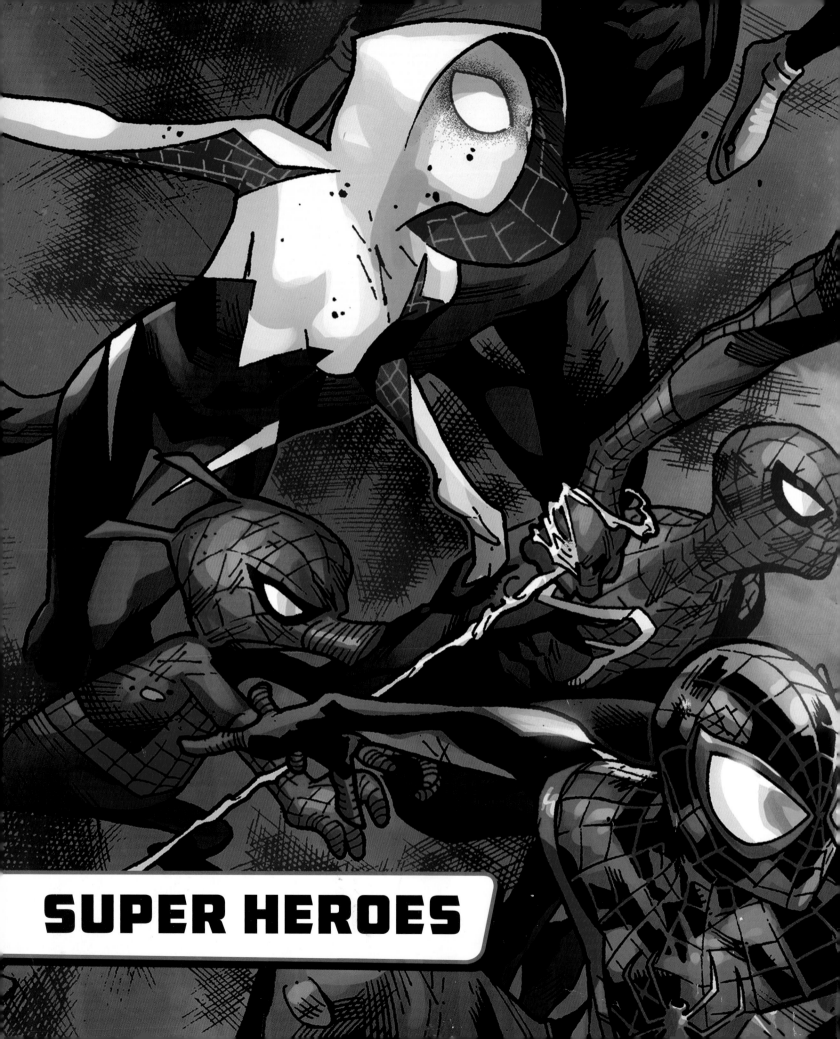

SUPER HEROES

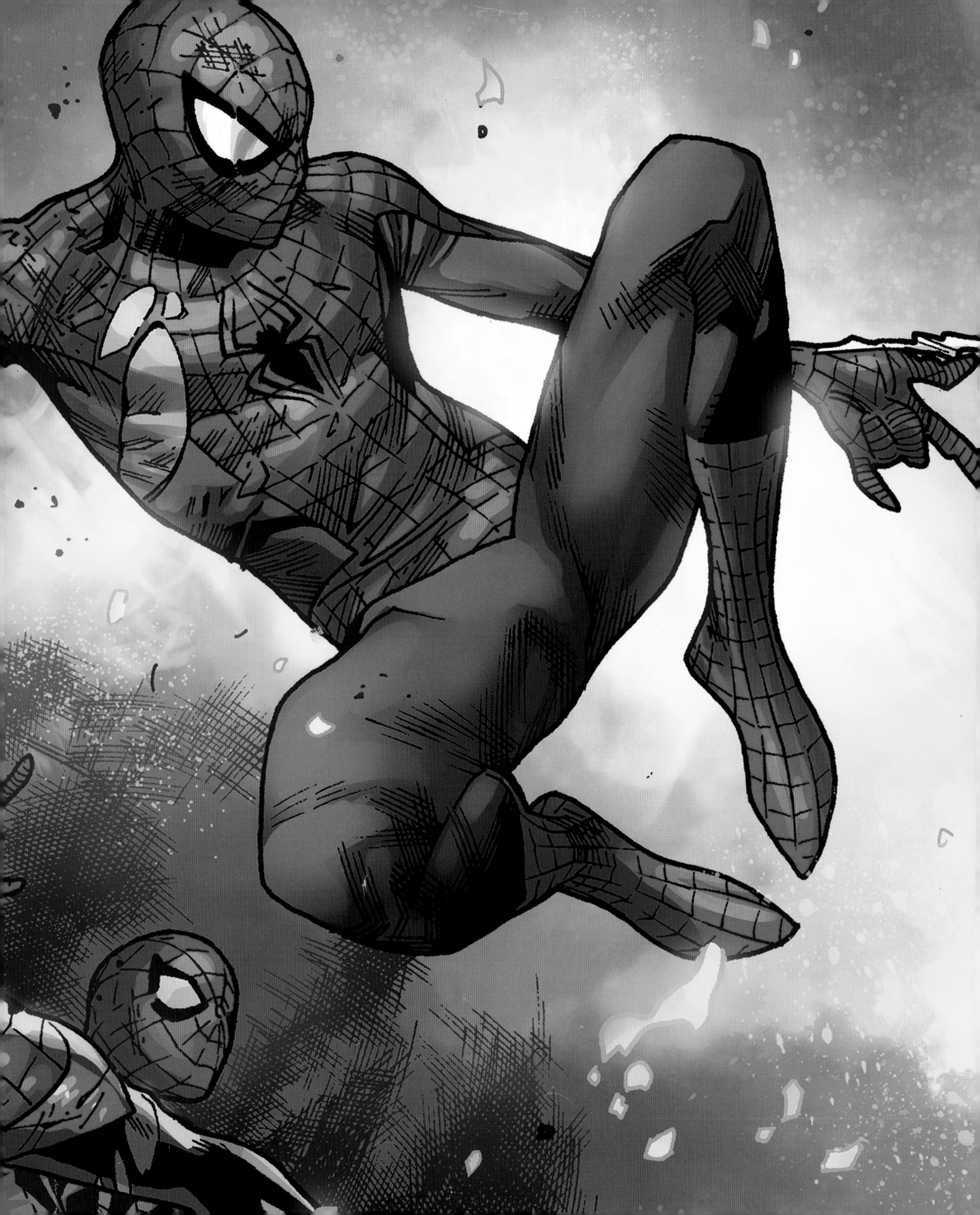

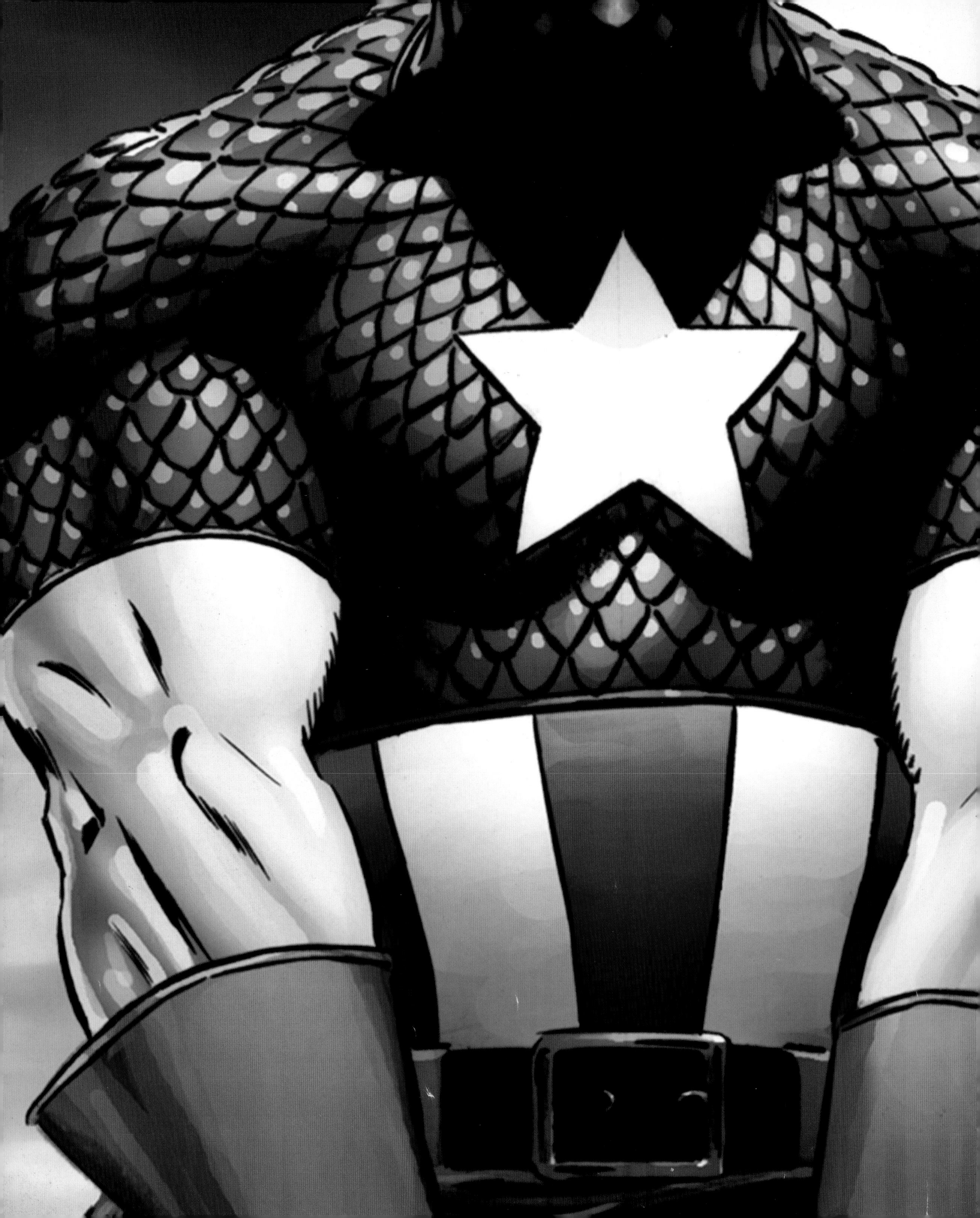

"My job is to make tomorrow's world better. Always has been... There'll always be *something* to fight for. And I'll *always* be a soldier."

"Reach out. Dare to dream the highest dreams and you will make a difference."

"It is up to *each and every one of us* to remind ourselves, and anyone who will listen, that *all* men and women are created *equal*."

"I can't surrender. I don't know how!"

"This nation was founded on *one principle* above all else: the requirement that we *stand up for what we believe*, no matter the odds or consequences."

"Look into my eyes, tyrant! They're the eyes of a man who would die for liberty!"

While battling **Nightshade**, the "Queen of the Werewolves," Steve Rogers is injected with **yet another serum**. It turns him into a **werewolf!**

6ft 2in (1.87m)
Steve Rogers' height, post-serum

240lbs (109kg)
Steve Rogers' weight, post-serum

1922
The year Steve Rogers was born

30mph (48kph)
Steve Rogers' max running speed, post-serum

4-F
Steve Rogers' reject classification when he first attempts to enlist in the military

WOW!

800
The weight in pounds Cap can bench-press (363kg).

TOP 5 STAND-IN CAPS

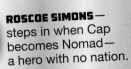

SAM WILSON (FALCON)—takes over when age catches up with Steve Rogers.

BUCKY BARNES (THE WINTER SOLDIER)—best buddy Bucky fills in when Cap is seemingly assassinated.

ROSCOE SIMONS—steps in when Cap becomes Nomad—a hero with no nation.

DAVE RICKFORD—a pawn used by Nick Fury to convince Steve Rogers to resume his role.

JOHN WALKER—takes up the role when Rogers resigns, before becoming the U.S. Agent.

Q: Why does Steve Rogers retire as Captain America?

A: When Cap faces the villain Iron Nail, the effects of the Super-Soldier serum are **neutralized** and Rogers **rapidly ages.** Sam Wilson, the Falcon, takes his place as Captain America.

TELL ME MORE!

Scrawny Steve Rogers wants to serve his country and fight the Nazis, but he is rejected for his poor physical condition. When Dr. Erskine invites him to join the U.S. military's Super-Soldier program, Operation: Rebirth, he doesn't hesitate!

THE WINTER SOLDIER
Bucky Barnes is believed killed when Baron Zemo's airplane explodes at the end of World War II. He returns years later, brainwashed as elite Russian agent the Winter Soldier. Steve Rogers helps his old friend recover his memories.

BETWEEN...

Marvel Comics rebooted World War II hero Captain America in *Avengers* #4 (March 1964). Cap returned with a new backstory—he had been frozen in Arctic ice since 1945!

...THE PANELS

Steve Rogers and **Sharon Carter** (Agent 13) fall in love but it **doesn't work out**. She's **brainwashed** by Dr. Faustus to **assassinate Cap!**

UNLUCKY IN LOVE

BACK FROM THE DEAD!

Cap is apparently assassinated after the superhuman civil war, but he **survives!** He is shot with a special time-travel weapon and has to **relive** major events in his life.

NOOOOO!!
As soon as Steve Rogers receives the Super-Soldier serum, Nazis **KILL** its creator, Dr. Erskine. Cap is left as the **ONLY MEMBER** of Operation: Rebirth—started to create an entire **ARMY!**

FAST FACTS

REAL NAME:
Steven Rogers

OCCUPATIONS: Army captain, director of S.H.I.E.L.D., illustrator

MAIN WEAPON: Virtually indestructible shield

STRENGTHS: Slow-aging, inspirational leader, expert fighter, physically perfect, great integrity

WEAKNESSES: His age (when the Super-Soldier serum wears off)

ALLIES: Winter Soldier, Falcon, Nick Fury, Avengers

FOES: Red Skull, Baron Zemo, Hydra, A.I.M.

SENTINEL OF LIBERTY

Captain America is an **inspiration** to U.S. servicemen in World War II, fighting **diabolical Nazi villains** and saving the world. Trapped in ice for decades, he is **revived** by the Avengers to **protect and serve** once more!

THE SEA KING

Namor is the ruler and protector of the underwater kingdom of **Atlantis** and has amazing **aquatic abilities.** Born to **a royal Atlantean mother** and **a human father,** Namor is frequently **at odds** with **"surface-dwellers,"** but he fights alongside them when he feels it's in **Atlantis' best interests.**

AAARRGHH!! Namor is virtually **INVINCIBLE** when in the ocean. Out of water, his **STRENGTH LESSENS,** and after a few days he could even **DIE!**

FAST FACTS

REAL NAME:
Namor McKenzie

NICKNAMES: The Sub-Mariner, The Avenging Son, Imperius Rex

STRENGTHS: Amphibious adaptations to live underwater; superhuman strength, speed, reflexes, and durability; flight; extended life-span; telepathy with sea life

WEAKNESSES: Vulnerable to dehydration and pollution; hot-headed

FOES: Attuma, Tiger Shark, Nitro, anyone he thinks threatens Atlantis

REALLY?!

Namor was once **married** to Marinna Smallwood—an **aquatic alien** member of Alpha Flight—until Norman Osborn **mutated** her into an uncontrollable **sea monster!**

ALTERNATE UNIVERSE

In the possible future of **Earth X,** Namor is responsible for the **demise of Johnny Storm** of the Fantastic Four. As penance, Franklin Richards **alters reality** so that one half of Namor's body is **always aflame!**

S.H.I.E.L.D. DECLASSIFIED

THE INVADERS
Namor fights on the frontlines of World War II against the Axis forces, teaming up with other early heroes as the Invaders. His wartime experiences give Namor a grudging respect for human heroes, especially Captain America (Steve Rogers).

HANDLE WITH CARE!

The **Horn of Proteus** is an Atlantean **artifact** capable of summoning **behemoths** from the deepest depths of the ocean to do the bearer's bidding. Namor has used the Horn to call on such beasts as **Giganto,** an enormous **sperm whale** with **legs and arms.**

INVISIBLE LOVE

Namor has long carried a torch for Invisible Woman (Sue Richards of the Fantastic Four), but Sue only has eyes for **MISTER FANTASTIC,** her hubby Reed!

"IMPERIUS REX!"

NAMOR'S BATTLE CRY

WOW!

60

Namor's top swimming speed in miles per hour (96.6kph). This is over 13 times quicker than the fastest human swimmer.

WHAT?!

Olympic swimmer Todd Arliss **injures his spine** in a publicity stunt and undergoes an experiment to **mix his DNA** with Namor's and a shark's. He turns into the aquatic, razor-toothed villain **Tiger Shark!**

NOOOOO!!

Possessed by the **PHOENIX FORCE**, Namor demolishes most of the nation of **WAKANDA** with a **TIDAL WAVE!**

WHEN GOOD GUYS GO BAD!

NAMOR'S CABAL
Namor secretly works with Iron Man, Mister Fantastic, Black Panther, Beast, and Black Bolt to prevent a clash of worlds destroying Earth. When the others reject his drastic solutions, Namor betrays them and joins a Cabal of ruthless villains!

NEPTUNE'S TRIDENT
The ruler of Atlantis often uses the trident as a standard, and it can also **manipulate water** and fire powerful **mystical beams**.

1 FRANKLIN RICHARDS—the son of Susan and Reed Richards can manipulate reality, molecules, time, and even see the future!

2 PROTEUS—warps reality, and can take over a human body as his host.

3 APOCALYPSE—can bring about (you guessed it!) the apocalypse!

BETWEEN...

The most powerful character in the Multiverse is the One-Above-All. Not only does he possess more power than any known entity, he is believed to represent the writers and artists of Marvel Comics!

...THE PANELS

TELL ME MORE!

The Multiverse must remain balanced or all will be destroyed! Master Order and Lord Chaos push and pull their servant, the In-Betweener, who must work to balance their desires. If all else fails, the Living Tribunal can intervene to keep the peace.

Nooooo!! The omnipotent **BEYONDER** uses Earth's heroes and villains as playthings! He creates "**SECRET WARS**" on his **BATTLEWORLD** (a planet of his own creation) and forces Super Heroes and Villains to fight each other!

ALWAYS WATCHING...

THE WATCHERS are an ALL-SEEING alien race who vow to observe the universe, but NEVER INTERVENE. UATU THE WATCHER gives occasional warnings to humanity, but still keeps COSMIC SECRETS. This leads to his MURDER and the countless mysteries hidden within his eyes being REVEALED!

ETERNITY— embodies time

TOP 4 COSMIC ENTITIES
They exist outside of everything and possess vast powers over space, time, and existence.

INFINITY— embodies the entirety of space

DEATH— can give and take life as she pleases
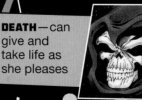

OBLIVION— embodies all that is nothingness

POWER PLAYERS

S.H.I.E.L.D. DECLASSIFIED

CYTTORAK, LORD OF OBLIVION

Cyttorak may be the strongest magical being in the Multiverse. Not only is his name so powerful that it is spoken as part of spells, but one of his gems is the source of the Juggernaut's powers. Cyttorak even has the strength to imprison Galactus, Devourer of Worlds.

TOP 5 POWERFUL GODS

BAST—ancient Egyptian Panther God of Wakanda

ZEUS—Godhead of Olympus

GAEA—Elder God and Mother Earth

AMATSU-MIKABOSHI—Shinto God of Chaos

ODIN—All-Father of Asgard

TOP 3 MIGHTY MYTHICAL MASTERS

YAO, THE ANCIENT ONE—the mystical master and teacher of Doctor Strange

LEI-KUNG THE THUNDERER—immortal martial arts mentor of Iron Fist

CHTHON—Dark Elder God; created vampires and responsible for the powers of sorceress Morgan le Fay.

TELL ME MORE!

The Vishanti (Hoggoth the Hoary, Oshtur, and Agamotto) are an ancient, magical trinity who have protected the Earthly dimensions since the dawn of time! They pen the mystical Book of the Vishanti that helps Doctor Strange become Sorcerer Supreme.

GRANDMASTER is a virtually immortal cosmic being. He travels the universe MASTERING GAMES of all kinds. He even challenges DEATH to a game, AND WINS!

AAARRGHH!!

Power Up!

COSMIC UPGRADE

Cosmic power can have a **DARK SIDE**! **JEAN GREY** is a powerful telepath, but after absorbing the **PHOENIX FORCE**, she becomes **PHOENIX**—wielding the power to obliterate or create **ENTIRE PLANETS**!

REALLY?!

The **Supreme Intelligence** may be a supercomputer, but it's one of the most **powerful beings** in the Multiverse! It is created by the Kree, an advanced alien race, but develops **a mind of its own**. Its ruthless logic then results in the **destruction** of the Kree homeworld!

These **all-powerful** masters of the **cosmic** and **mystical** realms balance the forces of good and evil, chaos and order, time and space. They could end the **entire Multiverse**—or **create a new one!**

Golden Avenger

Endo-Sym Armor

Silver Centurion

The Red/Gold Armor

WOW!

52

...and counting! The number of different Iron Man suits.

War Machine's Armor

Classic Gray Armor

Iron Destroyer Armor

Hulkbuster Armor

Stealth Armor MK II

Space Armor MK III

Iconic Armor

Model 42 Armor

Hydro Suit

HEAVY METAL

Tony Stark is the **billionaire owner** of tech company Stark Industries, a **playboy,** and **world-class genius!** His many **suits of armor** control a life-threatening injury and grant him **amazing powers** to fight for justice as **Iron Man!**

BETWEEN...

Marvel's Stan Lee wanted to create a character—a rich arms manufacturer—readers would dislike, and make him sympathetic. Iron Man duly debuted in *Tales of Suspense* #39 (March 1963)!

...THE PANELS

FAST FACTS

REAL NAME:
Anthony Edward Stark

STRENGTHS: Genius-level intellect, leadership, engineering skills, combat skills

WEAKNESSES: often needs tech to stay alive; alcohol problems; big ego

POWER SOURCE: Iron Man suits enhance durability and strength, fire repulsor blasts, and grant supersonic flight

FOES: Too many to mention!

ALLIES: War Machine/Iron Patriot (Jim Rhodes), Avengers, Mr. Fantastic

TELL ME MORE!

Critically wounded and held hostage by a warlord, Tony Stark and fellow prisoner Ho Yinsen construct a magnetic plate that prevents shrapnel in Tony's chest from reaching his heart. The magnet also powers a suit of armor...

BEST KNOWN FOR

CONTROL FREAKERY AND PARTYING

IDENTITY CRISIS!

Jim "Rhodey" Rhodes dons the Iron Man armor to protect Tony's secret identity, before stepping into his own identity as the heavily armed War Machine.

WOW!

7,673

The speed that Iron Man's Space Armor MK III can reach, in mph (12,348kph).

Power Up!

GOING TO EXTREMES

Tony enhances his system with **EXTREMIS NANOTECH**, enabling him to store his armor's under layer **IN HIS BONES.** He gains strength, agility, and can grow **NEW ORGANS!**

S.H.I.E.L.D. DECLASSIFIED

DIRECTOR STARK

Following the superhuman civil war, Tony Stark is appointed director of S.H.I.E.L.D. When he fails to anticipate and to prevent the alien Skrulls' invasion of Earth, his reputation is severely damaged, and the villainous Norman Osborn takes his place.

TOP 5

Iron Man Suits

1 **HULKBUSTER**—lets Tony go toe-to-green-toe with an out-of-control Hulk.

2 **IRON DESTROYER**—Uru-powered upgrade—handy when Thor's evil uncle attacks Earth.

3 **STEALTH ARMOR MK II**— equipped with "active camouflage"—you can't fight what you can't see!

4 **SPACE ARMOR MK III**— back-mounted rocket thrusters and an onboard A.I. called P.E.P.P.E.R. enable Tony to be a true Guardian of the Galaxy.

5 **HYDRO SUIT**—This pressure-resistant model allows Stark to get wet and wild in the depths of the ocean.

UNLUCKY IN LOVE

Playboy Tony is famous for his stormy love affairs. He has a knack for getting involved with beautiful women who have shady agendas, psychological issues, can't cope with him being Iron Man, or get killed!

WHEN GOOD GUYS GO BAD!

Caught in the Red Skull's "inversion wave," the bad aspects of Tony's character come to the fore. Choosing profit over heroism, Tony develops an Extremis 3.0 app and charges civilians outrageous sums to use its enhancing nanotech.

NOOOOO!!

TONY'S ARMOR develops a mind of its own and begins using **LETHAL FORCE.** Confronting his "living armor," Tony has a heart attack and the armor sacrifices its sentience to **SAVE HIM!**

RESCUE MISSION

An attack by Ezekiel Stane leaves Tony's some time girlfriend Pepper Potts with shrapnel in her chest. Tony saves her life by equipping her with special Iron Man suit, allowing her to become the hero Rescue!

KEY ARMORED FOES

CRIMSON DYNAMO
Everything is bigger in Russia, as proven by this walking Soviet tank. Bigger, but not necessarily better!

WHIPLASH
This highly talented techie takes a piece of Tony Stark's armor and adds his own deadly electrified whips.

SPYMASTER
The face behind the mask may change, but every single Spymaster spells major trouble for Tony.

BLIZZARD
Is it suddenly freezing cold, or is it just Blizzard's ability to generate sub-zero temperatures?

WHIRLWIND
Imagine a spinning top covered with razor blades and you've got this tornado-generating super-thug.

IRON MONGER
Munitions dealer Obadiah Stane tries to gain control of Stark Industries by attacking in his Iron Monger armor.

TELL ME MORE!

Hank Pym discovers Pym Particles. These allow him to shrink to ant-size (or even smaller), or grow to enormous heights! The serum can be taken as a pill or breathed in as a gas.

WOW!

100

Hank Pym's max size as Goliath/Giant-Man in feet (30.5 meters).

AVENGERS A.I.
The robot Ultron isn't Hank Pym's only disastrous invention. He also develops an anti-Ultron virus that evolves into a sentient A.I., calling itself Dimitrios. This becomes such a threat that Hank forms an Avengers A.I. team (Hank, Doombot, Alexis, Vision, Victor Mancha, and Monica Chang) specially to combat it.

"I'm not Ant-Man anymore."

"I'm not Giant-Man..."

HANK PYM— FUGITIVE

Hank's enemy **Egghead** frames him for stealing **nuclear secrets.** Egghead and the Masters of Evil then **break him out** during the trial, making things look **even worse** for Hank!

AAARRGHH!!
Hank's **BIGGEST MISTAKE** is creating the robot Ultron. Ultron **COMES ALIVE,** wants to kill the entire human race, and has a **CRUSH** on Hank's wife, Wasp!

WHAT?!

When Hank dumps his **shy Giant-Man persona** and becomes **brash vigilante Yellowjacket,** he doesn't tell his Avengers team or his **girlfriend Janet.** Yellowjacket kisses her and, to **everyone's amazement,** she agrees to **marry him!**

Q: How Does Hank Pym Control Ants?

A: Hank develops a **cybernetic helmet** to control ants. The helmet transmits **psionic and electronic waves** and has a broadcast range of **1 mile (1.6 km).** Hank first calls on ants for help when KGB agents try to **kill** him and **destroy** his research.

BACK FROM THE DEAD!

Hank and Ultron eventually **merge!** Hank realizes what he has become and seemingly **dies.** Months later, he's back, wearing Ultron as **armor!**

PYM'S PARTICLES

Hank Pym is a brilliant **scientist, robotics expert,** and a founding member of **the Avengers.** But whether shrinking as **Ant-Man** or hitting the heights **as Goliath,** he's never felt **at ease** being a Super Hero!

"...or Goliath..."

"...or Yellow-jacket!"

"I'M HENRY PYM!"

BAD DAY

Hank consumes so many Pym Particles that he can change size at will and even alter the size of any objects he touches! However, this proves bad for his health.

BEST KNOWN FOR

CHANGING HIS SIZE AND HIS HERO ID

FAST FACTS

REAL NAME:
Dr. Henry "Hank" Pym

ALIASES: Ant-Man, Goliath, Giant-Man, Yellowjacket, Wasp, Ultron

STRENGTHS: Brilliant scientist and inventor

WEAKNESSES: Insecure, jealous of other heroes, guilt complex, work puts strain on his health

ALLIES: Avengers, West Coast Avengers, Mighty Avengers, Tigra, Wasp

FOES: Egghead, Kang, Morgan Le Fay, Ultron

IDENTITY CRISIS!

Hank Pym is replaced by a Skrull imposter during the Secret Wars. The real Hank returns, only to see his wife Janet die, owing to the evil deeds of the Skrull agent. Hank takes on her Wasp Super Hero identity in her honor.

FAST FACTS

REAL NAME:
Janet Van Dyne

STRENGTHS: Changing size, superhuman speed, flight, bio-electric blasts

WEAKNESSES: Shrinking too small could trap her in the Microverse!

FOES: Yellowjacket (Criti Noll), Egghead

FAMOUS RELATIVE:
Dr. Hank Pym (ex-husband)

NUMBER CRUNCH!

5ft 4in (1.6m)
Janet Van Dyne's height

4ft 2in or less (1.3m or less)
Height when wings begin to sprout

0.5 in (1.3cm)
Janet's miniature height as Wasp

110lbs (50kg)
Wasp's weight

2–4 wings
Wasp's varying number of wings

38mph (63kph)
Wasp's approximate flight speed

REALLY?!

Hank Pym implants cells in Janet's head that allow her to grow **temporary antennae** and communicate with insects!

HANDLE WITH CARE!

Yellowjacket (Hank Pym) gives Janet the **Power Prism** and it takes control of her mind! The gem is really a **sentient being** with the power to manipulate energy.

"HI! I'm the Wasp! And you've just been STUNG!"

BAD DAY

Janet **divorces** Hank Pym when the effects of regularly **shrinking and growing** change his personality, making him **jealous and paranoid.**

WOW!

30
The weight Wasp can lift in tons at her max size.

BACK FROM THE DEAD!

The world believes Wasp has been **killed,** but after her emergency signal comes from the **Microverse,** the Avengers shrink down and **rescue her!**

AAARRGHH!!
During the **SKRULL INVASION,** Wasp gets trapped in the **MICROVERSE!** However, Hank and the Avengers presume she is **KILLED IN BATTLE** so don't think to look for her!

BEFORE...

In order to heal Janet from serious injuries, Hank Pym places her inside a cocoon to recuperate. When she emerges, Janet is more wasp than human, with massive wings, long antennae, and spindly fingers! Hank assures the concerned Avengers that Janet is in "perfect physical health!"

AFTER...

TELL ME MORE!

Thanks to Pym Particles, Wasp can grow and shrink at will, just like Ant-Man. Wasp's insect-like wings sprout when she shrinks below normal size, and they are absorbed by her body as she grows. She can also emit bio-electric blasts ("wasp stings") from her hands to stun opponents.

SUPER STING!

Janet Van Dyne joins forces with Hank Pym to avenge the death of her father, becoming the amazing **Wasp!** She is also a **founding member** of the **Avengers**, inspiring her teammates with courage and determination. She's tiny, but with a serious sting!

Q: How does Janet become the Wasp?

A: Janet's father, Vernon, uses a **gamma radiation beam** to search for alien life. A **Kosmosian criminal** follows the beam to Earth and murders Vernon. Janet wants to **avenge** her father, so Hank Pym transforms her into **the Wasp!**

Power Up!

TALL TALE
Janet spends most of her transformations as the **TINY WASP**, but after a **ROMANCE WITH HAWKEYE**, she decides it's time for a **BIG CHANGE!** She tries out the high life **AS A GIANT!**

Q: How does Scott become Ant-Man?

A: He steals the **old suit** of the original Ant-Man, inventor **Hank Pym**. Scott also steals Hank's Pym Particle formula to shrink to **ant size**.

Q: Why does Scott become Ant-Man?

A: Scott's young daughter **Cassie** needs a **heart op** but the surgeon has been kidnapped. **Desperate measures** are called for!

BEST KNOWN FOR

GETTING TO PLACES OTHER HEROES CAN'T REACH

THINK SMALL!

Super Heroes can come in **small sizes!** It's all very well being able to **punch out** a villain, don an **iron battle suit,** or wield a **magic hammer...** but sometimes, **big problems** call for a tiny hero—**Ant-Man!**

NOOOOO!!

Scott's daughter, Cassie, follows her father into the hero business as the size-changing **STATURE**, but is killed by a super-powered **DOCTOR DOOM!**

S.H.I.E.L.D. DECLASSIFIED

THE THIRD ANT-MAN
Ex-S.H.I.E.L.D. agent and criminal Eric O'Grady joins Norman Osborn's black ops Thunderbolts team as Ant-Man. After Osborn's crazed Green Goblin persona resurfaces, Eric is accepted by Steve Rogers' Secret Avengers. He helps the team to clean up the mess left by Osborn's dark time as U.S. security chief.

WOW!

1,760

Distance in yards that Ant-Man can talk to insects (1.6km). Of course, he needs to be wearing his cybernetic helmet!

YESSS!!
Ant-Man **SAVES** his daughter Cassie's life during her heart transplant by **SHRINKING** to microscopic size and attacking her **WHITE BLOOD CELLS!**

Ride 'em Ant-Man!
If Scott wants to get **someplace super-fast,** he just shrinks himself to bug size and jumps aboard **a friendly flying ant!**

"Truth is, I've always been kind of a lousy SUPER HERO."

FAST FACTS

REAL NAME:
Scott Edward Harris Lang

STRENGTHS: Gaseous Pym Particles in belt allow him to shrink to any size; helmet enables control of insects; wrist gauntlets fire bio-electric blasts; electronics expert; a good dad

WEAKNESSES: Low self-esteem, for a hero; only possesses the strength of a normal man; can be squashed

FRIENDS: Avengers, Fantastic Four

FOES: Taskmaster, Master of Evil

NEW START

Scott puts his **criminal past** to good use when he starts a private security firm—**Ant-Man Security Solutions**. He runs the company himself, with help from **a team of ants** and a former foe—bear-exo-skeleton-wearing **Grizzly!**

Clint's Sarcastic Sayings

1 "Cap, did you *TAKE LESSONS* on how to be a *CORNBALL*, or does it just *COME NATURAL?*"

2 "I like playing *DUMB*. It makes me *FEEL SMART. SOMETIMES.*"

3 "Figured you hadn't had one of these in a long time... *A PARTY* I mean, not birthdays. You gotta be at *LEAST EIGHTY* or something."

4 "*FLATMAN??* I don't believe it! You got a partner called '*RIBBON*'?"

5 "*FIRST SIGN* of madness. *TALKIN'* to yourself. *FISHING'S* the *SECOND.*"

"Well, here's another fine mess you've gotten us into *Hawkeye!*"

TEAM PLAYER

Clint is **not comfortable** taking orders, leading to **frequent spats** with Captain America. Despite the conflicts, Cap recognizes Hawkeye's **leadership potential** and appoints him to **head up** a team of **Secret Avengers** including Captain Britain, Venom, Valkyrie, and the original Human Torch.

Clint has dated **many** of his heroic colleagues, including the Wasp, Scarlet Witch, Spider-Woman, and **Black Widow**—who leads him into a shady world of **spying** before both reform and become **Avengers!**

CUPID'S ARROW

IDENTITY CRISIS?

Clint gets fed up with not having superpowers, so doses himself with Pym Particles and grows to giant proportions, becoming the **Super Hero Goliath!** It doesn't last, though—Clint realizes you don't need powers to be a hero!

FAMOUS LAST WORDS

"*COME ON AVENGERS! Let's end this OUR way!!*"

—JUST BEFORE HAWKEYE FLIES INTO A KREE WARSHIP'S ENGINE TO SAVE THE TEAM.

HOT SHOT!

Hawkeye is a **mainstay** of the **Avengers**, but he has a chip on his shoulder **bigger than the Hulk**—he's got **no superpowers!** Earth's Mightiest Heroes wouldn't be the same, though, without the purple-clad sharpshooter's wit and **ace archery skills!**

DOG'S DINNER

When Clint moves to Brooklyn, he **rescues a dog** named **Arrow** from a pack of criminals. Clint renames him **Lucky**, but the pooch's penchant for pizza earns him the nickname **Pizza Dog!**

FAMILY CONNECTIONS

Clint's brother Barney is content being a **small-time hustler** until Baron Zemo manipulates him into becoming the villain **Trickshot**. He joins the Dark Avengers, but villainy doesn't work out so well: He shows up on Clint's doorstep seeking forgiveness—**and a few bucks!**

FAST FACTS

REAL NAME:
Clinton Francis "Clint" Barton

STRENGTHS:
Master archer, expert marksman, martial artist

WEAPONS: His custom-made bow and a trick arrow for every situation

ALLIES: Black Widow, Iron Man, Captain America, Mockingbird

CLAIM TO FAME:
His arrows never miss!

TELL ME MORE!

Hawkeye may have the best eyes in the business, but after he uses a sonic arrow to defeat the villainous Crossfire, he goes deaf! It doesn't last forever though—his hearing is restored when Franklin Richards alters reality.

"When you talk to the *COPS* about this, tell 'em Hawkeye was the *GOOD GUY* willya? I don't need any more *BAD PRESS*."

WOW!

122

The number of arrow types Hawkeye uses (there could be even more—it's tough for him to keep count!).

TOP 7
Best Arrows

1. **EXPLOSIVE ARROW**— *KA-BLAM!*
2. **ROCKET ARROW**—blasts away the bad guys!
3. **BOXING GLOVE ARROW**— a knockout!
4. **PYM PARTICLES ARROW**— shrinks your target right off the battlefield.
5. **HACKING ARROW**—for when you can't remember your computer password.
6. **GLUE ARROW**—puts bad guys in a sticky situation!
7. **BOOMERANG ARROW**— really cuts down on restocking costs.

Power Up!

HAWKEYE'S "WINGS"
Since Hawkeye **CAN'T FLY**, he asks an engineer to build him an **ANTIGRAVITY SKY-CYCLE!** He then uses it to **FLY** into battle—**IN STYLE!**

BACK FROM THE DEAD!

Clint **sacrifices** himself to stop the Kree invasion, but is brought **back to life** when Scarlet Witch **alters reality**.

640

Thor's weight in pounds (290kg).
He's only 6ft 6in (2m),
but Asgardian muscle and
bone is incredibly dense.

GOD OF THUNDER!

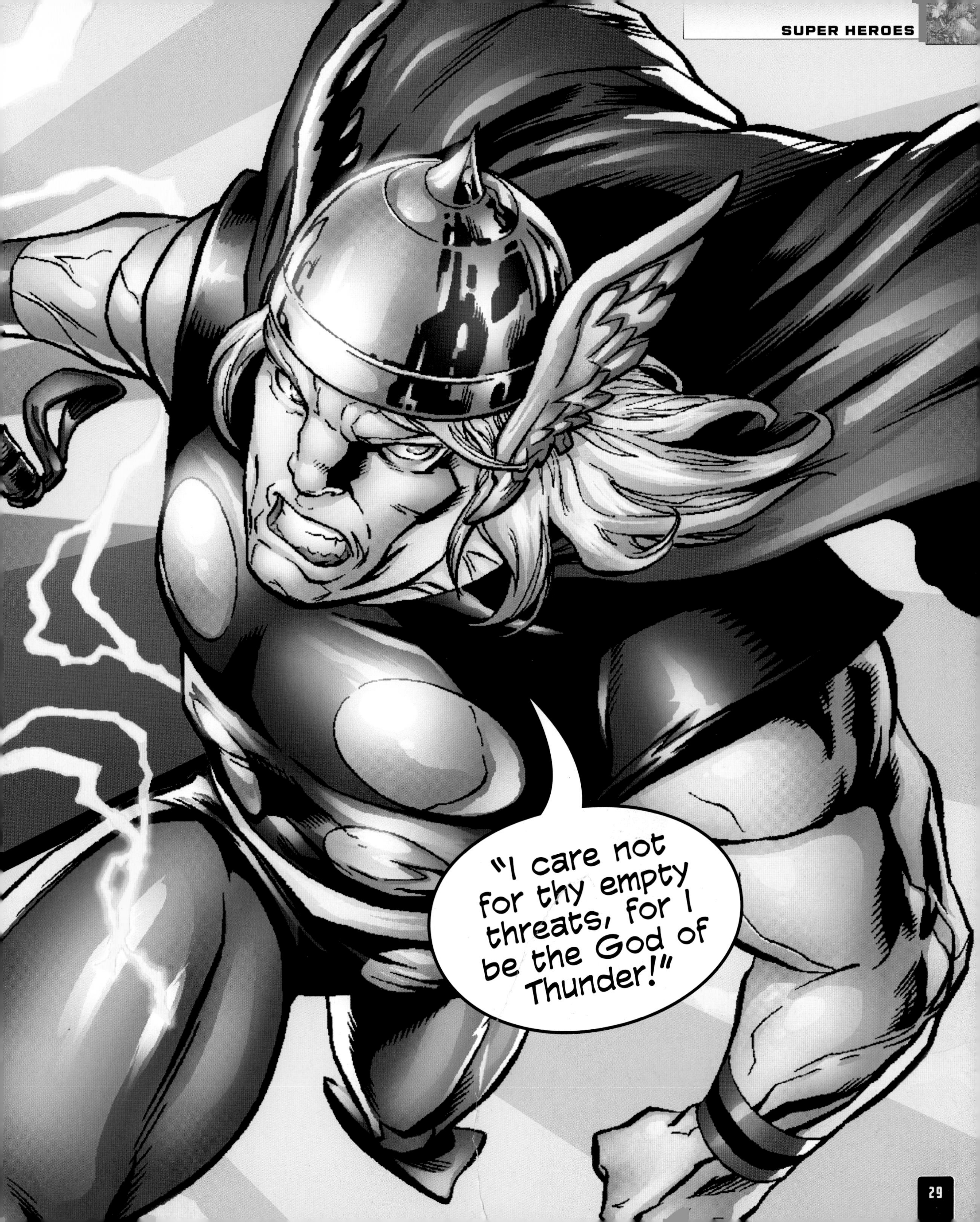
"I care not for thy empty threats, for I be the God of Thunder!"

FAST FACTS

REAL NAME:
Thor Odinson

STRENGTHS: Immensely strong, warrior skills, heroically handsome

WEAKNESSES: Needs his hammer, Mjolnir, to fly, manipulate weather, fire energy blasts

FOES: Loki, Malekith, Enchantress

ALLIES: Captain America, Warriors Three (Fandral the Dashing, Hogun the Grim, Volstagg the Valiant)

BACK FROM THE DEAD!

Tony Stark believes Thor is dead, so he creates a **clone** **version** from one of Thor's hairs! This violent version is named **Ragnarok**.

Oh, Brother!

Thor doesn't get along with his adopted brother, **Loki, God of Mischief.** Only brotherly love has stopped them killing each other—**so far!**

Name Game
Spider-Man's nickname for Thor is **Goldilocks!**

"The *legend* has come true."

By the will of the GODS, I am alive!

I am invincible! I am— THOR!!!"

WOW!

1,000,000,000

The weight of an arch Thor once destroyed, in tons.

KAPOW!

In battle, Thor can increase his strength **tenfold** by entering into a state known as **Warrior's Madness!**

Asgardians aren't **immortal.** Thor has eaten a Golden Apple of Idunn, which grants him long-lasting life!

REALLY?!

Thor's chariot is drawn by two flying goats named **Toothgnasher** and **Toothgrinder.**

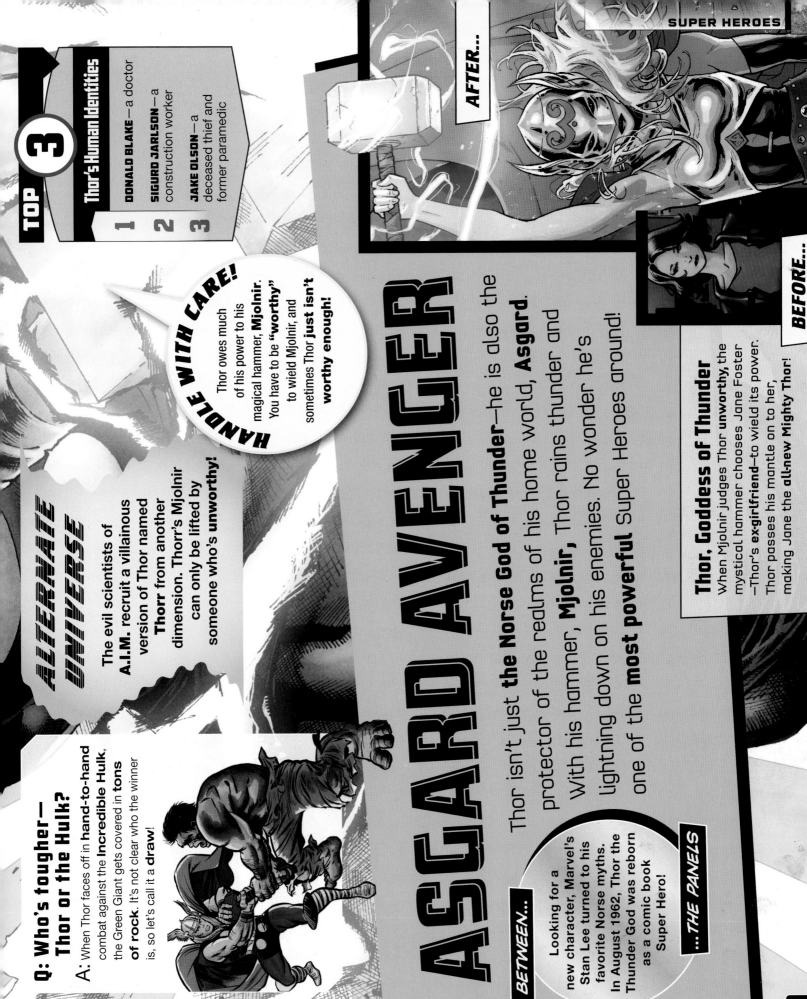

AFTER...

BEFORE...

TOP 3

Thor's Human Identities

1 DONALD BLAKE—a doctor

2 SIGURD JARLSON—a construction worker

3 JAKE OLSON—a deceased thief and former paramedic

HANDLE WITH CARE!

Thor owes much of his power to his magical hammer, Mjolnir. You have to be **"worthy"** to wield Mjolnir, and sometimes Thor **just isn't worthy enough!**

ALTERNATE UNIVERSE

The evil scientists of **A.I.M.** recruit a villainous version of Thor named **Thorr** from another dimension. Thorr's Mjolnir can only be lifted by someone who's **unworthy!**

Q: Who's tougher— Thor or the Hulk?

A: When Thor faces off in **hand-to-hand combat** against the **Incredible Hulk**, the Green Giant gets covered in **tons of rock**. It's not clear who the winner is, so let's call it a **draw!**

ASGARD AVENGER

Thor isn't just **the Norse God of Thunder**—he is also the protector of the realms of his home world, **Asgard.** With his hammer, **Mjolnir,** Thor rains thunder and lightning down on his enemies. No wonder he's one of the **most powerful** Super Heroes around!

BETWEEN...

Looking for a new character, Marvel's Stan Lee turned to his favorite Norse myths. In August 1962, Thor the Thunder God was reborn as a comic book Super Hero!

...THE PANELS

Thor, Goddess of Thunder

When Mjolnir judges Thor unworthy, the mystical hammer chooses Jane Foster —Thor's ex-girlfriend—to wield its power. Thor passes his mantle on to her, making Jane the all-new Mighty Thor!

HIGH FLYER

Hard work, fierce independence, and **phenomenal willpower** help Carol Danvers become **Captain Marvel**—one of Earth's greatest heroes. Whether she's soaring through space or facing foes, Captain Marvel's first priority is to **protect the planet.**

TEAM PLAYER

When Captain Marvel isn't joining up with **Guardians of the Galaxy,** she splits her time between female Avengers team **A-Force** and powerhouse squad the **Ultimates!**

REALLY?!

Captain Marvel's pet cat, **Chewie,** is actually a **Flerken**—an **extremely dangerous, egg-laying alien** who just happens to resemble Earth felines. Luckily, Chewie is just as **cuddly** as a typical kitty.

TELL ME MORE!

Carol Danvers is caught in the explosion of an alien device known as the "Psyche-Magnetron." Her genetic structure mingles with that of the heroic Kree alien, Mar-Vell, granting her superhuman abilities!

UPGRADED!

Thanks to genetic tampering by aliens, Carol gains a connection to a white hole—and the energies of a star! She becomes the cosmic hero Binary.

YESSS!!

Carol is a former **AIR FORCE CAPTAIN.** Her **MILITARY EXPERTISE** makes her the ideal candidate to lead a new **SPACE DEFENSE** program against alien threats with team **ALPHA FLIGHT.**

"Even with my back against the wall—*I DON'T GIVE UP!*"

FAST FACTS

REAL NAME: Carol Danvers

ALIASES: Ms. Marvel, Binary, Warbird

FOES: Deathbird, Yon-Rogg, Moonstone

ALLIES: Mar-Vell, Ms. Marvel (Kamala Khan), Rogue, Spider-Woman

POWERS: Flight, superhuman strength, durability, agility, fires energy blasts from hands

ARCHENEMIES

Captain Marvel frequently fights Shi'ar villainess, **Deathbird.** This menacing foe doesn't just boast razor-sharp **telescopic javelins**—she also knows and exploits Carol's **greatest weakness:** putting others' welfare **before her own safety.**

WOW!

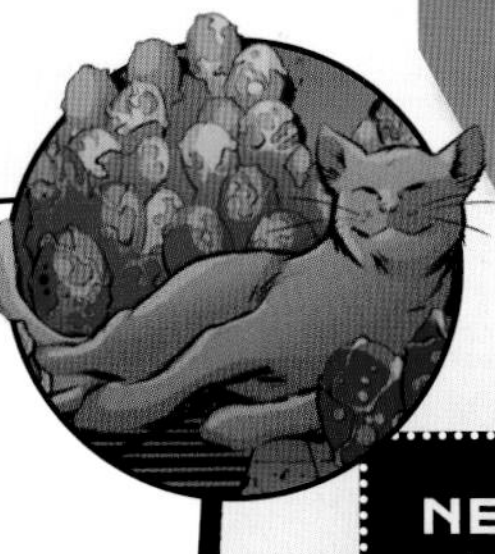

117

The number of eggs Chewie lays on Captain Marvel's spaceship. They hatch into kittens!

NEXT GENERATION

When teenager **Kamala Khan's** Inhuman **shape-shifting** abilities kick in, she's **inspired** by her hero Carol Danvers to become the **new Ms. Marvel** and **fight crime** in Jersey City!

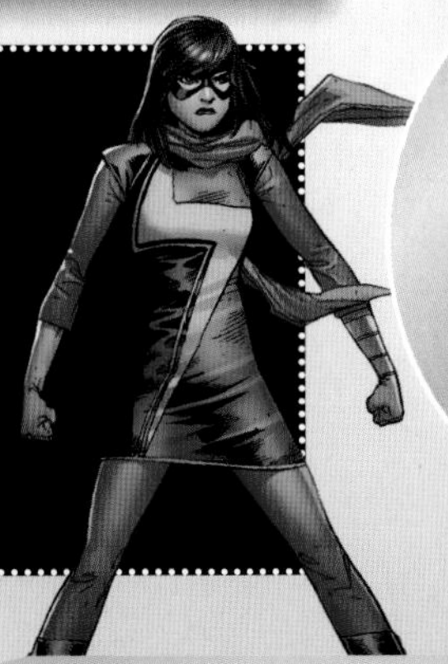

BETWEEN...

Writer Kelly Sue DeConnick's long stint on *Captain Marvel* was so popular that fans began calling themselves the "Carol Corps!"

...THE PANELS

NOOOOOO!!

In a long-awaited rematch, Captain Marvel defeats her Kree nemesis, YON-ROGG. But victory comes at a price—she LOSES most of her MEMORIES!

ALTERNATE UNIVERSE

In the Marvel Mangaverse, a nearly invulnerable Carol Danvers dons the costume, shield, and moniker of Captain America!

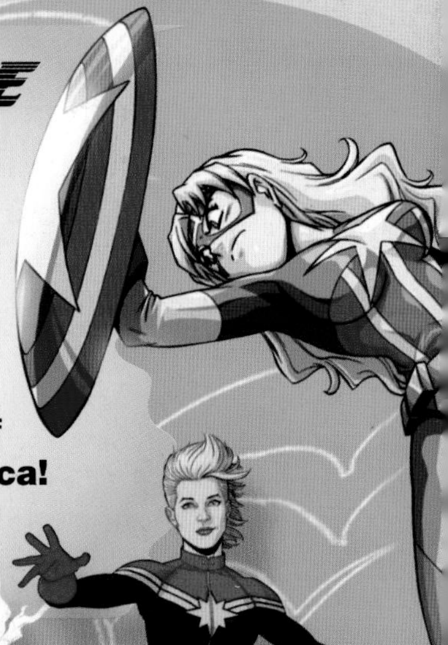

A young girl who idolizes Carol gives her the nickname "Princess Sparklefists." It's unlikely she will ditch "Captain Marvel" for that title any time soon...

BEFORE...

When Carol steps into the role of Captain Marvel, she **ditches** her lightning-bolt leotard for a **sleek new suit** that better represents her **military background** and **years of heroic experience**.

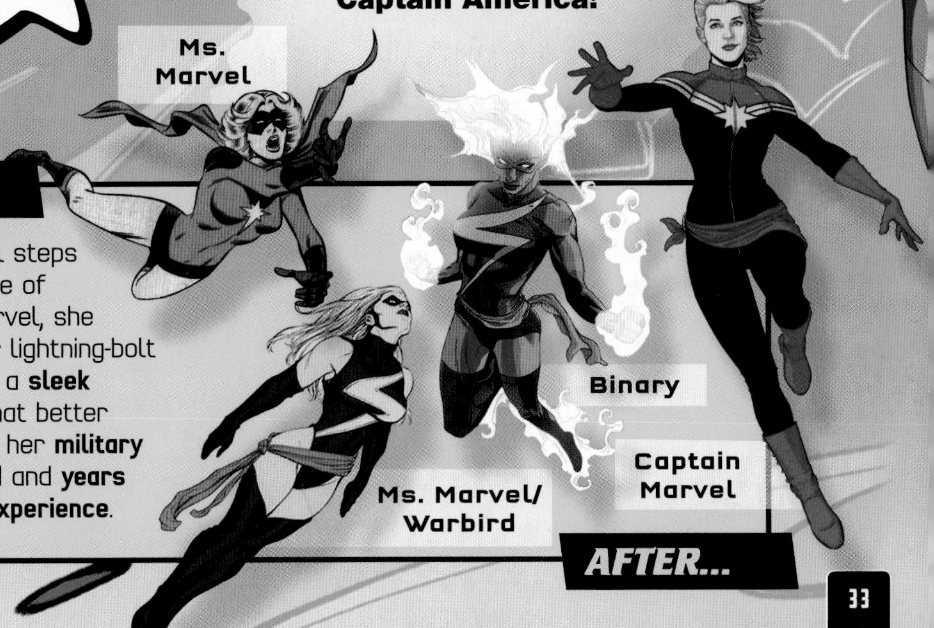
Ms. Marvel
Binary
Ms. Marvel/ Warbird
Captain Marvel

AFTER...

REALLY?!

The man who raised Natasha, **Ivan Petrovich,** becomes an **insane cyborg,** and she is forced to **destroy** him!

"If the world learns I am the *BLACK WIDOW,* it would mean the *END* of my private life!

I should have *CONSIDERED* that when I designed my *MASKLESS NEW COSTUME!*"

"My name is... Madame Natasha... but you... can call me *THE BLACK WIDOW!*"

WHEN BAD GUYS GO GOOD!

FRENEMIES
Black Widow is sent by the Russian KGB to spy on Stark Industries. She fakes a romance with Tony Stark, but he soon gets wise. Natasha switches sides and becomes one of Iron Man's most trusted allies!

NUMBER CRUNCH!

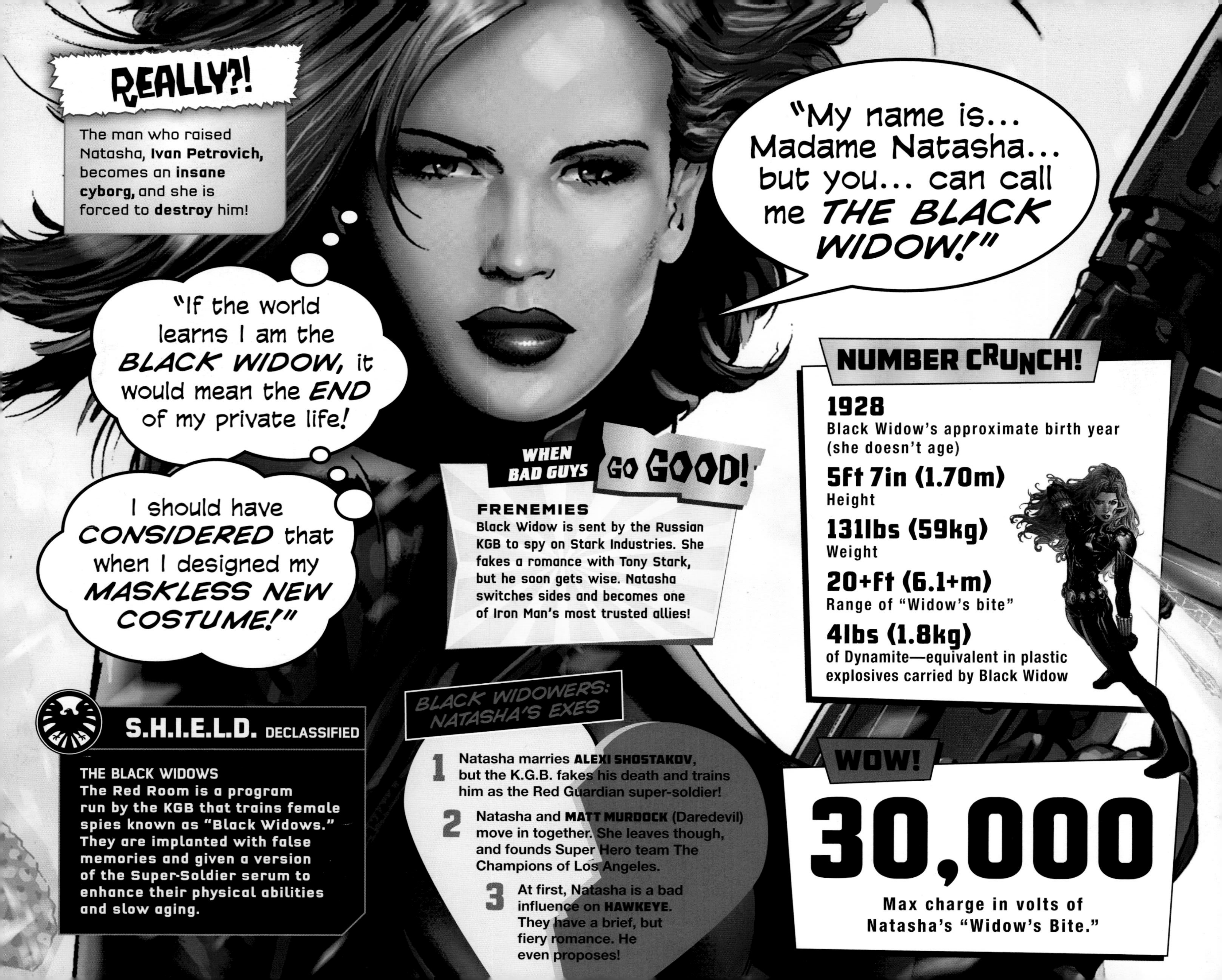

1928
Black Widow's approximate birth year (she doesn't age)

5ft 7in (1.70m)
Height

131lbs (59kg)
Weight

20+ft (6.1+m)
Range of "Widow's bite"

4lbs (1.8kg)
of Dynamite—equivalent in plastic explosives carried by Black Widow

S.H.I.E.L.D. DECLASSIFIED

THE BLACK WIDOWS
The Red Room is a program run by the KGB that trains female spies known as "Black Widows." They are implanted with false memories and given a version of the Super-Soldier serum to enhance their physical abilities and slow aging.

BLACK WIDOWERS: NATASHA'S EXES

1. Natasha marries **ALEXI SHOSTAKOV,** but the K.G.B. fakes his death and trains him as the Red Guardian super-soldier!
2. Natasha and **MATT MURDOCK** (Daredevil) move in together. She leaves though, and founds Super Hero team The Champions of Los Angeles.
3. At first, Natasha is a bad influence on **HAWKEYE.** They have a brief, but fiery romance. He even proposes!

WOW!

30,000

Max charge in volts of Natasha's "Widow's Bite."

FAST FACTS

REAL NAME: Natalia Alianovna Romanova (a.k.a. Natasha Romanoff)

STRENGTHS: Master martial artist and acrobat; a version of the Super-Soldier serum keeps her in peak physical condition

WEAKNESSES: Her dark and uncertain past

FOES: Hydra, Gynacon Corporation, Baron Von Strucker, Yelena Belova

TOP 4

Influences On Black Widow

1 HAWKEYE—convinces Natasha to defect to S.H.I.E.L.D.

2 CAPTAIN AMERICA—saves Natasha's life when she is a girl. Later recruits her to the Avengers.

3 IRON MAN—Natasha sides with Stark during the superhuman civil war.

4 BUCKY BARNES—trains Natasha as a Black Widow.

BACK FROM THE DEAD!

While on a mission, Natasha is poisoned and killed by the **Hand** ninjas! Stone—an ally of Daredevil's—magically brings her **back to life.**

Q: Who is Yelena Belova?

A: Belova is a recent graduate of the KGB's **Red Room,** with higher grades than Natasha. She works for terrorist group **Hydra,** who transform her into a powerful **Super-Adaptoid android**—then trigger her to **self-destruct!**

KAPOW!

Black Widow uses automatic weapons and knives, but she is famous for her **Widow's Bite** (electric bolts to disable her enemies) and the **Widow's Line** (a cable for swinging and climbing).

AARRGHH!!

Natasha thinks she's had a **GREAT CAREER** as a ballerina, but it's a **FALSE MEMORY** planted by **THE K.G.B.!**

SUPER SPY

The Black Widow is trained as a **lethal sleeper agent** by the K.G.B. and sent to the U.S. But her Russian spy career is short-lived—she **turns away from skulduggery** and uses her amazing espionage skills as **a heroic Avenger!**

The Black Panther is a hereditary title, but it must be earned through trials. When T'Challa is deemed unworthy by the Panther God, his younger sister, Shuri, steps up to lead the country as the new Black Panther.

HANDLE WITH CARE!

Black Panther gains many powers from the juice of the **Heart-Shaped Herb.** It is said that the herb will **kill** anyone not **worthy enough!**

AAARRGHH!!

ULYSSES KLAW wants Wakanda's **VIBRANIUM** and slays T'Chaka, T'Challa's father. T'Challa shatters Klaw's right hand and **EJECTS** the outsider from the country.

"It is not for nothing that I am called the *BLACK PANTHER!*"

CLAW OF THE JUNGLE

Ruler. Diplomat. Warrior. Avenger.

Black Panther is all of these— protecting the great African nation of **Wakanda** from the outside world, and using his intellect and power to **fight injustice** across the globe.

Power Up!

HEART AND SOUL

T'Challa shares a connection to the mysterious **PANTHER GOD.** This grants him enhanced senses and an **INSTINCTIVE CONNECTION** to his homeland, **WAKANDA.**

GOOD DAY

When Black Panther first meets **the Fantastic Four,** he shows off his skills by **defeating** each one of them!

REVENGE!

During a **universe-destroying** Incursion, T'Challa **takes revenge on Namor** for the destruction of Wakanda—by **abandoning the** aquatic hero on a dying planet!

BETWEEN...

Black Panther debuted in *Fantastic Four #52* (July 1966), making him one of comics' first black Super Heroes. Created by Stan Lee and Jack Kirby, the character gained his own title in 1973.

...THE PANELS

After a **long romance,** T'Challa and Storm **finally wed on the eve of the civil war,** but break up when the Phoenix Force **possesses** five X-Men, resulting in **Wakanda's destruction!**

LOVED—AND LOST...

ALTERNATE UNIVERSE

In the ravaged world of **Earth X,** T'Challa has been mutated by **Terrigen Mists** into a **true** humanoid black panther!

TOP 5

Black Panther Foes

1 **ULYSSES KLAW**—murders Black Panther's father and tries to steal Wakanda's vibranium ore.

2 **NAMOR**—destroys Wakanda with a huge tidal wave.

3 **MAN-APE**—eats the sacred White Gorilla and gains its powers.

4 **KILLMONGER**—wants to overthrow T'Challa and rule Wakanda.

5 **WHITE WOLF**—adopted by T'Challa's father; one-time leader of Wakanda's brutal secret police.

S.H.I.E.L.D. DECLASSIFIED

VIBRANIUM OF WAKANDA

T'Challa rules Wakanda, an isolated and advanced African nation. Wakanda is known for its technological innovation and its vast source of the rare and almost indestructible Vibranium ore. The metal is used to line Black Panther's suit and allows his claws to cut almost anything.

FAST FACTS

REAL NAME: T'Challa

HOME COUNTRY: Wakanda

STRENGTHS: Genius-level intellect, enhanced senses, Olympic-level strength and reflexes, skilled tracker, Vibranium suit

WEAKNESSES: Bright lights and loud noises can overpower his senses

RELATIVES: Storm (ex-wife), Shuri (younger sister and successor), T'Chaka (predecessor and father)

S.H.I.E.L.D. DECLASSIFIED

ELECTRIC ATTRACTION
Matt Murdock and Elektra Natchios are college sweethearts —until her father is murdered. Elektra becomes an assassin for hire! She reenters Matt's life when secret ninja organization the Hand tries to kill him.

IDENTITY CRISIS?

"Sometimes I think I was born to be Daredevil—and Matt Murdock is the identity that's not for real!"

"The name's **DAREDEVIL**... remember it!"

NIGHTTIME NINJA

By day, **blind Matt Murdock** works as an **attorney**. By night, he's **Daredevil**, protecting the **innocent** from crime and Super Villains! To law-abiding folks he's a **guardian angel**, but to the criminals of the underworld he's a **terror**!

WOW!

50

The maximum distance in feet (15m) Daredevil can track a person by smell through a crowd.

TELL ME MORE!

SUPER SENSITIVE
A childhood accident with radioactive chemicals leaves Matt blind but boosts his other senses to amazing levels. He can hear changes in a person's heartbeat that reveal they are lying! He also develops a "Radar Sense" that perceives the 3-D space around him and detects motion.

FAST FACTS

REAL NAME: Matthew (Matt) Michael Murdock

STRENGTHS: Incredible martial arts, superhuman senses, athletic skills

WEAKNESS: Legally blind

JOB: Trial lawyer

HOME TURF: Hell's Kitchen (New York City)

ALLIES: Spider-Man, Black Widow, Iron Fist, Foggy Nelson, Karen Page

FOES: Kingpin, Bullseye, Stilt-Man, Electro, Impossible Man

REALLY?!

Daredevil's sense of touch is so **fine-tuned** he can **read newsprint** just by **feeling it!**

BETWEEN...

When creating Daredevil, Stan Lee wanted a fresh new Super Hero formula. He focused on a hero with a great weakness, who had developed amazing powers to compensate.

...THE PANELS

BEST KNOWN FOR

HUNTING DOWN UNDERWORLD BOSS KINGPIN

NUMBER CRUNCH!

20mg
The amount of a substance needed in food for Daredevil to detect it.

12 years old
The age Matt Murdock loses his sight.

20ft (6m)
The maximum distance Daredevil can hear a heartbeat.

3 city blocks
The maximum distance Daredevil can smell gunpowder.

1 decibel
The lowest sounds Daredevil can hear (20 for average people).

KAPOW!

Matt's father is a **boxer** who wants his young son to stick to his studies. However, Matt disobeys and secretly becomes a **martial artist**, trained in **ninjitsu, kung fu,** and **karate** by mysterious mentor Stick.

TOP 3

Daredevil Fill-Ins

1 **IRON FIST**—poses as Daredevil while Matt is in prison, and during the Civil War.

2 **PETER PARKER**—dresses as Daredevil to protect Matt's identity in court, until another Daredevil imposter, actor Terrence Hillman, also shows up!

3 **FOGGY NELSON**—pretends to be Daredevil to romance Matt's on-off girlfriend Karen Page!

Q: Is Daredevil a lone wolf crime fighter?

A: No—he sometimes teams up with **Spider-Man**, who **patrols** some of the same areas. He turns down several invitations to join **the Avengers**, but finally comes aboard after urging from **Luke Cage**.

DAREDEVIL'S GUIDE TO SNAZZY COSTUMES

Stand Out!
A yellow suit with a single "D" insignia (later double) gives a distinctive look.

Keep It Simple!
Comfort is key for Super Heroes! This crimson suit is a practical choice.

Arm Y...
Guard ...
with th...
suit v...
whit...

Switch It U...
This black cost...
with red utility...
and gloves is...
to freak out...

HANDLE WITH CARE!

Matt's **cane** contains a ... **grappling hook** and ca... for climbing rooftops. It ... converts into a **fighting** ... and he can **throw i** ... incredible accur...

With their world on the brink of destruction, the Korbinites transform their most powerful warrior, Beta Ray Bill, into a cybernetic super-being. He travels the galaxy for aid and finds it in Asgard, where Odin gives him the Uru hammer Stormbreaker and similar powers to his son, Thor.

WOW!

183

...and counting! The number of known alien races in the Marvel Universe.

Q: What happens when a planet comes to life?

A: You get **Ego the Living Planet!** Using powerful humanoids created from his **own body,** Ego attacks other worlds and **absorbs them** into himself!

HANDLE WITH CARE!

If you're looking for the **most powerful** items in the universe, go see **the Collector,** Taneleer Tivan. An **Elder of the Universe,** he's one of the oldest known beings in the cosmos and spends his life collecting **items of boundless power.**

BLAST OFF!

There's a universe of **cosmic wonders** out there! Mighty alien heroes, **godly beings** with supreme powers, creatures the **size of planets**—there's a lot more to space than just **rockets and astronauts!**

GUARDIAN OF THE UNIVERSE

The **Uni-Power** is a manifestation of the universe itself! When **reality is in peril** it bonds with a host to become **Captain Universe**—a hero tasked with protecting **everything in existence!**

ALTERNATE UNIVERSE

The **Uni-Power** doesn't discriminate about its partners. On Earth-91110, it bonds with a **dog** named Casey to become **Captain Uni-Mutt!**

TELL ME MORE!

Eon is a cosmic entity hailing from his own dimension, the Eonverse. He creates the powerful Quantum Bands and appoints the Protectors of the Universe to wield them.

"YOU WON'T LIKE ME WHEN I'M *ANGRY!*"

"Hah! When Hulk *SMASHES* something, It stays *SMASHED!*"

"NOW HULK IS *EXTRA* MAD!"

"Yes, Hulk was Avenger once... *DIDN'T LIKE IT!*"

"HULK IS THE STRONGEST ONE THERE IS!"

"HULK is not SORRY. Hulk is HULK."
"HULK SMASH!"
"What nameless nightmare have I awakened to now??"

REAL NAME:
Dr. Robert Bruce Banner

ALLIES: Power Man,
Spider-Man, Iron Fist

FOES: The Leader, the
Abomination, Rhino

STRENGTHS: Almost
invulnerable, super-strong,
swift healing powers, can
resist mind control,
amazing jumping power

WEAKNESS:
Getting very mad!

RICK'S ROLES
Banner is blasted by the
gamma bomb and becomes
Hulk, but he saves **teenager
Rick Jones** from the same
fate! Rick has since been:
- **Hulk's friend**
- **Hulk's boss**
- **A mega-strong
  Rick Jones-Hulk**
- **A blue monster
  named A-Bomb**
- **A best-selling
  novelist!**

BAD DAY
Childlike and lonely,
Savage Hulk tries to
**"make friends with the
stars."** He leaps into
orbit, faints from **lack
of oxygen**—and **comes
down to Earth** with a
massive crash!

HRH THE HULK!
After crash-landing on the
planet Sakaar, the Hulk is
forced to fight as a gladiator
by its wicked ruler, the Red
King. The Hulk leads a
rebellion against him, and
is crowned king!

BIG TROUBLE!

A massive dose of **gamma rays** from an
experimental bomb changes the **DNA** of
scientist **Dr. Bruce Banner**. Now, whenever
he is overwhelmed by **anger** or **fear**,
Banner transforms into a **rampaging,
green-skinned giant**—the Incredible Hulk!

WOW!

150,000,000,000

The weight in tons of the mountain range Molecule Man drops on the Hulk! The Hulk catches it—proving he's an unbelievable powerhouse!

BETWEEN...

The Hulk's skin was gray in his very first appearance in *Incredible Hulk* #1 (May 1962). The color was hard to print correctly—so in the next issue he became "ol' greenskin!"

...THE PANELS

HULKING LINE UP

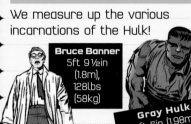

We measure up the various incarnations of the Hulk!

Bruce Banner
5ft 9½in (1.8m), 128lbs (58kg)

Gray Hulk
6ft 6in (1.98m), 900 lbs (408kg)

Green Hulk
8ft (2.4m), 1,400lbs (635kg)

MEGA MAKEOVER

The Himalayan nation of Llhasa is under threat from General Fang's armies. Hulk dresses up in a fur suit against the cold and puts Fang's armies to flight. They think he's the yeti!

TEAM PLAYERS

Super-shrink Doc Samson **separates** Bruce Banner from the Hulk. Banner then forms a team of **Hulkbusters** to **take down** Hulk!

REALLY?!

When Loki frames the Hulk for attacking a train, the bewildered behemoth **disguises** himself as a **robot** and gets a job **juggling animals** in a **circus**! The Avengers' first mission is to find him.

TOP 5

Hulk Incarnations

There have been a whole lotta Hulks! Here are just a few:

1. **SAVAGE HULK**—big, green, and childlike—unless he gets scared or angry.

2. **'JOE FIXIT'**—gray, mean, and cunning; a notorious Las Vegas gangster!

3. **WORLD BREAKER**—when the Hulk gets really, really angry!

4. **DOC GREEN**—Banner uses Extremis nanobots to repair his brain. Hulk becomes both big and brilliant!

5. **SAVAGE BANNER**—the Savage Hulk's mind, in Banner's body. Not very scary, to be honest!

KAPOW!

Hulk can cause a **sonic boom** by **clapping his hands**—and knock enemies **off their feet!**

MAESTRO HULK

100 years in the future, Earth is devastated by nuclear war. Hulk is **driven mad** by radiation and turns into the **Maestro**—an **evil**, bearded overlord!

NOT A SCRATCH!

The Hulk really is super-tough. In one single battle he is shot with:

- **a napalm rocket launcher**
- **an elephant gun**
- **an anthrax grenade launcher**
- **a shotgun firing 40,000,000-volt taser rounds**

He never even blinks!

TRUE LOVE

Jarella, **princess** of the subatomic kingdom of K'ai, loves **both** Bruce Banner and the Hulk! She could have been **the one**, but tragically she dies...

WHO'S THE DADDY?

For a long time, twins **Wanda** and **Pietro** believe that **Magneto** is their father! They eventually discover that their true parents are Romany travelers from Transia. The twins' mutant powers are the results of genetic experiments by scientist the **High Evolutionary** and his god-like power.

TELL ME MORE!

Wanda already has the potential to become an energy-manipulating mutant. However, the demonic Elder God Chthon then imbues her with magical abilities as well.

Power Up!

A WITCH IN TRAINING

To help control her powers, the witch **AGATHA HARKNESS** tutors Wanda in the art of sorcery. Magical knowledge combined with her superhuman abilities increases Wanda's power, but things **STILL GO WRONG!**

HEX POWER!

The Scarlet Witch can **reshape reality,** giving her **immense power.** You might think that would make her happy, but Wanda is a **complex soul**—unsure of **who her parents are,** troubled about her **lost children,** and vulnerable to **villainous manipulations.**

FAST FACTS

FULL NAME:
Wanda Maximoff

STRENGTHS: Mutant Hex power alters reality; sorcery training to control magical powers

WEAKNESSES: Influence of villains such as Doctor Doom can lead to destructive urges; training only 80 per cent effective

ALLIES: Vision, Quicksilver, Avengers, Wonder Man, Agatha Harkness

FOES: Doctor Doom, Chthon, Mephisto, Master Pandemonium

LOVE TRIANGLE

Scarlet Witch marries the android **Vision**, who is programmed with the brainwaves of dead hero **Wonder Man**. When Vision's programming is wiped and Wonder Man **returns from the grave,** Wanda starts dating him instead!

Yesss!!

Scarlet Witch becomes such a **powerful sorcerer** that she even manages to defeat the dread demon **Dormammu.**

DIVIDED LOYALTIES

Magneto saves young Wanda and her brother **Pietro** (Quicksilver) from a mob. They join his **Brotherhood of Evil** Mutants, battling the X-Men, but their hearts aren't in it and they join Captain America's new Avengers team instead.

Demon Doll

The demon **Chthon** tries to use the Scarlet Witch as a vessel for his **demonic doings.** The Avengers trap his **essence** in a **doll**, and the Scarlet Witch buries the doll beneath an **avalanche.** But you can't keep a demon like Chthon down **for long...**

TEAM PLAYER

Scarlet Witch becomes leader of Super Hero team Force Works. Her Hex mainframe computer predicts in advance where trouble is most likely to flare up.

"There is no defense against the Scarlet Witch's HEX!"

REALLY?!

Scarlet Witch loses her powers and memory and **almost marries Doctor Doom!** Iron Lad and the Young Avengers rescue her and they all travel back in time. Wanda gets her powers back, tries to **undo** the past harm she's done, and repower all mutants. Then Doctor Doom **steals her powers!**

TOP 3

Wanda Weird-Outs

1 Wanda has twin sons with her then-husband Vision. When they vanish, she goes mad, blames the Avengers, destroys Avengers Mansion, and kills several teammates, including Vision and Ant-Man (Scott Lang).

2 Wanda reshapes reality so that mutants rule, with Magneto in charge.

3 Wanda changes reality again so that most mutants are depowered.

PS: DOCTOR DOOM WAS REALLY TO BLAME!

AAAARRGHH!! Scarlet Witch doesn't know how powerful she is. She's **RESHAPED** reality, **CREATED** life, **DEPOWERED** heroes, and brought friends **BACK TO LIFE!** Who knows what she'll do next!

WORLD SAVIOR

The cosmic Phoenix Force possesses some of the X-Men, driving them on to rule the world. Scarlet Witch rejoins the Avengers to help expel the destructive Phoenix Force from Earth.

A HAPPY ENDING?

Wanda is a "Nexus Being"—a living focal point for Earth's mystical energies. Her power, combined with that of Doctor Doom, captures the Life Force and gives her back her sons, Wiccan and Speed.

BORN TO RUN

Blink and you'll **miss** these **lightning-quick** speedsters. Whether they're on the run from the law or **chasing fast-fleeing felons,** these super-powered sprinters know how to **finish first!** Catch 'em if you can!

BETWEEN...

The super-fast amnesiac calling himself "Buried Alien" is a nod to DC Comics' The Flash (Barry Allen). Could The Flash have run so fast, he'd been transported to the Marvel Universe?

...THE PANELS

REALLY?!

World War II hero the **Whizzer** obtains incredible **super speed** after being injected with the **blood of a Mongoose!**

"I'm freaking *QUICKSILVER!!!* and you can eat my freaking *DUST!*"

TOP 4

Super-Fast Feats

1 **QUICKSILVER**—sprints from Tibet to Indonesia in just a few seconds!

2 **SURGE**—runs from New York to Colorado in an afternoon!

3 **MAKKARI**—makes cyclones by running around in circles!

4 **SPEED DEMON**—runs straight up walls and across water!

Speed

Quicksilver

Speed Demon

Rocket Raccoon

ALTERNATE UNIVERSE

In the Marvel Zombies universe (Earth-2149), Quicksilver's extreme speed spreads the zombie virus across the globe like wildfire!

Natural Velocity
New Warrior **Speedball** is super-fast, but doesn't have super-speed! He uses **kinetic force fields** to travel at extreme velocities by **bouncing off** of solid objects.

WOW!

7,612

Quicksilver's top speed in mph (12,250kph).

Power Up!

GODLY GALLOPER
Quicksilver loses his powers, exposing himself to the Inhumans' gene-altering Terrigen Mist crystals. He briefly gains the ability to leap through time!

Q: How does Spitfire get her powers?

A: British MI-13 agent Lady Jacqueline Falsworth receives **a blood transfusion** from android the Human Torch, but with a side effect—she gains **super-speed!**

YESSS!

Quicksilver is so fast, he can attack opponents from multiple angles in a split second, and dodge anything they throw at him—he can even outrun Thor's lightning bolts!

SPACE RACE

Elder of the Universe the **Runner** invites **Quicksilver, Makkari, Black Racer, Captain Marvel, Speed Demon, Super Sabre,** and **Whizzer** to take part in a race to prove who is Earth's fastest. Makkari sets the pace, but the mysterious **"Buried Alien"** comes from nowhere to win!

WHO'S FASTEST?

ON YOUR MARKS...

ROCKET RACCOON: He might have a powerful brain, but he only has little raccoon legs!

SPEED DEMON: This fleet-footed felon will do anything to cross the line first!

SPEED: No matter what he says, this kid is not overtaking Quicksilver!

QUICKSILVER: Once Pietro Maximoff is in the lead, surely no one is catching the ultimate super-sprinter!

MAKKARI: It takes something special to slip past this Eternal speedster!

Makkari

NOOOOO!!
Light-speed lowlife **SPEEDFREEK** is battling the **NEW WARRIORS** when his partner, **NITRO THE LIVING BOMB,** destroys a school, sparking the superhuman civil war!

WITH GREAT POWER...

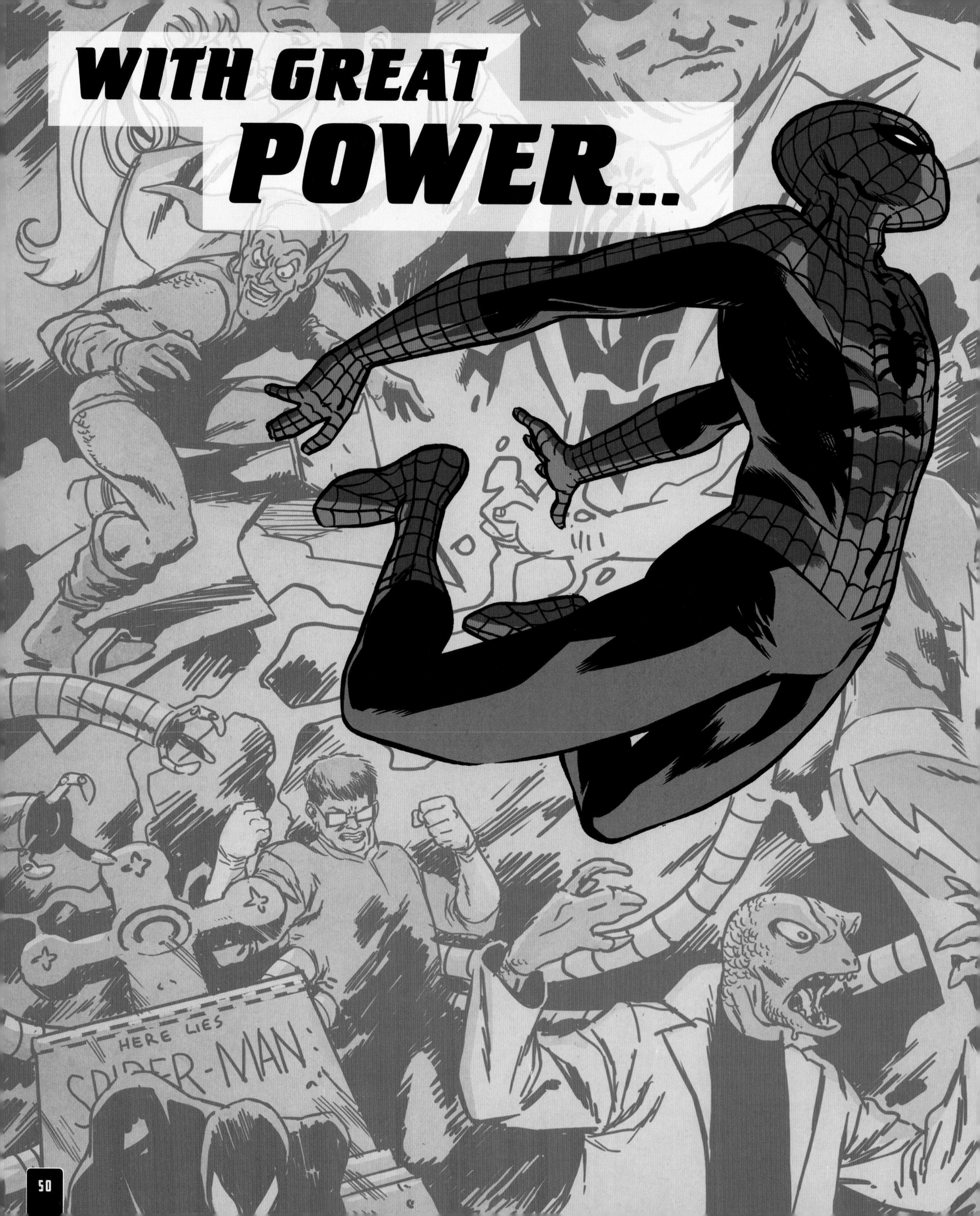
HERE LIES
SPIDER-MAN

WOW!

10,000+

The number of lives Spidey has probably saved.

COMES GREAT
RESPONSIBILITY

WEBSWINGER!

BETWEEN...

Debuting in 1962, Spider-Man was a new kind of hero—a teenager fans could easily identify with. As writer Stan Lee says in *The Amazing Spider-Man #9*, Spider-Man is "the Super Hero who could be—you!"

...THE PANELS

Q: How does Spider-Man create his webs?

A: Peter Parker can **climb like a spider,** but most of the time he isn't able to shoot **spider silk** naturally. Parker invents **web-shooters,** worn on both wrists and fueled by **web fluid.**

He's your friendly neighborhood Spider-Man, the **Wallcrawler,** the **Webswinger,** the **Webhead.** These are all names for the secret ID of Peter Parker, a shy student **transformed** into an amazing Super Hero by the **bite of a spider!**

NOOOOO!! Spidey loses his powers when he comes down **WITH A COLD!** He's unmasked by Doc Ock, but no one believes **PUNY PETER** could really be Spider-Man!

HELLO MARY JANE!
"Face it tiger, you just hit the jackpot!"—Mary Jane first meets Peter on a blind date arranged for him by Aunt May. And so begins Peter and MJ's long, on-off romance. At one point they even get married!

S.H.I.E.L.D. DECLASSIFIED

DAWN OF THE SPIDER-MAN
After his parents are killed in a plane crash, Peter Parker is raised by his Aunt May and Uncle Ben. A radioactive spider-bite gives Peter incredible powers, and he becomes a TV star. Everything changes when a criminal kills Uncle Ben! Peter blames himself and vows to use his powers to protect the innocent from now on.

ALTERNATE UNIVERSE

Spider-Monkey (Peter Parker) is a "webswinger" from Earth-8101. The friendly neighborhood primate joins the spider-army of Spider-Man—who is Otto Octavius!

"My **SPIDER-SENSE** is tingling."

DASTARDLY DEED!

Chameleon and Green Goblin try to drive Spidey crazy by using **androids** to impersonate Mary and Richard Parker, Peter's dead **mom and dad!**

TELL ME MORE!

Peter Parker's spider-sense gives him a tingling sensation at the base of his skull when danger is near. This instinct also helps him swing across New York City, without even having to look where he's going!

REALLY?!

When Spider-Man loses his costume, **Johnny Storm** loans him a Fantastic Four uniform and a **brown paper bag** for a mask. The bag says **"Kick Me"** on the back!

TOP **3**
Spider-Men

1 **SPIDERY SPIDER-MAN**— Peter is kissed by the Spider-Queen (Adriana Soria) and is transformed into a full-on spider by her mutagenic enzymes!

2 **SPIDER-HULK**—Spidey is zapped with a biokinetic energy ray while battling the Hulk. He absorbs the Hulk's energy and turns big and green!

3 **SIX-ARMED SPIDER-MAN**— Peter experiments with a formula to restore him to normal (without spider powers), and grows four extra arms!

A DEAL WITH A DEMON!
To save **Aunt May** from death, Peter makes **a deal** with the **demon Mephisto**. The demon **re-arranges history**, saving Aunt May's life, but Peter's marriage to Mary Jane is also **wiped from reality!**

BETWEEN...

Stan Lee has joked that J. Jonah Jameson, fiery Editor-in-Chief of the *Daily Bugle*, New York City mayor, and chief thorn-in-the-side of Spider-Man, is actually based on himself!

...THE PANELS

FAST FACTS

REAL NAME: Peter Benjamin Parker

BASE: New York City

STRENGTHS: Highly-intelligent; proportional reflexes; spider powers; spider-sense; generates web with web-shooters

WEAKNESSES: Enemies exploit his love of friends and family; vulnerable to power loss

FOES: Norman Osborn (Green Goblin), Doctor Octopus, Vulture, Electro, Jackal, Kingpin

ALLIES: Fantastic Four, Avengers, X-Men, Black Cat, Daredevil, Firestar

FAST FACTS

REAL NAME:
Jessica Miriam Drew

STRENGTHS: Spider powers, energy blasts, mood-altering pheromones, flight, resists poisons

WEAKNESSES: Prone to losing powers, hates rats

FOES: Hydra, Morgan le Fay, Charlotte Witter

FAST WORK

In London, Jessica evades capture by a Scotland Yard detective by ripping up a lamppost and **throwing it at him!** To stop it from killing him, she then zooms in front of her own projectile and pushes him **out of the way!**

"From now on Spider-Woman **FIGHTS BACK!**"

Q: Is Spider-Woman related to Spider-Man?

A: Only through the web of life! Jessica Drew's origins have nothing to do with Peter Parker's radioactive spider bite.

WHEN GOOD GUYS GO BAD!

...AND GOOD AGAIN!

When Spider-Woman loses her powers, a Hydra agent promises to restore them if she joins S.H.I.E.L.D. as a double agent. Spymaster Nick Fury encourages her to take the deal—and topple Hydra from within!

KAPOW!

Jessica's body naturally produces **bio-electrical energy**, which she channels into a powerful **"venom blast."**

ID PARADE

There's been more than one Spider-Woman...

Super Hero special agent and Avenger.

JESSICA DREW

Former government agent, now powerful psychic Madame Web.

JULIA CARPENTER

Spider-human hybrid controlled by Doctor Octopus to attack other Spider-Women, gain their powers, kill Spider-Man.

CHARLOTTE WITTER

Teenager who defeats Charlotte Witter.

MATTIE FRANKLIN

S.H.I.E.L.D. DECLASSIFIED

SPECIAL AGENT SPIDER
Spider-Woman is a seasoned secret agent, going deep undercover for S.H.I.E.L.D., tracking down alien threats for S.W.O.R.D., and serving on the Secret Avengers team alongside ex-boyfriend Hawkeye, espionage expert Black Widow, and mad scientist M.O.D.O.K.!

REALLY?!

During a Super Villain prison break, Spider-Woman joins the New Avengers. But she's no hero—she's the **Skrull Queen Veranke!** The shape-shifting Queen is planning a **secret invasion of Earth!**

SPIDER SCIENCE!

Spider-Man isn't the **only** wall-crawler in town! Jessica Drew certainly hasn't had an easy life, but she chooses to protect ordinary folks as the Super Hero **Spider-Woman!**

AAARRGHH!!

Jessica's hand-to-hand skills come from her time with **TERRORIST ORGANIZATION HYDRA**. It takes years for Jessica to shake the **FALSE MEMORIES** Hydra uses to control her.

Magical mayhem
Spider-Woman has made a frequent enemy of legendary sorceress **Morgan le Fay**—even traveling back through time to clash with the wicked magician!

ALTERNATE UNIVERSE

The Jessica Drew of the Ultimate Universe is actually an **altered clone** of Peter Parker, alias Spider-Man!

BETWEEN...

A pregnant Jessica stars on the cover of *Spider-Woman #1* (November 2015). The Marvel team wanted to explore her success in combining the roles of Super Hero sleuth and mother-to-be!

...THE PANELS

TELL ME MORE!

Jessica's scientist parents, Jonathan and Miriam Drew, are seeking to "improve" human DNA with spider abilities. When Jessica falls gravely ill, Jonathan gives her experimental injections of their spider serum to save her life, and she gains super-spider powers.

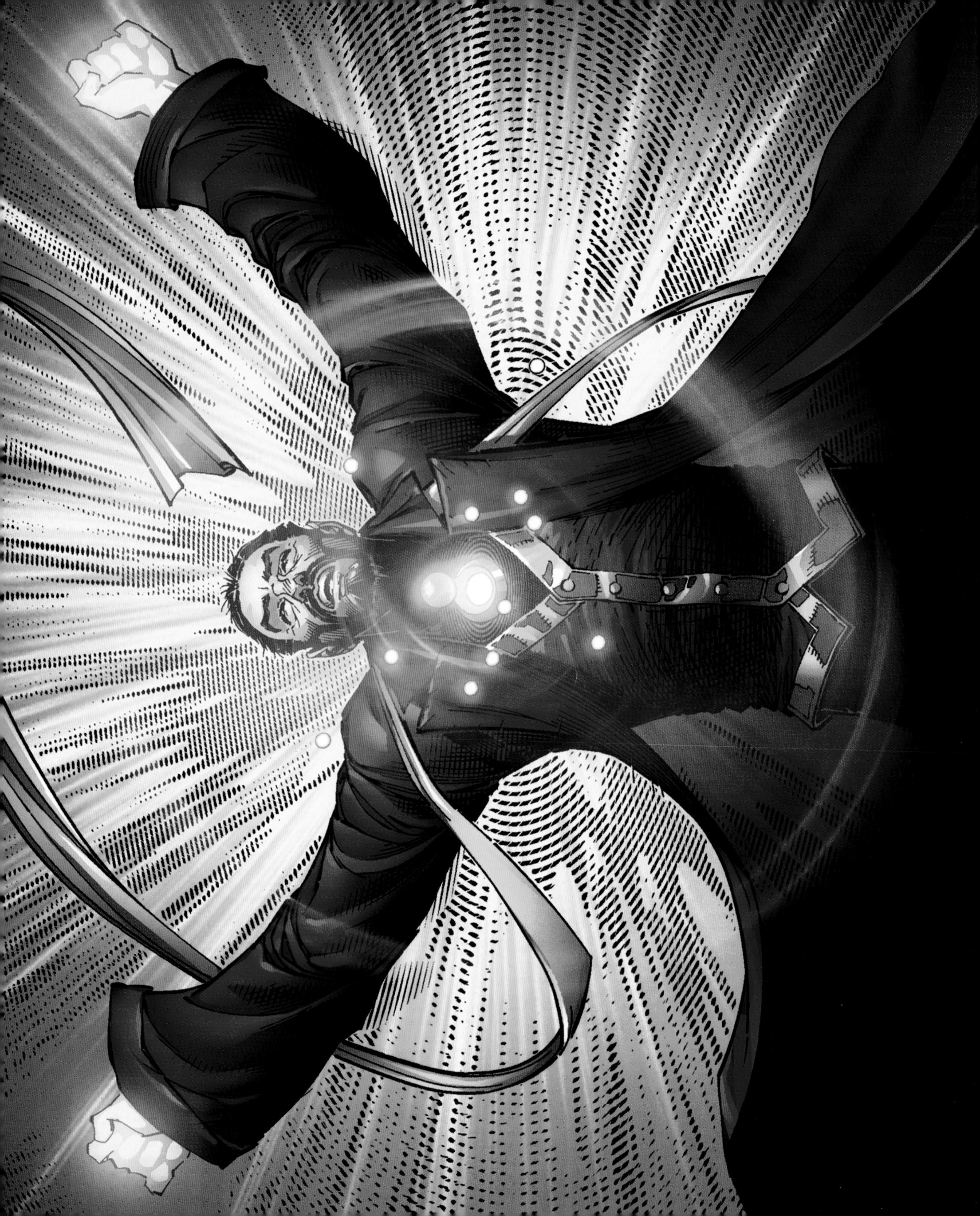

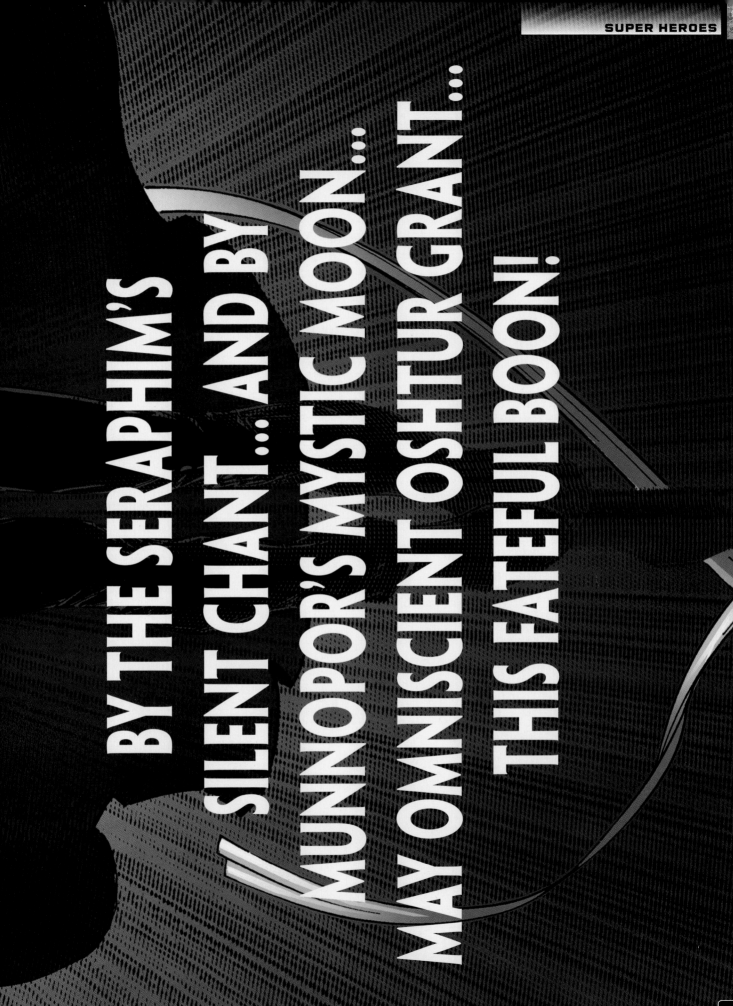

BY THE SERAPHIM'S SILENT CHANT... AND BY MUNNOPOR'S MYSTIC MOON... MAY OMNISCIENT OSHTUR GRANT... THIS FATEFUL BOON!

Dr. Strange forms the heroic Defenders, a team with no official roster or charter, to guard Earth from intergalactic and supernatural threats.

Q: How does Doctor Strange learn magic?

A: Stephen Strange is a brilliant, but arrogant, surgeon—until he **injures his hands.** Desperate to find a cure, he tracks down legendary mystic the **Ancient One** in the Himalayas. The Ancient One is Earth's **Sorcerer Supreme** and he chooses Strange as his apprentice!

FAST FACTS

REAL NAME: Dr. Stephen Vincent Strange

ALIASES: Sorcerer Supreme, Master of the Mystic Arts

STRENGTHS: A hugely powerful magician, with a library of spells and a collection of magical artifacts

WEAKNESSES: Limited fighting ability and strength (he's only human)

ALLIES: Avengers, Defenders, Clea

FOES: Baron Mordo, Dormammu, Shuma-Gorath, Nightmare

CLOAK OF LEVITATION

Want to fly? This cloak is what you need! It obeys Doctor Strange's commands, even when he's not wearing it!

WHEN GOOD GUYS GO BAD!

ENTER THE RED RAJAH!
A magical ruby known as the Star of Capistan takes control of Doctor Strange! He becomes the Red Rajah and tries to magically brainwash everyone in Manhattan!

REALLY?!

Doctor Strange often battles **occult threats,** but he also manages to save Earth from a **Skrull invasion fleet.** Using the **Images of Ikonn** spell, he creates a **huge illusion of Galactus** that sends the aliens packing!

FACE THE STRANGE!
Doctor Strange is famous for his **disco stage-magician look,** but when the demon **Asmodeus** steals his appearance, Strange **revamps his style** with a skintight outfit, Super Hero-style hood, and chest symbol!

STRANGE MAGIC

Doctor Strange is the **Sorcerer Supreme,** Earth's mightiest magician. Other heroes battle Super Villains and alien invaders—Strange **protects** our planet from **demons, warlocks,** and **spooky entities** from **mystic dimensions!**

"Where mankind is **MENACED** by magic... there must Dr. Strange go to **COMBAT** it!"

S.H.I.E.L.D. DECLASSIFIED

THE SANCTUM SANTORUM
Doctor Strange's home—his Sanctum Sanctorum—houses his collection of magical items and books and is protected by powerful enchantments. It stands on a place of mystical power in New York's Greenwich Village.

Astral Travel!
One of the **mystic arts** Doctor Strange has mastered is **astral travel**—his spirit can leave his body and **travel unseen** across the world.

Weakness:
His astral form can be **seen by spirits** (and the Hulk!), and his **body is helpless** while his spirit is away!

BETWEEN...

How did Doctor Strange get his name? His adventures first appeared in *Strange Tales* (beginning #110, July 1963), so creator Steve Ditko named him after the comic!

...THE PANELS

TELL ME MORE!

Doctor Strange receives spells, magical items, and help from three ancient godlike beings named the Vishanti. They are Oshtur the Omnipotent, Agamotto the All-Seeing, and Hoary Hoggoth.

TOP 5

Strange Spells!

1 IMAGES OF IKONN
A powerful illusion spell that has even terrified the mighty Galactus!
[USEFULNESS: 10/10]

2 CRIMSON BANDS OF CYTTORAK These glowing magic ribbons can even imprison the Hulk!
USEFULNESS: 9/10

3 THE SEVEN RINGS OF RAGGADOR Blue energy rings that protect Doctor Strange from harm!
USEFULNESS: 7/10

4 WINDS OF WATOOMB
This whirlwind can whisk Strange across the world —or blow enemies away!
USEFULNESS: 7/10

5 FLAMES OF THE FALTINE
These green fiery bolts strike fear into foes!
USEFULNESS: 6/10

Q: Who is Wong?

A: He's Doctor Strange's **manservant,** equally handy at martial arts, magic, **and cooking!** He's been Strange's faithful servant for years, despite being scarred, kidnapped, and even **turned into a vampire!**

AAAARRGHH!!
Dr. Strange's brother, **VICTOR,** dies. Trying to revive him, Strange uses a spell from the evil **VAMPIRIC VERSES.** Vic returns as troubled vampire hero **BARON BLOOD.**

SUPERNATURAL!

These **spooky sorts** really put the **"super"** into **"supernatural!"** They come from **mystical dimensions**; they possess powers **beyond human understanding**; and, if you're not careful, **they're coming after you**!

"I am the spirit of *VENGEANCE*. *NOTHING* will stop me..."

NEED HELP?!
Looking for a **hero** to battle a supernatural threat? If *Doctor Strange* is busy, try *Doctor Voodoo*, who has also held the title of **Sorcerer Supreme**!

VAMPIRE HERO
BLADE'S mother is bitten while giving birth, giving Blade **IMMUNITY** to full vampirism. He becomes a Daywalker—a vampire who is impervious to sunlight. Blade battles vampire villains, like Dracula.

FAST FACTS

SUPERNATURAL SAVIORS: Ghost Rider, Blade, Caretaker, Werewolf By Night

FEARSOME FOES: Dracula, Nightmare, Blackheart, Master Pandemonium, Satannish

SOMEWHERE IN BETWEEN: Daimon Hellstrom

PARTY ANIMAL!
Jack Russell is a normal(ish) teenager—until he turns into the **Werewolf By Night.** A pity it has to happen in the middle of his **18th birthday party!**

DEMON HOST
Master Pandemonium's limbs have been **replaced by demons**, granting him command of **dark forces**. He also controls the **Rakasha**, a horde of demons that actually live in his body!

FRIGHT NIGHT

Nightmare is the demon lord of a dream dimension. He haunts the sleeping minds of wicked humans upon his horse **Dreamstalker**. If Nightmare has his way, all humanity will fall into an eternal slumber full of frights!

Ghost Riders have the ability to manifest and control **hellfire-infused chains**, often with sharp **hooks** and **sickles** attached.

A Ghost Rider's greatest weapon is his **Penance Stare**, an **incapacitating** gaze that forces his enemy to experience every **pain** he or she has ever inflicted on an **innocent** person.

Q: Daimon Hellstrom: Hero or villain?

A: A bit of both! The **Son of Satan** looks down on mere mortals. When it suits him, he allies with **heroes** like the **Defenders**. And when a wicked mood strikes? He hangs with Baron Zemo as a **Master of Evil!**

WHAT?!

There have been **many** Ghost Riders and some **don't use** motorcycles. Transportation includes a **hot rod**, a **horse**, a **bear**, and even a **shark!**

AAAARRGHH!!

DRACULA, Lord of the Vampires, makes a deal with **DOCTOR DOOM**, and tries to turn the U.K. into a **VAMPIRE STATE!!**

YECCH!

Satannish is an immensely powerful demonic being who most often appears to humans as a green-skinned, horned monstrosity with a second, toothy face in his stomach!

WEIRD AND WONDERFUL

When **the world** is swarming with **mutating mists** and portals to **bizarre realities,** things are bound to get a little... strange. From **amphibian thunder gods,** to a Super Hero **alien duck,** let's meet the oddest dwellers in the universe!

"I've become something greater than either SPIDER or PIG... I've become a SPIDER-HAM!"

REALLY?!

Spider-Ham is a **mild-mannered spider** who is bitten by a **radioactive pig.** He turns into an **anthropomorphic** (humanlike) **porker!**

Living **cartoon hero** Slapstick is an honorary **New Warrior.** He'll **mash** you with his **mallet** if you insult his teen teammates!

TOP 5

Spider-Ham's Enemies

1 BULLFROG—humanoid, thieving frog.

2 BUZZARD—humanoid, con-man possum.

3 KINGPIG—humanoid, porcine crime boss.

4 RAVEN THE HUNTER—humanoid, big-game-hunting raven.

5 HOGZILLA—a giant, reptilian pig!

BUZZWORTHY

Scientist Fritz von Meyer's attempt to control a **mutated bee colony** backfires when the insects **devour** him... but his consciousness **lives on** through Swarm—a **sentient mass of living bees.**

AAAARRGHH!! The first time Swarm **CLASHES** with Spider-Man, the webslinger gets him to **BUZZ OFF** by coating his spider-suit in **BUG SPRAY!**

WEIRD WILDLIFE

HOWARD THE DUCK
Born on planet Duckworld, where intelligent life evolved from waterfowl.

PET AVENGERS
Team of furry, feathered, and fanged Super Hero animals.

SQUIRREL GIRL
Part-human, part-squirrel mutant, aka Dorothy Green.

Squirrel Girl's best friend, **Tippy-Toe** the squirrel, is way smarter than the average rodent. Tippy-Toe not only helps defeat Super Villain **M.O.D.O.K.**, she can use the Great Lakes Avengers' **blender** to make herself **acorn smoothies!**

YESSS!

Squirrel Girl doesn't just talk to squirrels! She's defeated **Doctor Doom, Fin Fang Foom, Bi-Beast,** and even **persuaded** Galactus not to **devour the Earth!**

HOW TO MAKE A DRAMATIC ENTRANCE BY HOWARD THE DUCK
Get stolen from your home planet by wicked Thog the Overmaster.
↓
Fall to Earth.
↓
Encounter the monstrous swamp beast, Man-Thing.
↓
Get attacked by Bessie the Vampire Cow.

Q: Does Howard the Duck have superpowers?
A: As well as some talent for magic, Howard is a master of the **ancient martial art** of Quack-Fu.

TEAM PLAYERS
Howard teams up with beautiful model **Beverly Switzler** to fight foes like **Turnip Man, Count Macho,** and the gigantic **Gingerbread Man!**

ALTERNATE UNIVERSE

Moon Boy is a **small, furry humanoid** with an unusual best buddy—a **bright red T-Rex** named Devil Dinosaur! Moon Boy rescued him as a **baby** on their primitive home planet of **Dinosaur World.**

Can't touch this!
The Man-Thing's **semiliquid** body is made of **roots** and **slime.** It is almost **indestructible**—so foes who try to hurt him with hammers, pickaxes, and laser pistols will be **disappointed!**

SUPER VILLAINS

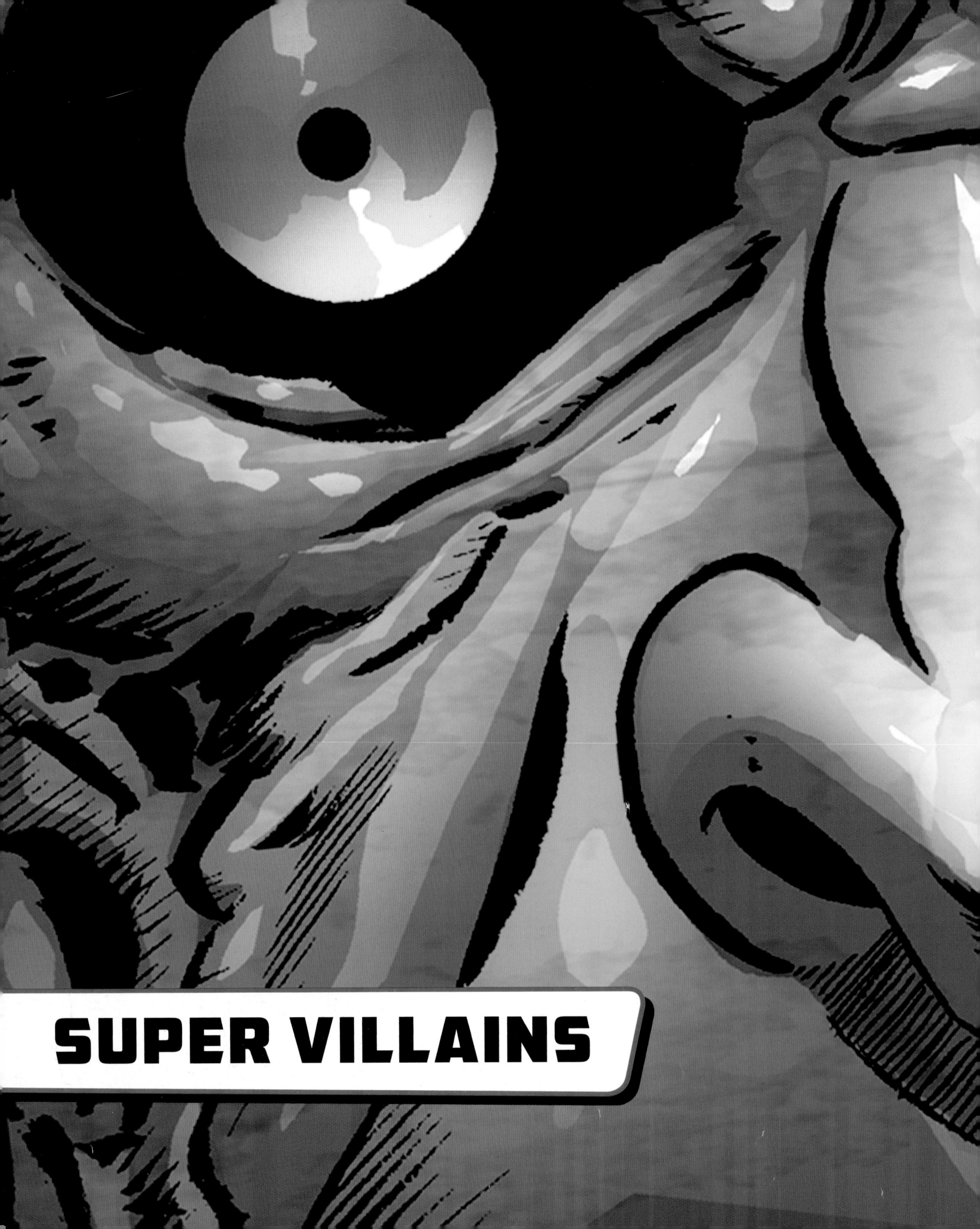

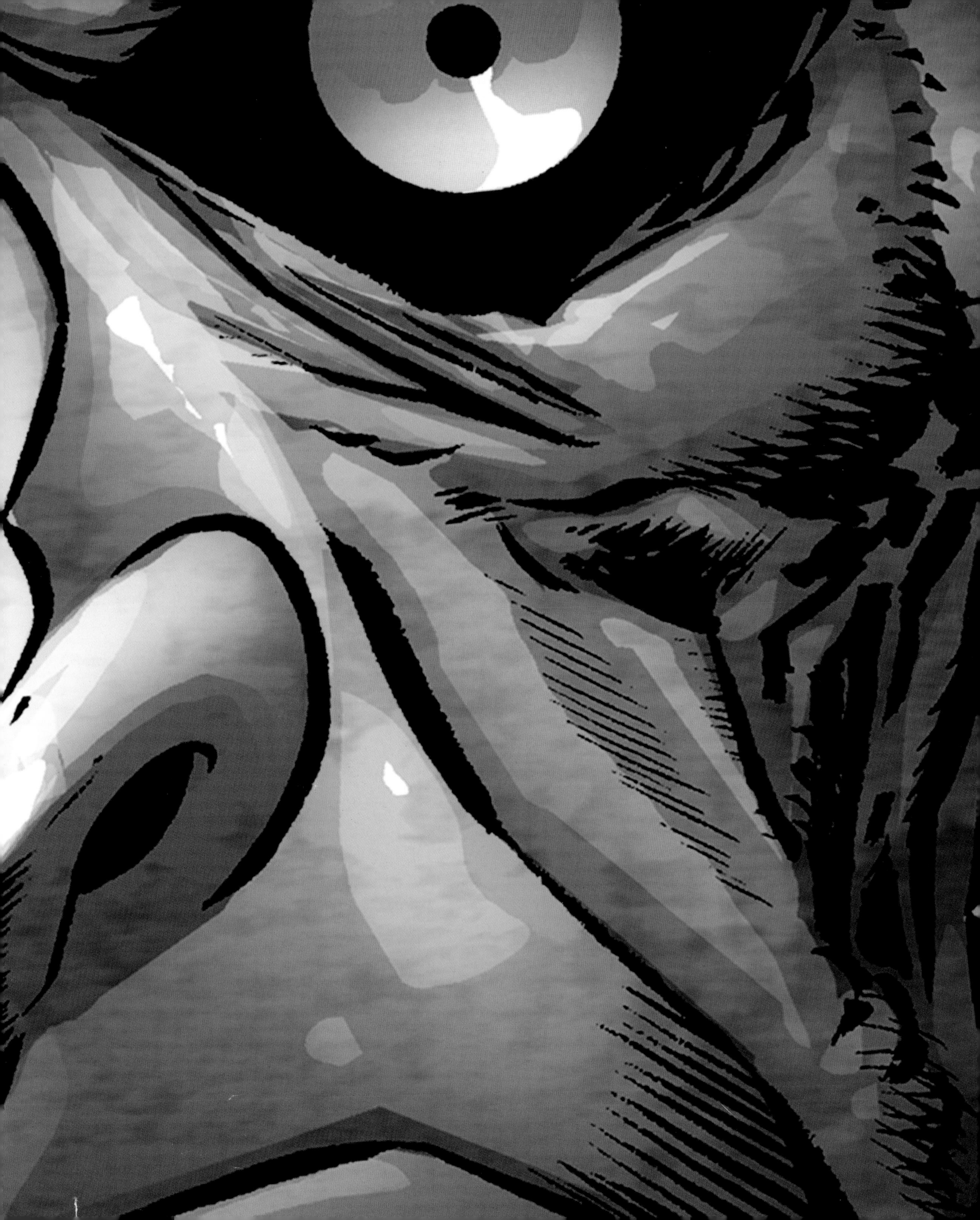

FAMILY CONNECTIONS

Thanos has **big family problems!** His brother **Starfox** helps the Avengers defeat him, his adopted daughters **Moondragon** and **Gamora** reject him, his granddaughter **Nebula** steals his Infinity Gauntlet, and he tries to kill **Thane**, his only son! Even **Thanos's mother** tries to kill him, so he **returns the favor!**

MOMMY

"...Interesting."
Thanos's last word when he realizes that Drax the Destroyer has punched through his chest and taken out his heart!

TITAN OF TERROR

Thanos is a threat to **every living thing** in the **universe!** The mad Titan is obsessed with **conquering worlds** in order to inflict immeasurable **death and destruction!**

ENERGY DIET

Thanos does not need to eat or drink. He can get by on ambient cosmic energy alone.

BACK FROM THE DEAD!

Thanos has been turned to stone, suspended in amber, and **Drax** has even removed his heart. Then **Death** resurrects him—and he becomes **almost invincible!**

TOP 5

Thanos's Gadgets

1 **FORCE FIELD GENERATOR**—to protect against projectiles

2 **ROBOT DRONES**—minions to perform any number of jobs

3 **TIME PROBE**—time machine for complicated schemes

4 **FLYING SPACE THRONE**—for teleportation and inter-dimensional travel

5 **THE SANCTUARY**—mobile space station

S.H.I.E.L.D. DECLASSIFIED

THE INFINITY GAUNTLET

The Infinity Gauntlet gives power over time, space, and reality itself. Thanos's tremendous strength and psychic powers, together with this cosmic artifact, make him almost unstoppable.

TEAM PLAYER

In his quest for the **Infinity Gems**, Thanos forms the **Black Order**, a group of deadly aliens, to help him **conquer** and **destroy** worlds.

HANDLE WITH CARE!

Thanos absorbs the power of the **Cosmic Cube,** then discards it. Wrong move! The Cube still has some power left—and **Captain Mar-Vell** uses it to defeat him!

GRUDGE MATCH

Few can take on **the mad Titan** and win, but he meets his match in **Drax the Destroyer.** Drax is a genetically engineered being with one purpose—**to destroy Thanos!**

BEFORE...

AFTER...

Thanos spends his youth **madly in love** with a woman he meets on Titan, and he destroys **countless worlds** to impress her. The mystery woman reveals herself as **Death** in disguise, but Thanos **still loves her!**

"Let the universe cower in *FEAR!*"

Two of a Kind

Thanos is in love with Death, but she doesn't feel the same way. He seeks the Infinity Gems just so he can cause as much destruction as possible—and finally make her happy!

WOW!

100,000,000

The estimated number of people that Thanos has killed—but the total could be even higher!

FAST FACTS

RACE: Mutated Eternal (a race of genetically altered humans)

HOMEWORLD: Saturn's moon, Titan

STRENGTHS: Telepathy, energy projection, super strength, intelligence—he can do almost anything!

WEAKNESSES: He's so evil, the whole universe wants to defeat him!

ALLIES: Death

FOES: Guardians of the Galaxy, Drax the Destroyer, Avengers, Adam Warlock

AAARRGHH!!

When **ODIN** creates the **DESTROYER** armor to save humanity from some future foe, he doesn't expect Loki to steal its **POWER** and use it against **THOR!**

GOOD DAY

Loki turns a **tree** into a **tiger** to attack Thor's girlfriend Jane Foster, puts a **force field** around **Mjolnir** (so Thor can't use it), makes **people disappear**, turns New York City into **ice cream**, and stops **an atomic bomb** exploding—all in one day!

MISCHIEF MAKER!

Loki is the shape-shifting **God of Mischief**—one of the **greatest sorcerers** in all of Asgard. With this **trickster,** you can be sure of just one thing —he's out for **number one!**

BETWEEN...

Loki first stirred up trouble in August 1949 as the main villain of *Venus* #6, a fantasy romance comic book about the Earthly adventures of the goddess of love.

...THE PANELS

BEFORE...

Loki is a master of magic and illusion, and he has taken on many forms, including several versions of himself. These include Kid Loki, Young Loki—even Lady Loki!

TELL ME MORE!

Prophecies link Loki to Ragnarok—the Norse word for the end of everything. As well as trying to overthrow his adoptive father, Odin, and tormenting his brother, Thor, Loki also nearly destroys Asgard many times over!

Young Loki

Kid Loki

Lady Loki

AFTER...

REALLY?!

Loki can even trick **himself!** Kid Loki traps his older, more evil self within a **magpie** named **Ikol.**

FAST FACTS

REAL NAME: Loki Laufeyson

STRENGTHS: Cunning, sorcery, astral projection, shape-shifting, inter-dimensional travel

WEAKNESSES: Lust for power, too clever by half—nobody likes a wiseguy!

FOES: Anyone who stands in his way—often Thor and the Avengers

DREAM JOB: Supreme ruler of Asgard

Q: Why does Loki hate his adoptive father, Odin?

A: Loki cannot forgive Odin for killing his **Frost Giant father, Laufey**—even though Laufey **abandoned** Loki as a baby!

"The Age of Odin and his sons is ending... Fire and chaos are coming. **AND I AM THE LORD OF CHAOS!**"

BEST KNOWN FOR TORMENTING HIS BROTHER, THOR, AND TRYING TO DESTROY ASGARD!

Old West outlaw

Teenage trickster

YESSS!! **LOKI** uses an illusion to keep the **FIRE DEMON SURTUR** at bay until his brother, **THOR**, and his father, **ODIN**, can join him and **SAVE ASGARD!**

WOW!

50

The weight in tons that Loki can lift.

WHEN BAD GUYS GO GOOD!

LOKI THE WORTHY
To stop the Red Skull, Scarlet Witch and Doctor Strange cast an inversion spell—turning bad guys good! Loki gets so good, he's worthy to wield Thor's hammer, Mjolnir!

Worthy to wield Thor's hammer

FAST FACTS

REAL NAME:
Nathaniel Richards

STRENGTHS: Futuristic battle armor, high intelligence, skill with technology, combat expertise, political manipulation, slowed aging

WEAPONS: Battle armor fires energy blasts, provides super-strength, enhanced durability; can summon any weapon from the timestream with a finger-snap

FOES: Fantastic Four, Avengers

TOP 7 ITEMS IN KANG'S TROPHY ROOM

CAPTAIN AMERICA'S SHIELDS

THOR'S MJOLNIR

DOCTOR OCTOPUS'S TENTACLES

ULTRON

SILVER SURFER'S SURFBOARD

MAGNETO'S HELMET

WOLVERINE'S ADAMANTIUM SKELETON

REALLY?!

Kang **changes his own timeline** to remove being bullied as a child. Young Nathaniel, seeing Kang as his **villainous fate,** joins the Young Avengers as **Iron Lad!** But after the death of his friend **Cassandra Lang,** he changes into the evil **Kid Immortus!**

IDENTITY CRISIS!

Too many Kangs spoil the timestream! Traveling through time creates loads of alternate Kangs, so Prime Kang sets out with two other Kangs to remove all the others from existence!

S.H.I.E.L.D. DECLASSIFIED

CUNNING OPERATOR
When Kang heads to a new time, he takes on a new persona and blends in well with that era's society and culture. He politically maneuvers or aggressively attacks, with one aim—to conquer!

"All of *HISTORY* is my weapon... I fight with *TIME* itself. You are its *PLAYTHINGS.* I am its *CONQUEROR.*"

WOW!

7,000
The span of years that Kang travels—from Ancient Egypt to the year 4,000. He may journey even farther!

TIME-TRAVELING TYRANT

Born on an **alternative Earth** in the year 3000, Super Villain **Kang** rebuilds Doctor Doom's old **time machine** with one purpose: to conquer all of **space and time!**

TOP 4
Kang Characters

1 **PHARAOH RAMA-TUT**—uses future technology to conquer Ancient Egypt and tries to make Invisible Woman his queen!

2 **VICTOR TIMELY**—mayor of Timely in 20th-century Illinois. Tries to destroy the Avengers with a robotic Spider-Man.

3 **THE SCARLET CENTURION**—tricks the Avengers into hunting Super Heroes and Villains for him!

4 **IMMORTUS**—a possible future version of Kang seeking mastery over all of time.

BEST KNOWN FOR

CONQUERING, TIME TRAVEL, AND HIS BLUE FACE

Kang wants to marry **Princess Ravonna Redslayer** and add her kingdom to his empire, but she declines. Kang **refuses to execute** the princess, so his furious army **kidnaps her!** Kang teams up with **the Avengers** to rescue his lady love.

PRINCE CHARMING

AAARGHH!!! Kang kidnaps the **APOCALYPSE TWINS**, raising the pair with the aim of using them to resurrect the **FOUR HORSEMEN OF DEATH** and cause the **END OF EVERYTHING!**

Q: Why is Kang's face blue?

A: Kang's technologically advanced battle armor makes it *look* like his face is blue! Actually, he is a normal human being from the future.

FAMILY CONNECTIONS

Kang is rumored to be a distant descendant of **Reed Richards** (Mister Fantastic) and possibly of the scientist and sorcerer **Doctor Doom.**

4

The number of times Skull's body is destroyed, only for him to return!

SIN

YECCH!

The Red Skull steals Professor X's body and grafts a piece of the X-Men leader's brain into his own brain to gain some of the prof's psychic powers!

TELL ME MORE!

Adolf Hitler personally manages the training of Johann Shmidt to turn him into the "perfect Nazi." He gives him a hideous red skull mask and, as the Red Skull, Shmidt becomes the Third Reich's secret second-in-command, carrying out Hitler's most evil missions!

FAMILY CONNECTIONS

The Red Skull brings up his daughter, **Sin,** to be a **killing machine.** As a test, he pits her in combat against **Baron Zemo,** planning to choose the victor **as his heir.** Although Sin seemingly **kills the Baron,** the Red Skull **rejects her...** but she soon **claims his mantle!**

DASTARDLY DEED!

Crossbones and **Sin** help the Red Skull assassinate Captain America after the superhuman civil war. **The Winter Soldier** captures Crossbones, but **Sin escapes**—and stabs Cap's beloved, **Sharon Carter!**

FAST FACTS

REAL NAME:
Johann Shmidt

HOME NATION: Germany

STRENGTHS: High intelligence, master military strategist, master of disguise, skilled unarmed combatant and marksman

WEAKNESSES: He's too evil! A lot of Super Villains refuse to ally with Skull because he's a Nazi

ALLIES: Adolf Hitler, Arnim Zola, Crossbones, Doctor Faustus, Hydra, Sin

FOES: Captain America, Avengers, the Winter Soldier

S.H.I.E.L.D. DECLASSIFIED

SKULL AND CROSSBONES
Young neo-Nazi Brock Rumlow dreams of working for his hero, the Red Skull. This comes true when, as Crossbones, he is recruited as Skull's main henchman. Crossbones is an expert martial artist and marksman; he also briefly gains the power to shoot blasts of fire from his face.

FACE OF EVIL

The Red Skull is one of the **most evil men in history.** He **changes his form** and his identity. He's defeated. **He's even killed.** But he always returns with another **dastardly plot!**

"And now a toast...to UNENDING CONQUEST!"

BAD TO THE BONE

The Red Skull is so nasty that even Adolf Hitler is scared of him!

BACK WITH A BANG

After **decades in hibernation,** the Red Skull is revived by **A.I.M.,** but he steals their **Cosmic Cube!** This gives him the power to **change reality.** Luckily, he doesn't have it for long!

CAUGHT IN TWO MINDS

K.G.B. General **Aleksander Lukin** shoots the Red Skull to steal his **Cosmic Cube.** Skull's body dies, but he uses the Cube to trap their minds together— **inside Lukin's body!**

TOP 3

Skull Subordinates

1. **ARNIM ZOLA**—Hitler's personal physician, the man responsible for the Red Skull's frequent body changes.

2. **CROSSBONES (BROCK RUMLOW)**—the Red Skull's head henchman

3. **SIN (SINTHEA SHMIDT)**—Skull's evil daughter and heir.

BEFORE...

THE DUST OF DEATH
Skull's personal chemical weapon kills on contact with the skin—but not before the victim's head tightens and shrivels into a bright red skull!

AFTER

Osborn's business partner, Prof. Mendel Stromm, discovers a formula to enhance human strength. Osborn frames Stromm for stealing and gains control of their company and what will become the Goblin Formula.

GOOD DAY

When Osborn shoots the Skrull Queen Veranke live on TV, he is hailed a hero for ending the Skrulls' Secret Invasion of Earth. The U.S. president even makes the cunning villain head of S.H.I.E.L.D.!

WHEN BAD GUYS GET WORSE!

Osborn becomes U.S. security chief and renames S.H.I.E.L.D. H.A.M.M.E.R. He also dons one of Tony Stark's Iron Man suits and names himself the Iron Patriot, leading a new team of Dark Avengers. Osborn hopes to present himself to the world as a combination of Iron Man and Captain America, but his evil side soon resurfaces!

GOBLIN GOONS

The Goblin Nation are followers of the Green Goblin, wearing Goblin-themed garb and using Osborn's Goblin technology.

TOP 5

Goblin Formula Effects

1 SUPERHUMAN STRENGTH —as well as enhanced speed, reflexes, and endurance!

2 REGENERATION—heals quickly: Osborn has even grown back lost limbs and organs!

3 SUPERIOR INTELLIGENCE —Osborn was already smart, but the formula makes him a genius!

4 INSANITY—Osborn must wear drug patches on his skin to keep sane, though they don't always seem to work very well!

5 ALTERED APPEARANCE —Norman may look the same in this universe (he wears a mask when Green Goblin), but other people are not so lucky!

INSANE AND LOVING IT!

Norman Osborn is the unbelievably wealthy chief of tech company **OsCorp**. He's been **head of U.S. security**, but he's really motivated by **greed** and an unquenchable **thirst for power**. Oh, and he **really hates** Spider-Man, too!

WOW!

$1 million

Daily Bugle's bounty for Spider-Man's capture on behalf of Norman Osborn.

FAST FACTS

FULL NAME: Norman Virgil Osborn

ALIASES: Green Goblin, Iron Patriot, Goblin King

STRENGTHS: Ruthless businessman, cunning strategist, skilled in chemistry, electronics, engineering, and genetics

WEAKNESSES: Goblin Formula has alarming side effects that undermine his schemes

ALLIES: Makes brief alliances with other villains, but he's only looking out for himself!

ENEMIES: Spider-Man, Iron Man, Captain America, Avengers

"Now... just between me and you, here's my little *SECRET*. Here's what it all *MEANS*...

S.H.I.E.L.D. DECLASSIFIED

OSBORN'S DOWNFALL
U.S. security chief, Osborn organizes an illegal attack on Asgard, which is floating in the sky above Broxton, Oklahoma. Not one but two Captain Americas—and many other heroes—try to foil his plan, but Asgard is destroyed. By now, it is clear to everyone that Osborn is crazy with power and he is sacked in disgrace.

BEST KNOWN FOR POWER-MAD SCHEMES AND PLOTTING SPIDEY'S DOOM

FAMILY CONNECTIONS
One complicated, messed-up family!

NORMAN OSBORN
Criminally insane patriarch

HAROLD "HARRY" OSBORN
Son of Norman and wife Emily, who dies after Harry is born. Troubled Harry follows in Norman's freaky footsteps as Green Goblin and joins his Avengers team as American Son.

GWEN STACY
Mother of Goblin-Formula-infected twins Gabriel and Sarah after secret affair with Norman. Gwen wants Norman to keep away from her kids. Killed by Norman as Green Goblin, who blames Peter Parker.

GABRIEL STACY
Joins Norman's Dark Avengers team as the second American Son. Goblin Formula eventually drives him insane.

SARAH STACY
Daughter Sarah tries to use her abilities for good!

...The bad guys *ALWAYS* win."

YECCH!

After losing control of H.A.M.M.E.R. and suffering repeated defeats, Norman becomes the Goblin King. His "realm" becomes the New York City sewer system!

"Venom wants to PLAY!"

AAAARRGHH!! The Venom symbiote busts Eddie Brock out of jail and leaves behind **AN OFFSPRING**. This bonds with Brock's cellmate, violent **CLETUS KASADAY**, who becomes the **RAMPAGING VILLAIN CARNAGE**.

Q: What is a Symbiote?

A: It's one of a species of **alien parasites** called the **Klyntar**. A symbiote **sets out to be good,** but if it bonds with a less-than-perfect host, it becomes **vicious and violent.**

WHEN GOOD GUYS GO BAD!

Eddie Brock is a respected journalist until he pens an exposé blaming an innocent man for a crime that is later solved by Spider-Man. Brock blames Spidey for his downfall, making him an ideal host for the sneaky Venom symbiote!

BEST KNOWN FOR

POSSESSING SPIDER-MAN'S POWERS—ALONG WITH SHARP TEETH AND A TERRIBLE TONGUE

Q: How does Spidey get rid of the symbiote?

A: With the help of **Reed Richards,** Spider-Man discovers that the symbiote can't stand loud noises, such as **the clanging of church bells.**

ALTERNATE UNIVERSE

A **pig version** of Venom named **Pork Grind** faces off against Peter Porker, the **Spectacular Spider-Ham!**

VENOM

The Venom symbiote bonds with Eddie Brock to create one of Spider-Man's most deadly foes.

CARNAGE

Criminal Cletus Kasaday is the symbiote's host in this crazy and very deadly partnership.

TOXIN

Ex-cop Pat Mulligan succeeds Eddie Brock as Toxin and becomes an ally of the Avengers.

ANTI-VENOM

This mindless creature forms from the remnants of the Venom symbiote in Eddie Brock's blood.

Power Up!

CHANGEUP
Exposed to crime Mister Negative's inverting touch, Eddie Brock's skin transforms part of the Venom symbiot into Anti-Venom, capable of "curing" Spider-Man of his powers—and much more, too!

S.H.I.E.L.D. DECLASSIFIED

AGENT VENOM
War hero Corporal Eugene "Flash" Thompson loses his legs fighting in Iraq and the government selects him to be Agent Venom—a super agent harnessing the power of a subdued Venom symbiote. He is outfitted with a "kill switch" in case he loses control!

BAD DAY
Trapped on **an alien Battleworld** in a tattered costume, Spider-Man dons what he believes to be a suit of **alien fabric,** but he soon discovers that **the suit is alive!**

HOMESICK SUIT
Flash Thompson's control over his symbiote suit becomes increasingly erratic after he joins the Guardians of the Galaxy. The symbiote even hijacks the Guardians' ship and takes it to its home planet!

VENOMIZED!

Spider-Man thinks his **cool black suit** is just an **alien costume**—until it begins to **control him!** He gets rid of this **symbiote,** but it moves on, creating the **villain Venom**—and **even worse foes.**

COST-EFFECTIVE
One of the **major perks** of the Venom symbiote? A **self-replenishing supply** of webbing. No risk of **running out mid-swing** between two skyscrapers.

ARMS CRISIS!

Otto Octavius was the genius son of a brutal construction worker. He becomes a top scientist, but his **power-mad ambitions** lead him to become the villainous **Doctor Octopus** and a **bitter foe** of **Spider-Man!**

HANDLE WITH CARE!

Otto's four mechanical **titanium** tentacles can each perform a different task simultaneously.

AAAARRGHH!!

KAINE, a crazy clone of Peter Parker, appears out of nowhere and **BUMPS OFF** Doc Ock! The poor doctor had just **SAVED** Peter's life!

NUMBER CRUNCH!

360°
Spinning rotation of each tentacle's pincers

245lbs (111kg)
Otto's weight

50mph (80kph)
Speed when walking on tentacles

5in (13cm)
Diameter of Otto's tentacles

6–25ft (1.8–7.6m)
Distance Otto's arms extend

61mph (98kph)
Speed Otto's tentacles can strike

WHAT?!

Prison doctors remove Doc Ock's tentacles. Little do they know... he can **mentally control** his arms! He gets them back—simply by sending the **thought impulse**: "Return to your master!"

WHEN BAD GUYS GO GOOD!

SUPERIOR SPIDEY!
Doc Ock's health is failing. Before he dies, he swaps minds with Peter Parker, so Peter dies in Doc Ock's body and Ock takes over Spider-Man's body. Doc Ock becomes the "Superior Spider-Man," aiming to be a better hero than Peter Parker ever was!

WOW!

900

The distance in miles (1,448km) Otto can telepathically control his tentacles.

FAST FACTS

REAL NAME:
Dr. Otto Octavius

ALIASES: Doctor Octopus, Doc Ock, Master Planner

ALLIES: Sinister Six, Masters of Evil, Charlotte Witter

ENEMIES: Spider-Man

STRENGTHS: Intellect (gifted in science and engineering), four mechanical tentacles

WEAKNESSES: Poor eyesight, failing health

REALLY?!

Doc Ock rents a room from Peter Parker's Aunt May. When he learns she's set to inherit a nuclear reactor, Otto tries to **marry her!**

GOOD DAY

Sometimes Doc Ock **really scores!** During their first encounter at Bliss Private Hospital, Doc Ock beats Spider-Man so badly that Spidey **wants to retire!** When the Fantastic Four decline to fight him, Doc Ock appears to have **won...**

UPGRADED!

Doc Ock upgrades from four to eight tentacles and then tries to control all the electronics in New York City!

TELL ME MORE!

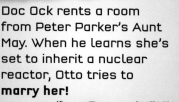

Doc Ock doesn't always battle Spidey alone... he forms the Sinister Six—himself plus Vulture, Electro, Kraven, Lizard, and Mysterio—to try to destroy the web-slinger!

"With such power and my brilliant mind, I'm the **SUPREME** being on Earth!"

BEFORE...

"Mad scientist" Doc Ock has a suitably loopy fashion sense that changes with the times without ever achieving cool!

Otto begins his villainous career in a green jumpsuit and unflattering "bowl" haircut.

He then attempts classy, with a white suit and sunglasses. Still the same bad haircut!

More recently, Otto has sported a flowing trench coat and weird slicked-back hair.

AFTER...

REALLY?!

When the **renegade heroes of Nextwave** visit the town of Shotcreek, they discover that it's being attacked by **Rorkannu** and **his army of Mindless Ones**. Rorkannu could be Dormammu's **long-lost twin brother...**

Q: Who are the Mindless Ones?

A: These **one-eyed brutes** inhabit the fringes of the **Dark Dimension** and destroy everything they can with their stony fists and eye-beams. Dormammu sets up **magical barriers** to stop them from **destroying** the entire **Dark Dimension!**

DOUBLE TROUBLE

DORMAMMU & LOKI
This devious duo cook up a plan to get the Avengers and Defenders fighting over the mystic **Evil Eye of Avalon.** When Loki betrays Dormammu, the Dread One **ensnares him** with magic—but then the Scarlet Witch **traps Dormammu** in the Evil Eye!

Umar Loves Hulk!
Umar likes her men tall, green, and angry! When Hulk is close to destroying Earth, she takes him to the Dark Dimension as her new husband. She gets a "handsome" new king, and the Hulk has fun smashing Mindless Ones!

FAMILY CONNECTIONS

Clea

Doctor Strange

Umar

Dormammu's **sister, Umar,** is sometimes his ally and sometimes his rival! Umar has a **daughter** named **Clea.** Unlike her mother and uncle, Clea rejects evil. She falls for **hunky Doctor Strange** when he visits Dormammu's Dark Dimension!

BACK FROM THE DEAD!

Dormammu and his sister Umar have a **love-hate** relationship! Dormammu kills Umar —but she is brought back by the power of **a wishing well!**

AAARRGHH!!
Doctor Strange stops **THE MINDLESS ONES** from invading Dormammu's domain and makes him promise to leave Earth alone. Dormammu **SWEARS REVENGE!**

FAST FACTS

REAL NAME: Dormammu

ALIASES: The Dread One, Lord of the Dark Dimension

SPECIES: Faltine (magical entities from another reality)

STRENGTHS: Total mastery of magic; can draw on the power of his worshippers and the magical energies of the Dark Dimension itself!

WEAKNESS: Ruling one dimension just isn't enough!

FOES: Doctor Strange, the Ancient One, Clea, Celestials, Eternity

"No mere mortal can overcome **DORMAMMU!**"

TOP 5
Dormammu Defeats

1 **DORMAMMU**—challenges Doctor Strange to a fight in front of the other Lords of the Netherworld, but is outwitted by the Sorcerer Supreme.

2 **DORMAMMU**—attacks the mighty cosmic being Eternity and, after a battle that nearly destroys the universe, is crushed between two planets!!

3 **DOCTOR STRANGE**—tricks Dormammu into going through a portal to Earth, thus breaking his mystic oath to leave the Earth alone! Violating this oath drains his power!

4 **DORMAMMU**—traps the Earth spirit Gaea and tries to conquer Earth, but Umar helps Doctor Strange banish him from our world!

5 **DOCTOR STRANGE AND CLEA**—lead a rebellion against Dormammu and Clea takes his Dark Dimension throne!

BETWEEN...

Marvel's Stan Lee made up the name Dormammu as something cool for Dr. Strange to say when spell-casting. Fans wanted to know more, and the Dread One debuted in *Strange Tales* #126 (November 1964).

...THE PANELS

TELL ME MORE!

Plokta, a demonic Dark Dimension entity, creates the Mindless Ones from the souls of people trapped in an apartment block in Birmingham, U.K.!

Power Up!

ABSORBING THE ENEMY
When **UMAR AND BARON MORDO** take over the Dark Dimension, a mysterious Faltine helps **CLEA** fight them. It is actually **DORMAMMU** in disguise! He absorbs Mordo and Umar and becomes **EVEN MORE POWERFUL!**

DREAD LORD

This flame-headed, **mystical ruler** of the hellish **Dark Dimension** is pure evil. **Dormammu** is obsessed with **conquering Earth** and destroying its Sorcerer Supreme, **Doctor Strange!**

BARONS OF BAD

FULL NAME:
Baron Heinrich Zemo

BIRTHPLACE: Castle
Zemo, Germany

STRENGTHS: Scientific
genius, slowed aging,
expert marksman and
swordfighter

WEAKNESSES: Obsessive
hatred for Captain America,
crazy for power

ALLIES: Masters of Evil,
Baron von Strucker, Red
Skull

FOES: Captain America,
Nick Fury and his Howling
Commandos, Fantastic
Four, Invader

Q: What's with the mask?

A: During **World War II**,
Heinrich Zemo is Hitler's
greatest **scientist**. After
Heinrich's **death ray** kills
hundreds of Germans, he
becomes such a **hated
figure** in his own country that
he starts wearing a **purple
hood** to conceal his identity!

Q: Why does Zemo age so slowly?

A: **Compound X!** Heinrich
invents this serum to preserve
his **youth** and keep him in
prime physical condition.
His son Helmut **bathes** in it!

GOOD DAY

Heinrich **captures Cap**
and ties him to a **plane**
which explodes over
the **Arctic.** Heinrich
believes he has **finally
killed** his archenemy!
But Cap survives,
after being **frozen in
ice** for decades...

AAARRGHH!!
Heinrich is **DAZZLED**
by light reflecting off of Captain
America's shield and misfires his
weapon—bringing a **DEADLY
LANDSLIDE** of **ROCKS**
crashing down on himself!

BARON
HEINRICH ZEMO

*"I warn you... it is
DANGEROUS to pry
into Zemo's secrets!"*

HANDLE WITH CARE!

Heinrich develops an indestructible
glue, Adhesive X, to immobilize
Allied troops. When Captain America
breaks a vat of Adhesive X with his
shield, the glue **spills** all over
Heinrich's head and **sticks** his hood
permanently to his face!

There is more than one **Baron Zemo** and **both** are bitter foes of **Captain America!** Baron **Heinrich** Zemo is an **evil genius** and **war criminal,** and his son, **Helmut,** is a **lawless opportunist** on a mission to **avenge his father!**

FAST FACTS

FULL NAME:
Baron Helmut Zemo

BIRTHPLACE: Leipzig, Germany

STRENGTHS: Slowed aging, expert combatant, more cunning than his dad

WEAKNESSES: Overconfidence—taking over the world is never easy!

ALLIES: Songbird, Moonstone, Atlas, Masters of Evil, Thunderbolts, Hydra

FOES: Captain America, Bucky Barnes, Norman Osborn, Doctor Doom, Avengers

YEGGH!

Helmut tries to boil Cap in a vat of Adhesive X. The Baron's face gets splashed with glue and ends up **horribly scarred,** looking like **drippy melted wax!**

HANDLE WITH CARE!

Helmut gets hold of **twin gems** named "moonstones," which are actually **Kree lifestones.** They allow him to travel across **space and time,** and **between dimensions.** When the stones get cracked, however, they hurl Helmut through a **time vortex!**

FAMILY CONNECTIONS

Helmut's wife, Hieke, is a villain known as the **Baroness.** She once claimed to be a **reincarnation** of Heinrich Zemo in a **woman's body…** and it may even be the truth! The happy couple adopt **25 children,** the **Kinder,** whom they **brainwash** to **hate** Captain America!

BARON
HELMUT ZEMO

*"**GUIDE** my hand, my father—as I avenge your **DEATH!**"*

BAD DAY

Helmut and his **Masters of Evil** team are the first to destroy the **Avengers' Mansion.** But his triumph is shortlived—Helmut is defeated in battle and appears to **fall to his death** from the **roof…**

The underworld will now be run like a *BUSINESS*... and the *CHAIRMAN OF THE BOARD* will be ... *THE KINGPIN!*

 TELL ME MORE!

Kingpin Wilson Fisk may look fat and out of shape, but he is actually 420lbs (191kg) of solid muscle! Fisk is also a martial arts master—he regularly beats up a gang of burly bruisers as part of his fitness program. Mess with him at your peril!

HANDLE WITH CARE!

The Kingpin's **jeweled walking stick** contains a nasty surprise—its inbuilt **disintegrator ray** can **vaporize** an opponent!

TOP **5**

Kingpin's Flawed Henchmen

1 ELEKTRA
PROS: a highly trained ninja assassin
CONS: has a thing for Kingpin's nemesis, Daredevil

2 BULLSEYE
PROS: an incredibly accurate assassin
CONS: better at killing than following orders

3 NUKE
PROS: a Captain America-style super-soldier
CONS: goes out of control and devastates Manhattan

4 TYPHOID MARY
PROS: a mutant with amazing psychic powers
CONS: dangerously crazy and seriously unpredictable

5 SANDMAN
PROS: his ability to turn to sand is a powerful weapon
CONS: keeps getting outsmarted by Spider-Man

NOOOOO!!! **PETER PARKER** reveals that he is actually **SPIDER-MAN** and **THE KINGPIN** sends a sniper to shoot him. The bullet hits **AUNT MAY** instead!

TOP CRIME BOSSES

KINGPIN

A hugely powerful, ambitious, and ruthless criminal genius

THE ROSE

Kingpin's son Richard Fisk tries to take over dad's operation

HAMMERHEAD

Violent, retro-styled mobster with a steel-plated head

SILVIO "SILVERMANE" MANFREDI

Aging Maggia boss who turns himself into a cyborg to cheat death

COUNT NEFARIA

Gains the powers of Whirlwind, Living Laser, and Power Man

MADAME MASQUE

The daughter of Count Nefaria, her gold mask hides a scarred face

TOMBSTONE

Lonnie Lincoln files his teeth to points, making him even more scary

JUSTIN HAMMER

Criminal genius specializing in financial wheeling and dealing

THE HOOD

Parker Robins gains superpowers from the demon Dormammu

MR. NEGATIVE

Controls the Darkforce to shape-shift and also brainwash people

HEADBANGER!
The **gangster** Hammerhead **takes out** enemies with his reinforced **steel skull!**

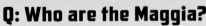

Q: Who are the Maggia?

A: **The Maggia** originated in southern Europe and is now a **major power** in the U.S. underworld. Members promise to **keep silent** about group activities, on **pain of death.** There are three rival Maggia "families," each led by a notorious mobster: the **Silvermane** family, the **Nefaria** family, and the **Hammerhead** family.

WHO'S THE BOSS?

These **crime lords** are cunning, ruthless, and command gangs of henchmen, making them **dangerous foes.** Some even find ways to **boost their power,** becoming Super Villains able to battle the champions of justice **one-on-one!**

MAGICAL MENACES

From **demons** and **godlike beings** to **evil magicians,** the universe is **constantly under threat** from sorcerous villains. All that stands between Earth and **certain destruction** is a handful of courageous **mystic heroes,** armed with a library of **awesome spells!**

REALLY?!

The sorceress **Morgan le Fay** first meets **Doctor Doom** and **Iron Man** in the time of **King Arthur**—and mistakes the time-traveling duo for **armored knights!** The evil Morgan and "Lord Doom" **join forces,** but are defeated by "**Sir Iron Man!**"

BETWEEN...

The demon Thog the Nether-Spawn was once defeated by Marvel Comics writer Steve Gerber! Steve wrote *Man-Thing* #22 (October 1975), in which he and Man-Thing save the universe from Thog!

...THE PANELS

BAD DAY

Magician Baron Mordo is a student of the wise Ancient One, but, **hungry for power,** he plots to **kill his master.** Doctor Strange **saves the day**—and becomes Mordo's mortal enemy!

Power Up!

BLACK MAGIC
Villains Baron Mordo and Dormammu both **HATE** Doctor Strange, so they make a deal: Dormammu gives Mordo unlimited magical power—so he can **DESTROY** the Sorcerer Supreme!

AAARRGHH!!

The sorcerer **BELASCO** plans to sacrifice **SHANNA THE SHE-DEVIL** to bring the evil **ELDER GODS** back to Earth. Shanna's boyfriend **KA-ZAR** saves her—so the Elder Gods imprison him in Limbo!

Power Up!

DEMON HULKBUSTER!

Doctor Strange tries to use the demon **ZOM** to stop a rampaging Hulk, but **SETS ZOM FREE!** Zom takes over the Hulkbuster armor and seems unbeatable—until his spirit is captured by Strange's loyal assistant, **WONG!**

AAARRGHH!!

CHONDU THE MYSTIC has had a lot of bodies! His mind is put into the hero **NIGHTHAWK**, then into a **FAWN**, before he ends up in a **TENTACLE-ARMED MONSTER BODY!**

TOP 5

MERLIN WANNABES

Several magicians have claimed to be the legendary Merlin!

MERLYN—an Omniversal Guardian and advisor to Captain Britain.

MAD MERLIN—a villain who battled Thor while pretending to be Merlin, and later fought the X-Men as "Warlock" and "Maha Yogi."

COSMIC MERLIN—a mysterious figure who once helped Captain Britain.

ALIEN MERLIN—fought the Avengers, and turned out to be an evil shape-shifting Dire Wraith!

ALBION—this member of the Knights of Pendragon may actually be a reincarnation of the legendary wizard!

Enchantress

HOW ENCHANTING!

Asgardian sorceress Enchantress uses her power and beauty to get her way. She often tricks the Executioner into helping her, but her main target is Thor, whom she thinks should rule Asgard—with her by his side!

TEAM PLAYER

Enchantress disguises herself as the hero **Valkyrie** and recruits a **woman-only team of Avengers**. Naming themselves the **Lady Liberators**, they take on the Avengers to prove they are **just as strong** as Earth's Mightiest Heroes!

DOUBLE TROUBLE

CALYPSO & KRAVEN

Voodoo priestess Calypso is obsessed with helping Kraven the Hunter kill Spider-Man. She uses a magical drum and mind-bending poisons to weaken Spidey, but Kraven lets him go when he realizes Calypso is using magic—Kraven likes a fair fight!

FAST FACTS

MONSTERS: Carrion (Malcolm McBride), Lizard (Dr. Curtis Connors)

MATTER MANIPULATORS: Graviton (Franklin Hall)

ENERGY BEINGS: Klaw (Ulysses Klaw), Living Laser (Arthur Parks)

SUPER SCIENTISTS: Grey Gargoyle (Paul Duval), Molten Man (Mark Raxton)

HANDLE WITH CARE!

Klaw **assassinates** Black Panther (T'Chaka), but **loses** to his sucessor, T'Challa. To become stronger, he swaps his hand for a **sonic blaster** and jumps into a sonic conversion device, becoming a being of **living sound.**

TOP 6
SCIENTIFIC SUPERPOWERS

GREY GARGOYLE—turns victims to stone for one hour with a touch of his right hand.

THE LIZARD—regrows severed limbs and telepathically controls other reptiles.

MOLTEN MAN—emits heat and harmful radiation.

GRAVITON—power over gravity; he can fly, and crush opponents into the ground!

KLAW—made of living sound; creates other objects made of pure audio.

LIVING LASER—made entirely of photons; uses his own body as a weapon.

Power Up!
FUN WITH LASERS!

Tony Stark believes **ARTHUR PARKS** has been killed in an explosion. In fact, Tony's Iron Man suit has accidentally **CAPTURED** Arthur's scattered particles. Arthur then re-forms as the **LIVING LASER!**

NUMBER CRUNCH!

575lbs (261kg)
Weight gained by Paul Duval when he becomes Grey Gargoyle

550lbs (249kg)
Lizard and Molten Man's weight

500°F (260°C)
Maximum temperature Molten Man can withstand

70mph (113kph)
Lizard's tail whip speed

40 tons
Heaviest weight Molten Man can lift

STONE COLD VILLAINY

Chemist **Paul Duval** spills a potion on his hand, turning it to **living stone.** He gains the ability to **transform his entire body** into living stone, and turn others into **statues** with a **single touch!** In stone form, Duval gains vast **strength** and **durability** as the indestructible criminal **Grey Gargoyle!**

BEFORE...

ARMED AND DANGEROUS!

After Dr. Curtis Connors loses his arm in the military, he becomes obsessed with reptiles that can regrow limbs and develops a serum using their DNA. The serum regrows his arm, but turns him into the giant Lizard!

AFTER...

YECCH!

The original "living corpse" known as Carrion (a clone of Jackal, Miles Warren) creates a tentacled Spider-Amoeba using Peter Parker's DNA. Spider-Man throws the monster at Carrion—and it eats him!

BAD SCIENCE

Viruses, chemicals, serums, radiation, toxic pollutants, alien alloys... By **scientific slipup** or **risky experiment**, these **dangerous substances** can turn normal people into **misfits, monsters, and super-powered villains!**

WHEN GOOD GUYS GO BAD!

IF YOU CAN'T BEAT 'EM—JOIN 'EM!
At first, kindly Dr. Curtis Connors tries to resist the Lizard inside. Eventually, he uses the Lizard as an excuse to do evil. He even transforms his son into a lizard sidekick!

WOW!

186,282

The speed Living Laser can travel in miles per second (299,792km per second).

TELL ME MORE!

Scientist Mark Raxton develops a liquid metallic alloy from a radioactive meteor, but spills it on himself and transforms into the villainous Molten Man. His step-sister, Liz (Harry Osborn's wife), helps him reform, but he doesn't lose his fiery temper!

TOP 10

Bad Scientists

1 M.O.D.O.K. — creates Red Hulk and Red She-Hulk.

2 TINKERER — creates the whip-like, spiked, poisonous tail of the villain Scorpion.

3 PROF. SPENCER SMYTHE — invents various Spider-Slayer robots to attack Spider-Man.

4 JACKAL — creates clones to challenge, confuse, and menace Spidey!

5 DR. KARL MALUS — invents a control collar to make Werewolf By Night attack Spider-Woman.

6 MAD THINKER — his Awesome Android mimics the physical properties of anything it touches.

7 EGGHEAD — invents a machine to turn ants against Ant-Man!

8 WIZARD — his antigravity disks send three of the Fantastic Four floating away like balloons!

9 MORBIUS — creates an experimental serum that accidentally turns him into a "living vampire."

10 CALVIN ZABO — his "Hyde formula" enhances strength, but induces violent rages.

BEST KNOWN FOR

BEING TOO CLEVER FOR THEIR OWN GOOD—AND EVERYONE ELSE'S!

WOW!

750

Evil humanoid supercomputer M.O.D.O.K.'s weight in lbs (340kg).

NOooooo!!

WIZARD captures Carnage and tries to turn him into his own EVIL AGENT. He transfers the symbiote into the body of DR. KARL MALUS, but the plan soon goes HORRIBLY WRONG!

IDENTITY CRISIS?

The Jackal creates a virus that gives everyone in Manhattan spider powers, robbing Spider-Man of his advantage—and his unique identity!

UPGRADED!

When Spencer Smythe's son, Alastair, ends up in a wheelchair, he builds a hideous biomechanical exoskeleton to not only walk, but also destroy Spider-Man—becoming the Ultimate Spider-Slayer!

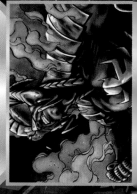

AAARGHH!!

J. Jonah Jameson pays Prof. **Spencer Smythe** to create a **ROBOT** with spider-powers so that Jameson can capture **SPIDEY** himself!

FAST FACTS

EVIL AND LOVING IT:
M.O.D.O.K, Jackal, Dr. Faustus, Mister Hyde, Leader, Mad Thinker, Wizard

SCIENTISTS DOING BAD THINGS: Tinkerer, Prof. Spencer Smythe, Egghead, Red Ghost, Dr. Karl Malus

MAKING AMENDS: Morbius, Maximus

DASTARDLY DEED

Smooth-talking psychiatrist Dr. Faustus tries to drive Captain America nuts. Cap thinks he's back fighting in the dark days of World War II—until Faustus's mind-bending drugs wear off!

HANDLE WITH CARE!

The **Tinkerer** is the most sought-after inventor in the **criminal underworld!** His clients include Hobgoblin, Beetle, Mysterio, Big Wheel, and the Constrictor. He also develops Trapster's arsenal, Grim Reaper's **scythe**, and Diamondback's **throwing diamonds!**

Calvin Zabo—a clever, physically unremarkable medical research scientist.

Mister Hyde—a villain so formidable that Baron Zemo recruits him for his Masters of Evil.

Q: Who are M.O.D.O.K's 11?

A: When M.O.D.O.K. plans to steal a living star and sell it to A.I.M. (then Hydra's scientific wing) for a cool $1 billion, he gathers a team of villains to help: Mandarin, Chameleon (Ultra-Adaptoid in disguise), Spot, Living Laser, Puma, Mentallo, Monica Rappaccini, Armadillo, Rocket Racer, and Nightshade.

LAB RATS!

Every villainous **organization** bent on **world domination** or destruction needs its own evil **genius** to design **doomsday devices,** build superweapons, or **enslave minds!** And sometimes these masterminds go into business for themselves!

BEFORE...

Scientist Calvin Zabo develops a formula to transform himself into Mister Hyde. He gains 200lbs (91kg) of muscle and bone in just 30 seconds and turns into a grotesque, muscular fiend!

BIG-HEADED!

Being exposed to gamma rays covers laborer Samuel Sterns with boils, swells his head, turns him green, and makes him a science genius! As the Leader, he dreams of controlling the Hulk and conquering the world.

IF LOOKS COULD KILL

You **can't always spot** a Super Villain from his or her **appearance**, but these rogues' rough-around-the-edges features are a dead giveaway. They all possess **looks** that could **kill**—sometimes literally!

FAST FACTS

VILLAINOUS VISAGES:
M.O.D.O.K., Gorgolla, 8-Ball, Xemnu, Terror, Karkas, Arnim Zola, the Headmen, Mojo

LETHAL LOOKERS:
Basilisk, the Orb, Skein, the Needle, Doctor Bong

TOP 3

Calling Cards of Pool-Themed Criminal, 8-Ball

1 **INVENTS** a hovercraft shaped like a pool rack.

2 **FIGHTS DO-GOODERS** with a jet-propelled cue-stick and ball bombs.

3 **NAMES** his henchmen after other pool balls!

SPECIAL MOVES

When **Doctor Bong** strikes his **bell-shaped helmet** with his metal ball hand, he can create **powerful vibrations, stun foes,** or even trigger his **teleportation device.**

AAARRGHH!!!
Eight-legged **MOJO** is not just really **UGLY**— on Earth, his whole body acts as an **ANTI-LIFE FORCE** that causes everything to **SHRIVEL UP** and **DIE!**

SPECIAL MOVES

The immortal **Terror** was an ordinary human, until he slew a demon and was cursed to take on its **spiky skin** and **decaying form.** When he **loses a body part,** he exudes an **acid** that loosens a body part from another person and **sticks it** to his **own** body!

WOW!

6

The number of long spikes on Terror's face. He breaks them off to use as weapons and then regrows them!

YECCH!

One of evil scientist **M.O.D.O.K.**'s many doomsday plans revolves around a **living supercomputer** built from his own **cloned brains!**

WHAT?!

She-Hulk defeats the **furry criminal alien Xemnu** by convincing a much bigger alien that Xemnu is a **teddy bear** for it to play with!

TEAM PLAYER

Elderly tailor **Josef Saint** loses an eye in a mugging, but discovers he can **paralyze people** with his remaining one! He renames himself the **Needle** and joins the **Night Shift** villain group.

Power Up!

THE EYES HAVE IT

Basilisk's **GLEAMING RED EYES** project energy beams that can **FLASH-FREEZE** or **SUPERHEAT** his foes and also **LEVITATE** Basilisk and move him through the air!

MONSTER MASH

It's behind you! From **killer crabs** and **city-sacking beasts** to a **creepy monster** that appears out of a **painting** —many of these creatures are the **stuff of nightmares.** That's **bad news** for even the **toughest** of Super Heroes!

REALLY?!

A pilot crashes on **Easter Island** in the Pacific and learns a terrible secret! The **giant statues** for which the isle is famous are actually **rocky-skinned aliens** named **Lithodia Rexians,** and they are planning to **take over Earth.** Even worse, when the pilot tries to warn people, they think he's **crazy!**

Titano

Gomdulla

S.H.I.E.L.D. DECLASSIFIED

ISLAND ISOLATION
Weird beasties of all kinds roam free on Monster Isle, off the coast of Japan. The Fantastic Four in particular use this jumbo-sized wildlife preserve to keep creatures they've captured from doing any more damage!

WOW!

18,000,000,000

The weight of the Apocalypse Beast in tons. This 3-mile-high (4.8km) multi-eyed alien is the terror of Tokyo!

6 MONSTER-DEFEATING TECHNIQUES

1 **FLYSWATTER**—shape-shifter alien Zogg turns into a housefly and gets squished!

2 **TERMITES**—a swarm nibbles the wooden alien Groot to kindling!

3 **OFF SWITCH**—Gomdulla can be deactivated by pressing a button on his right foot!

4 **GLACIER**—Titano is stuck solid when he gets trapped in Arctic ice!

5 **ANTS**—Grottu, King of the Insects, is foiled when his own "followers" turn against him.

6 **QUICKSAND**—Troublesome Googam is helpless when he gets stuck in mud!

TOP 5 Awesome Creatures

1 **FIN FANG FOOM, HE WHOSE LIMBS SHATTER MOUNTAINS AND WHOSE BACK SCRAPES THE SUN**—a fire-breathing alien dragon-beast.

2 **IT, THE LIVING COLOSSUS**—a statue that comes to life and smashes up Moscow and Los Angeles!

3 **GOMDULLA THE LIVING PHARAOH**—a massive mummy with a very bad attitude!

4 **ZZUTAK, THE THING THAT SHOULDN'T EXIST**—a monster that emerges from a painting created with magic pigments!

5 **TITANO, THE MONSTER THAT TIME FORGOT**—a giant crab from the ocean depths!

THEY AREN'T ALL BAD!
The alien **Googam,** the robotic **Electro,** the primate **Gorgilla,** and the dragon **Fin Fang Foom** are freed from captivity and **give up** their **villainous ways.** When they aren't busy at their day jobs, they fight menaces like the **extra dimensional warlord Tim Boo Ba** as the heroic **Fin Fang Four!**

"That's right, Earthlings... cower before the all-powerful Goom!"

DASTARDLY DEED!
Human-mutants known as the **Deviants** are obsessed with creating **ever-more-horrible monsters.** The Deviant **priest-scientists** enjoy making bizarre mutants to use as **living weapons!**

FAMILY CONNECTIONS
When **big-toothed** alien **Goom** is **arrested** for trying to conquer Earth, he leaves his son **Googam** behind in a cave. Googam soon emerges and tries to **take over the world,** but he proves **just as hopeless** as his dad!

GOOGAM

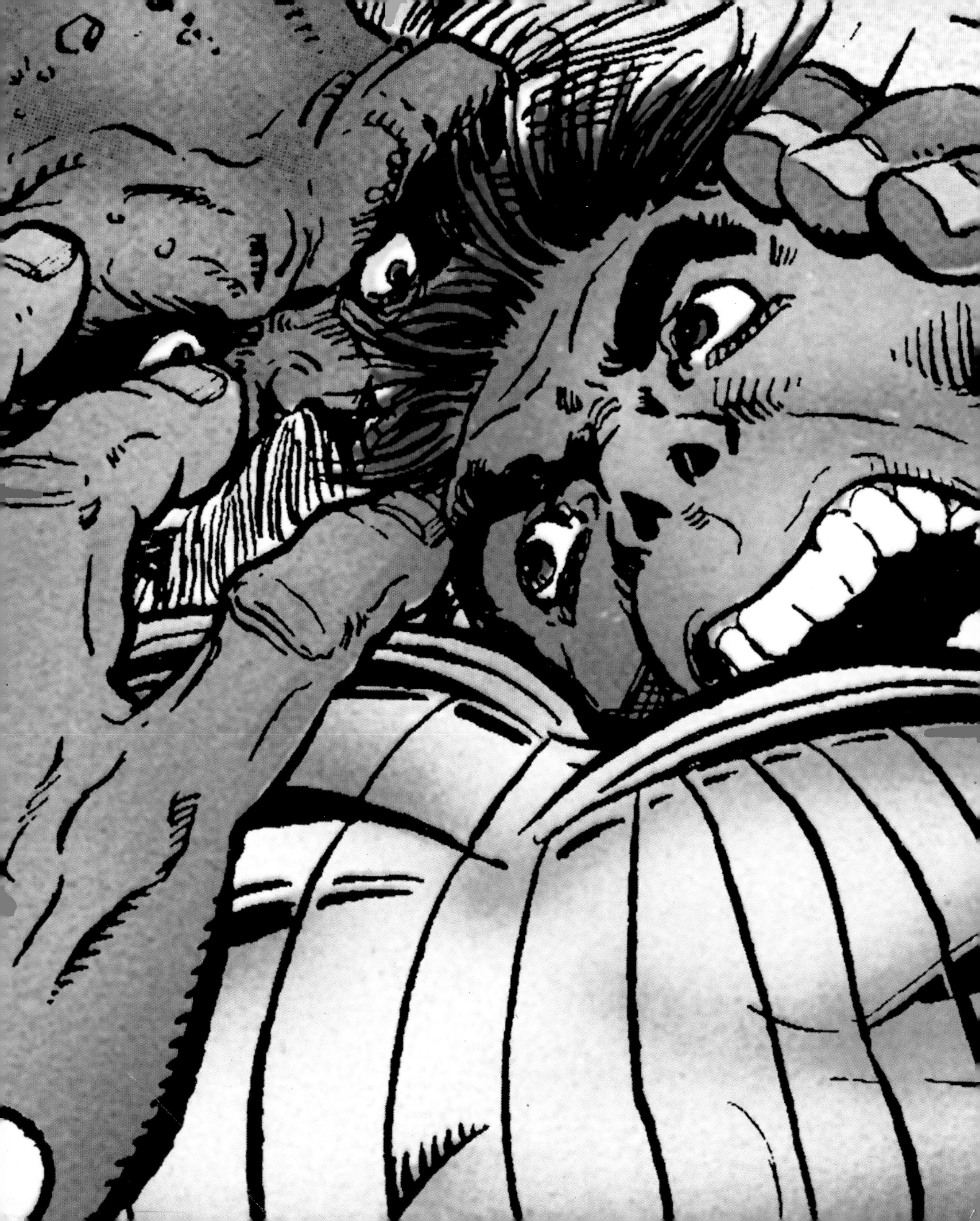

CLASSIC CLASHES

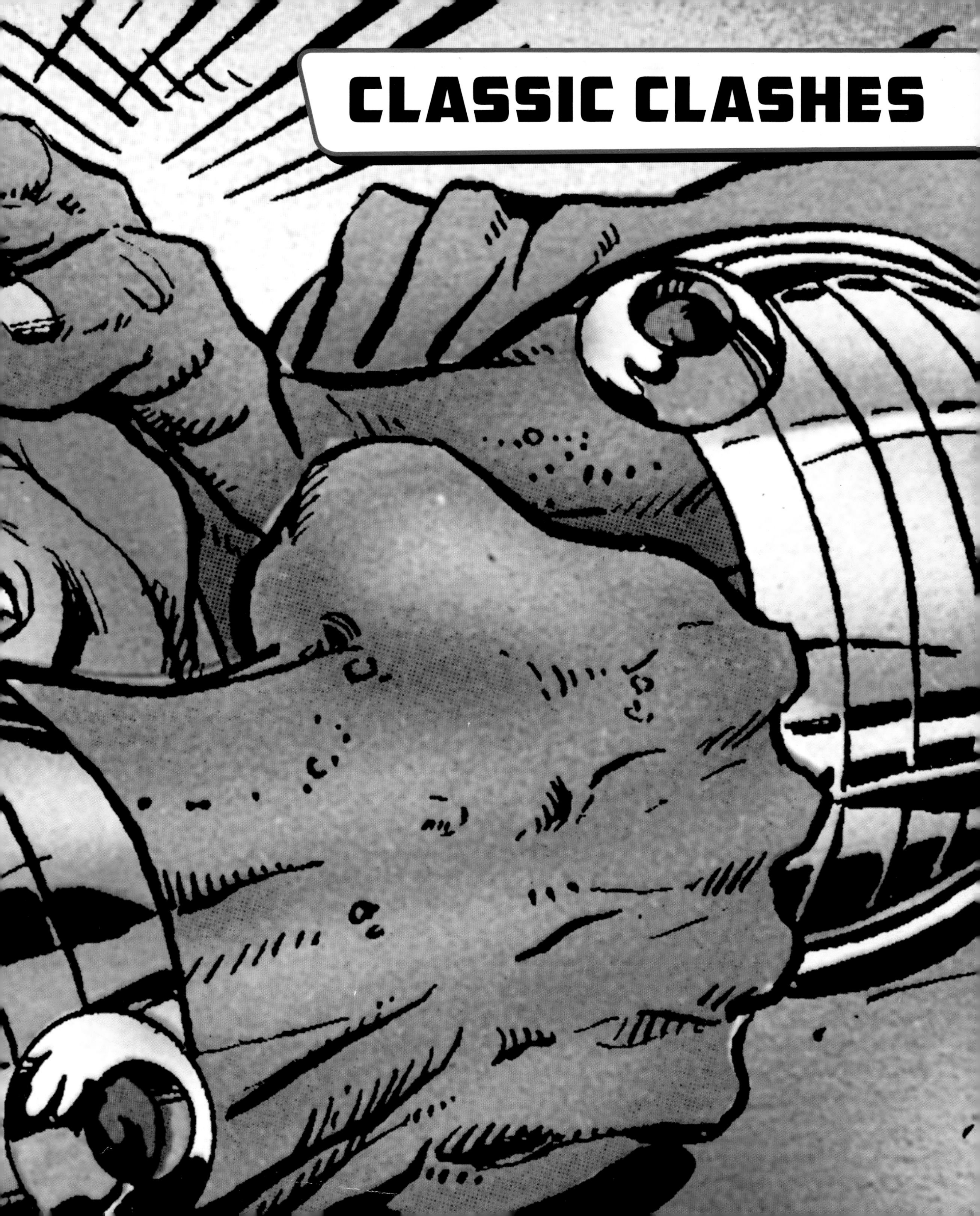

TOP **5**

Hulk's Major Clashes

1 **HULK VS. ABOMINATION** —Abomination attacks a science building, but the janitor, Bruce Banner, turns into Gray Hulk and doses his foe with toxic waste that melts his face!

2 **HULK VS. IRON MAN**— in enhanced Hulkbuster armor, Shellhead tries to stop a world-breaking Hulk on the warpath.

3 **HULK VS. SKAAR AND HIRO-KALA** —it's a bruising first family reunion for father Hulk and the twin warrior sons that he abandoned.

4 **HULK VS. RED HULK** —these bitter, equally matched enemies have a bone-crunching brawl outside the White House.

5 **HULK VS. THING** —an epic rematch across New York, which needs all the Avengers' help to subdue Hulk.

HULK VS. ABOMINATION

Scientific genius alter ego	■ Russian spy alter ego
Mutated by gamma rays	■ Mutated by gamma rays
Can revert to his human form	■ Permanent transformation
Loses human intellect when Hulk	■ Retains his human cunning
Free agent	■ Often used as a pawn by others
Anger increases his strength	■ Fixed maximum strength level

FIGHTS WON: 13   **FIGHTS WON: 0**

HULK WINS!

YECCH!

Who's big, bad, and green? Not who you think. Reptilian-like Abomination has a craggy face, scaly skin, bat ears, ridged back, talons, and split feet. He's not named Abomination for nothing!

BAD DAY

"ARGHHH! IT'S LIKE HITTING A STONE WALL!" The Hulk after punching the tough mass of muscle that is the Thing!

Power Up!

KLUH DESTROY!
Kluh is a Hulk incarnation who emerges when the Hulk is overwhelmed by **SADNESS**. This monstrous menace **TRASHES** the Avengers and only wants to wreak **DEATH** and **DESTRUCTION!**

YECCH!
In a battle between the Ultimate Hulk and Wolverine, the Green Giant pulls his opponent in two—and **throws** the top half miles away. Wolvie will have to spend **months** crawling back to his legs!

Ouch! How do you defeat a furious Hulk? Crawl **into his ear!** One of the Avengers' **smallest** members, the Wasp, climbs in and **zaps** his skull repeatedly with her **sting** power!

TEMPER, TEMPER!

The rampaging Hulk has fought **almost everyone**—from **malevolent monsters** and **earthbound enemies** to **cosmic crusaders.** Yet no matter what they throw at him, the result is the same... you **can't keep Hulk down!**

TOP 4
HULK VS. RHINO BATTLES
Some of the Hulk's wackiest battles have been with this horn-headed henchman!

NOOOOO!!
Hulk declares war on the Illuminati—and he seems unstoppable in his **WORLD-BREAKER** form! It only ends when Hulk **BEGS** Iron Man to use an **ORBITAL LASER** on him—before he destroys the planet!

WHEN GOOD GUYS GO BAD!

WELCOME TO THE TEAM!
Mutant overlord Apocalypse offers to remove **shrapnel** from Hulk's brain if he will serve him. Hulk agrees—and is turned into an armored agent of destruction named War, one of the villainous Horsemen of Apocalypse!

Justin Hammer hires Rhino to **kidnap** Bruce Banner, but he is **KNOCKED OUT** by the Green Giant! Winner: Hulk!

The Leader **possesses** Rhino's **mind** and uses him to fight the Hulk—**IN SPACE!** Winner: Hulk!

SPIDER SMASH!

ALTERNATE UNIVERSE
In an alternate world where the **Spider-Queen** rules Manhattan, the arachnid ruler turns the Hulk into one of her **creepy** servants— the bizarre Spider-Hulk!

Rhino gets a job as a **shopping-mall Santa,** but is attacked by Hulk. **Winner: No one**—a little girl tells them to **STOP FIGHTING!**

The Hulk signs up with a **pro baseball team**—but Rhino is playing for the **opposition** and they end up in **A BIG FIGHT.** Winner: Hulk!

99

BATTLING BROTHERS

Thor and **Loki** take brotherly rivalry to a whole **other level!** It's a power struggle between the heroic **God of Thunder** and the villainous **God of Mischief.** Who will win? **All bets are off!**

"If it's a war you truly desire, Thor—then Loki can happily provide."

"You will pay for what you have done! NOTHING will save you!"

NOOOOO!!

NOOOOO!!

OUTNUMBERED!

Thor is cursed by Hela, Queen of Hel, to be immortal, but unable to heal. Loki sends every villain he can find after his brother—reducing him to an immortal puddle!

REDEMPTION

Loki manipulates Norman Osborn into leading an attack on Asgard. When the city is almost destroyed, Loki realizes he has gone too far. He tries to help the Avengers, only to be killed by the hero Sentry's villainous alter-ego, the Void!

Loki **TRIES TO KILL** Kevin Masterson, son of hero **THUNDERSTRIKE.** Furious, Thor drains Loki's life force—breaking Asgardian law and forcing Odin to **BANISH** his favorite son!

Loki is **BANISHED,** but he wants to battle his brother. To bring Thor to him, he **TRICKS HULK** into causing a train wreck. Thor hunts the trickster down—and walks right into his trap!

TOP 5

Ways to defeat LOKI

1 **ATTACK** him with thunder and lightning
2 **ASSEMBLE** the Avengers
3 **CONVINCE HIM** to fight without magic
4 **TELL ODIN** to force him to stop causing trouble
5 **TEAM UP** with a more powerful magician

TOP 5

Ways to defeat THOR

1 **TRICK HIM** with magic
2 **TELL ODIN** he's being a naughty boy
3 **ATTACK** while he's in one of his human forms
4 **TEAM UP** with a powerful Super Villain
5 **SEPARATE HIM** from his magical hammer, Mjolnir

THOR VS. LOKI

THOR		LOKI
6ft 6in (2m)	•	6ft 4in (1.9m)
640lbs (290kg)	•	525lbs (238kg)
Asgardian	•	Frost Giant
Thunder & lightning	•	Powerful magic
Mjolnir & Belt of Strength	•	Norn Stones
Military skills	•	Cunning & trickery
Hand-to-hand combat	•	Illusions

Thor wins... providing he can get his hands on the trickster!

REALLY?!

Loki turns Thor into a **frog!** This doesn't stop Thor from **hopping all the way to Asgard** and putting Loki in his place!

KAPOW!

Loki creates multiple images of himself to fool Thor, but the Thunder God twirls Mjolnir at the speed of a propeller and blows all the phony Lokis off a cliff!

BAD DAY

Odin is tricked by Loki into banishing Thor from Asgard and taking half of his power away. Loki then gets villain the Tomorrow Man to attack the weakened Thunder God!

DASTARDLY DEED!

If you can't beat up your big brother, try enlisting someone with the Power Cosmic! The Silver Surfer is trapped on Earth for eternity, so Loki offers to free him—if he destroys Thor!

TELL ME MORE!

The reason the brothers fall out is mainly Loki's fault— he's jealous that their father Odin and the other Asgardians like Thor more than him. Loki doesn't help by calling himself the God of Mischief!

WHAT?!

Mandarin wants machines to house the dangerous alien spirits in his rings, so he kidnaps Tony Stark to make them. Tony saves the world by convincing the Mandarin's minions that the Mandarin is insane with power.

WHAT YOU COULD DO WITH THE MANDARIN'S RINGS...

- Turn Iron Man into iron dust with **REMAKER**
- Crush enemies into the ground with **DAIMONIC**
- Keep meddling heroes at bay with **INFLUENCE**
- Turn up the heat with **INCANDESCENCE**
- Trap a foe in a tornado with **SPIN**
- Shock your friends with **LIGHTNING**
- Turn roadblocks to rubble with **SPECTRAL**
- Create illusions with The **LIAR**
- Keep everyone in the dark with **NIGHTBRINGER**
- Freeze foes solid with **ZERO**

DRAGON ALLY

With the help of Makluan dragon **Fin Fang Foom**, one of the Fantastic Four's **most threatening foes**, the Mandarin conquers a sizable chunk of **mainland China**.

TELL ME MORE!

Raised in poverty in China, the Mandarin ventures into the forbidden Valley of the Spirits, where he discovers an abandoned spaceship containing ten rings. They were forged by the dragon-like aliens of Maklu IV.

TONY'S A WINNER!

Despite the **MANDARIN'S WILES** and the **POWER OF HIS RINGS**, he never gets the better of **IRON MAN** for long! Maybe this Super Villain just tries **TOO HARD!**

When the Mandarin's hands are severed, he reintegrates his rings into his body by embedding them in his spine!

YEGGH!

YESSS!! Mandarin has complete mastery over his **CHI**, or vital life-force. When imprisoned by the Chinese government, he survives without food or water—**FOR YEARS!**

BETWEEN...

The Mandarin is one of Tony's oldest foes, debuting in *Tales of Suspense* #50 (February 1964), one year after Iron Man premiered in the same title.

...THE PANELS

"I propose a duel, Iron Man. You against me, *ONE ON ONE.*"

BEHIND THE IRON MASK

Mandarin seeks to **destroy Stark Industries** for years before he discovers that Tony Stark is Iron Man. At one point, the Mandarin **rips off Iron Man's faceplate** only to be **fooled by a rubber mask!**

EXTREME MEASURES

Iron Man Tony Stark has a **big problem** when Mandarin seeks out scientist **Maya Hansen,** Tony's former girlfriend, and attempts to **eliminate** most of the world's population using her **Extremis technology.**

ALTERNATE UNIVERSE

In the **animal-filled alternate reality** of Spider-Ham, the Mandarin is a **ring-tailed lemur** known as **Mandaringtail!**

POWER STRUGGLE!

The Mandarin is Iron Man's **most persistent foe.** This evil genius doesn't go toe-to-toe with **ol' Shellhead** by suiting up in armor. His **ten rings** allow him vast control over **energy and matter!**

GRUDGE MATCH

Green Goblin Norman Osborn and his crazy Goblin dynasty are responsible for the **greatest tragedies** in **Peter Parker's life.** Spider-Man has overcome the Green Goblin **many times**, but there's always a **new Goblin** in town!

BAD DAY
Peter Parker is exposed to the **Goblin Formula** by Norman Osborn. Peter is the only person to resist the **formula's madness...** so far!

REALLY?!
The Green Goblin doesn't always want to **destroy** Spider-Man. Norman actually tries to **brainwash** Peter into becoming his **son!**

TROUBLE WITH HARRY
Norman Osborn's son **Harry** is Peter Parker's friend at university. Things turn sour when Harry **unfairly** blames Spider-Man for his father's death and becomes a **second Green Goblin** to avenge him.

WHEN BAD GUYS GO GOOD!

NEVER TOO LATE
Troubled Green Goblin Harry Osborn defeats Spider-Man and sets a bomb to blow them both up. M.J. arrives with Normie, Harry's little son, and Harry realizes what he's done. He saves M.J., Normie, and Spidey just before the bomb explodes!

TELL ME MORE!
Green Goblin Norman Osborn kidnaps Peter's girlfriend Gwen Stacy and throws her off a bridge. Spidey swears revenge and pursues the Green Goblin. In the fight that follows, the Goblin dies, accidentally impaled on his own Goblin Glider.

"You see, Parker? I always knew I could defeat you *ANY TIME* I wanted..."

TOP 8
Goblins

AAARRGHH!! Sometimes Spider-Man **LOSES** his battles. After the former **SCARLET SPIDER BEN REILLY** assumes the role of Spider-Man, he's killed by the Green Goblin.

1 **THE GREEN GOBLIN**—Norman Osborn, the first Green Goblin and inventor of the Goblin Formula.

2 **THE SECOND GREEN GOBLIN**—Harry Osborn continues his father Norman's legacy.

3 **THE THIRD GREEN GOBLIN**—Harry Osborn's psychiatrist, Bart Hamilton.

4 **THE HOBGOBLIN**—Roderick Kingsley follows Norman Osborn's journals to become the first of many evil Hobgoblins.

5 **THE FOURTH GREEN GOBLIN** and the **SIXTH HOBGOBLIN**—ex-journalist Phil Urich.

6 **MENACE**—Lily Hollister, the occasional girlfriend of both Norman and Harry Osborn.

7 **THE GREY GOBLIN**—Gabriel Stacy needs extra Goblin Formula injections to combat accelerated aging.

8 **CARLIE COOPER**—one of Peter Parker's girlfriends. She discovers a cure for the Goblin Formula!

TOP 5
Goblin Gadgets

PUMPKIN BOMBS Exploding jack-o'-lanterns!

GOBLIN GLASSES Mess with Spidey's senses!

GOBLIN GLOVES Shoot blasts of Goblin sparks!

SONIC TOADS AND ELECTRIC FROGS Little sound and energy bombs!

GOBLIN GLIDER Smashes into people and fires lasers!

Q: Is Norman Osborn always evil?
A: No. When the Green Goblin is thrown against **electrical wiring** while fighting Spidey, the shock gives him **amnesia**. Norman **forgets** his villainous past and even **becomes kind!**

BEFORE

UPGRADED! The Goblin Glider isn't the Goblin's first ride. He originally rode upon a rocket-powered broom!

AFTER

WOW!
300
The top speed of the Green Goblin's glider in miles per hour (483kph).

NEVER-ENDING WAR

Liberty versus **tyranny**, freedom versus force, heroism versus hatred... **Captain America** and **the villainous Red Skull** have waged a **battle** between **good and evil ever since** a **World War II**—and they don't look like **calling it quits** anytime soon!

TEAM PLAYER

Red Skull forms the **Skeleton Crew** to take on Captain America and the Avengers. However, **regular infighting** keeps the team from **reaching their potential**, and the crew wind up in jail!

UPGRADED!

The Red Skull creates Sleeper Robots for the Nazis after their defeat in World War II. He plans to join them together into one giant robot, travel to the North Pole, and then explode the planet's core!

THOOM! THOOM! THOOM! THOOM!

NEVER TOO OLD!

When the Red Skull's **aging process accelerates**, he uses a poison to make Captain America rapidly age, too—hoping to **take Cap to the grave with him!** With only hours to live, Cap **defeats Skull** in hand-to-hand combat—giving him time to find a cure, while **Red Skull dies of old age!**

HANDLE WITH CARE!

Red Skull re-creates a powerful **Cosmic Cube** that can alter the **fabric of reality**—and uses it to **swap bodies with Cap!**

"I damn you Captain America for what you are! We are *DEADLY OPPOSITES* you and I..."

"You **HAVEN'T BEATEN ME** yet, Skull!"

MASTER OF DISGUISE

The Red Skull becomes U.S. **Secretary of State** under the alias **Dell Rusk**. He plots to release **a biological weapon,** the **Red Zone plague,** at Mount Rushmore. Once again, it's a **race against time** for Cap to foil **yet another nefarious plan!**

XESSS!!

When Cap is **CAPTURED** by the Red Skull, the Skull's ally, villainous computer wiz and robotics expert **MACHINESMITH,** downloads all of Cap's memories— and uses them to **FRAME CAP FOR TREASON!**

WHEN GOOD GUYS GO BAD!

TELEVISION TROUBLE

To save New York from the Red Skull's diabolical plans, Captain America vows to serve the villain for one day! His promise is secretly televised, and Cap is branded a traitor!

ALTERNATE UNIVERSE

In the **Ultimate Universe (Earth-1610),** the Red Skull is not a World War II enemy of Captain America, but **his own son!** After his father's death, he is raised and trained on an army base to **succeed Steve Rogers,** but instead he becomes the villainous Red Skull!

BACK FROM THE DEAD?

At the end of World War II, Cap and Skull **battle in Hitler's bunker—** and the Red Skull is **seemingly killed** by a cave-in! An experimental gas keeps Skull alive for decades in **suspended animation,** and he returns **more evil than ever!**

REAL NAME:
Wilson Fisk, alias Kingpin

OCCUPATION: crime boss

SKILLS: sumo wrestling, martial arts, but usually relies on henchmen to do his dirty work

"We need each other, Daredevil... **WE** are the power in this city."

BAD DAY

Fisk uses his knowledge of Matt Murdock's **secret identity** to expose Daredevil to the F.B.I., but his **trumped-up** evidence against Murdock **backfires** and lands them both in jail!

BETWEEN...

Hell's Kitchen is a real-life area of New York City once notorious for crime and violence. It first appears in the Marvel Universe in *Daredevil #1* (April 1964).

...THE PANELS

WHO BEATS WHO?

DAREDEVIL
HEIGHT: 6ft (1.9m)

WEIGHT: 200lbs (91kg)

STRENGTHS:
Superhuman senses, martial arts, legal eagle

KINGPIN
HEIGHT: 6ft 7in (2.1m)

WEIGHT: 450lbs (204kg)

STRENGTHS:
Sumo wrestling skills, legions of henchmen, powerful connections

Despite Kingpin's considerable size and weight advantage, we're going to have to call this one a **draw!**

AAARRGHH!! Daredevil's on-off girlfriend, **KAREN PAGE**, reveals Daredevil's identity to **KINGPIN** who uses the knowledge to make the hero's life a **NIGHTMARE!**

DOUBLE TROUBLE

MURDOCK & FISK

Matt Murdock and Wilson Fisk are both cooling their heels in Ryker's Island prison when they realize that outside forces are trying to pit them against each other. With Bullseye's help, Fisk breaks himself and Murdock out of jail to battle those responsible!

TRAGEDY!

Matt Murdock's college sweetheart, **Elektra**, goes bad and works as an assassin for Kingpin. When she refuses to kill Matt's law partner and friend, **Foggy Nelson**, she is murdered by Kingpin's henchman **Bullseye**. This incident fuels Matt's **hatred** for Kingpin for years.

BEST KNOWN FOR

FIGHTING IN COURT AND ON THE STREETS

KITCHEN DEVILS!

The two most **powerful influences** in New York City's **Hell's Kitchen** are Daredevil, Matt Murdock, and gang boss the Kingpin, Wilson Fisk. They battle for **control of their turf**, one hoping to **protect it,** and the other to **control it.**

HEARTBREAKER!

If you want to **destroy your enemy,** start with their **heart!** Wilson Fisk gets nutty psychic **Typhoid Mary** to romance Matt Murdock and then **dump him.**

AAAARRGHH!!

The monstrous **ABOMINATION** holds his own against Hulk, but he's no match for the ruthless **RED HULK!** The scarlet giant shoots him with a special gun designed to **KILL HULKS!**

ATOMIC POWER!
Rick Jones is a faithful sidekick to the Hulk, Mar-Vell, and Captain America, but after the **Intelligencia** transform him into an **Abomination-like monster** named **A-Bomb,** he stops being so helpful!

YESSS!!

RED HULK declares himself the **RULER OF THE U.S.,** so **THE HULK** knocks him down to size and off his feet with a huge **THUNDER-CLAP!** Green Hulks really are **THE BEST!**

S.H.I.E.L.D. DECLASSIFIED

THE TRANSFORMATIONS OF BETTY ROSS
Bruce Banner's ex-wife Betty Ross is transformed twice by gamma radiation. First she is turned into the winged and wicked Harpy by the evil M.O.D.O.K. Later, after she dies, the Leader uses gamma rays to bring her back as the furious Red She-Hulk.

REALLY?!

Like his Biblical namesake, super-shrink **Doc Samson** draws his power from his **hair!** The longer his **gamma-green** locks grow, the **stronger** he becomes!

ALL-NEW HULK
Amadeus Cho is already a teenage **super genius,** but when a rampaging **sea monster** interrupts his day at the beach, he reveals his **all-new** super-powered gamma form—and becomes the **totally awesome Hulk!**

HULKS SMASH!

The Incredible Hulk isn't the only **muscle-bound monster** created by gamma radiation—there's a **whole family** of bizarre beings you really **don't want to make angry!**

SHE-HULK
Bruce Banner's cousin Jen Walters

RED SHE-HULK
Bruce's former wife, Betty Ross

RED-HULK
Betty's father and Hulk's enemy, General Thaddeus "Thunderbolt" Ross

SAVAGE SHE-HULK
Hulk's daughter Lyra from an alternate future

SKARR
Hulk's long-lost son

WOW!

238,835

The distance Red Hulk can cover in a single bound, in miles (384,400km). He once jumped all the way to Earth from the moon!

BEFORE...

BRAINSTORM
Gamma radiation causes Samuel Sterns to turn into the Leader— a criminal super-genius with a jumbo skull and gamma-powered brain. He tries to up his intelligence and brain size even more, but his experiments mutate him into a giant monster!

...AFTER

SMASH BROTHERS
The Hulk clan **have their differences,** but when they're faced with the menace of **gamma-powered dragon Fin Fang Foom,** the Hulk, Red She-Hulk, A-Bomb, and She-Hulk agree on one thing: it's time to **smash back!**

TITANIC TUSSLE

In the **red corner,** the fearless felon with a **big heart,** and **even bigger fists—Titania!** In the **green corner,** the mean, muscular hero with **a heck of a temper—She-Hulk!** **Let battle commence!**

BEST OF ENEMIES

Titania and the **Absorbing Man** get revenge on **She-Hulk** by infecting her with **mind-controlling microscopic nanites!** Now under their control, She-Hulk joins her enemies on a **rampage through New York!**

WINNER: TITANIA

S.H.I.E.L.D. DECLASSIFIED

TITANIA
Mary "Skeeter" MacPherran is an unpopular teen who dreams of being a glamorous Super Hero. When she is kidnapped to Battleworld during the Secret Wars, Dr. Doom offers to give her superpowers—and she becomes the mighty villainess Titania, obsessed with proving she's stronger than She-Hulk!

GRUDGE MATCH

KRASH!

LUCKY ESCAPE
In their very first fight on Battleworld, Titania knocks She-Hulk down, then gets loads of other villains to help finish the heroine off while she is helpless! If Shulkie's friends hadn't burst in to save her, she would've been a goner!

Winner: TITANIA *(but she cheated!)*

A PERFECT MATCH
While she was on the Beyonder's Battleworld, Titania met the love of her life: bald bad guy Crusher Creel, the Absorbing Man. This villainous couple sometimes consider quitting crime—but never do so for long!

Power Up!

BREAKER OF MEN
In order to cause chaos and destruction, Asgardian villain the **SERPENT** summons the seven hammers of the worthy to Earth. Titania picks one up and becomes the mighty **SKIRN, BREAKER OF MEN!**

DOUBLE DATE!

Luke Cage

Absorbing Man

Titania and the **Absorbing Man** try to rob **a fancy restaurant,** but they bump into She-Hulk on a dinner date with **Luke Cage.** The couples fight, and the Absorbing Man accidentally **knocks Titania out** with his whirling ball and chain!
Winner: SHE-HULK!

"It's not the first blow that counts. It's the **LAST.**"

BETWEEN...

She-Hulk works at the Goodman, Lieber, Kurtzberg, and Holliway law firm. Martin Goodman, Stan Lee (formerly Lieber), and Jack Kirby (formerly Kurtzberg) are three legends of Marvel!

...THE PANELS

A KNOCKOUT BLOW

Titania gets the Infinity Gem of Power from the Champion of the Universe, enabling her to beat She-Hulk with ease. Shulkie turns back into Jen Walters to escape, steals the Gem—and knocks Titania out with a single punch!
WINNER: SHE-HULK!

COURT IN THE ACT!

She-Hulk is in the **U.S. Supreme Court,** arguing against the **Mutant Registration Act,** but **Titania** keeps causing trouble outside! In fact, she's spoiling for a fight! She-Hulk clobbers her three times—while managing to **keep track** of the legal proceedings!
WINNER: SHE-HULK!

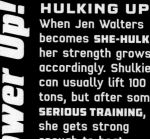

Power Up!

HULKING UP

When Jen Walters becomes **SHE-HULK,** her strength grows accordingly. Shulkie can usually lift 100 tons, but after some **SERIOUS TRAINING,** she gets strong enough to beat **HERCULES** in an arm-wrestle!

TELL ME MORE!

Lawyer Jennifer Walters is shot by a gang she is prosecuting in court, and her quick-thinking cousin, Bruce Banner, saves her life with a transfusion of his own gamma-radiated blood. Jen soon discovers that she can hulk out, too. But unlike Bruce, she remains intelligent when she changes into She-Hulk!

RESULT!

SHE-HULK: 3 TITANIA: 2

Atlantis, ruled by Namor the Sub-Mariner, is a sunken city the size of a small continent located somewhere in the Atlantic Ocean. It is home to the Atlanteans—a bluish cousin of humans who are able to breath underwater—but is coveted by the savage Mermen of Lemuria, led by Attuma.

WHO BEATS WHOM?

Don't let Attuma's **massive physique** fool you—the bigger they come, the harder they fall, and the **faster they sink!** While these guys are fairly evenly matched in fighting skills, **Namor** can **battle on** for far longer. Couple this with his ability to fly, and the Sub-Mariner is a **likely winner!**

"So long as Namor stands Atlantis shall be denied you-- FOREVER!"

TOP 6

How to Rule Atlantis

1 **GATHER** a ruthless Mermen army

2 **ENSLAVE** Atlanteans with hypnotic lights

3 **INFILTRATE** the Atlantean government

4 **FORCE** Namor to surrender by holding the surface world hostage

5 **STEAL** an unstoppable alien robot

6 **FIND** an enchanted hammer that gives you superpowers

BETWEEN...

Namor and Attuma have been battling each other for more than 50 years! The malevolent Merman first appears in *Fantastic Four* #33 (December 1964), when his barbarian hordes invade Atlantis.

...THE PANELS

DUEL IN THE DEEP

AAAARRGHH!!

ATTUMA creates an evil alliance with **TIGER SHARK** and **DR. DORCAS**. Namor takes on all three; he **LOSES** and is taken prisoner.

HANDLE WITH CARE!

Attuma finds an **ancient magical hammer** and becomes **Nerkkod, Breaker of Oceans.** He conquers the waves, destroys Atlantis, and finally **defeats Namor!**

"DEATH TO SUB-MARINER!! Only Attuma will wear the crown of Atlantis!!"

YESSS!!

Using **BRUCE BANNER'S BLOOD,** Attuma **GAMMA-RADIATES HIMSELF** and captures Atlantis—until Namor gets Hulk to **SMASH ATTUMA** back to normal!

GOOD DAY

When **Attuma attacks Atlantis,** Namor's girlfriend, **Lady Dorma,** begs the **Fantastic Four** for help. They **hold off the Mermen army,** allowing Namor to **defeat Attuma,** but keep their presence a **secret**—Namor's **big ego** can't handle his sometime enemies **saving his gills!**

Namor the Sub-Mariner and his **archenemy Attuma** wrestle for control of the submerged **City of Atlantis.** The **massive Merman** will do **whatever it takes** to depose King Namor and finally **rule the oceans!**

Q: What makes Mermen and Atlanteans different?

A: Both can **breathe underwater** and have **bluish skin.** Mermen look more fishlike and are **more barbaric.** Atlantean society is **more advanced**—politically, scientifically, **and magically.**

Atlanteans

Merman

HEAVY HITTERS

If one of this bunch hits you, you're **not getting up!** Most heroes and villains **pack a powerful punch,** but these folks are the **biggest bashers** and the **most thunderous thumpers** around!

AAAARRGHH!!

HULK can beat heavy hitters like the Thing, Thor, and Wolverine, but even he's been **KNOCKED BACK!** When Spider-Man is imbued with the **POWER COSMIC,** he punches Hulk **INTO ORBIT!**

TOUGH STUFF

Hulk tries to rescue his friend **Rick Jones** from the **Wrecker.** However, a misunderstanding puts him on a **collision course** with the **Fantastic Four**—and an **epic showdown** with fellow power-puncher, **the Thing!**

TELL ME MORE!

Heavy-hitters Thor and Hercules are good friends, but also rivals. While they both wield a mean weapon with mighty strength, Herc just can't keep up with Thor's god-given speed and lightning blasts!

HULK BUSTING

If you want a crack at **Tony Stark,** you better make sure he's not wearing his **Hulkbuster armor.** With it, Shellhead can lift **175 tons**—it's made to **bust Hulks,** after all!

Power Up!

COMING THROUGH! A gem from the magical **CYTTORAK** turns Cain Marko into the nearly indestructible **JUGGERNAUT.** This human battering ram is super-strong and can **CRUSH MOUNTAINS!**

YESSS!!

The Midgard Serpent wraps its planet-sized body all the way around the Earth, but **Thor** is so strong that he removes it—with a fishing rod!

S.H.I.E.L.D. DECLASSIFIED

CAPTAIN MARVEL
Captain Marvel Carol Danvers' superstrength is matched only by her iron will. Her ability to absorb energy means that the more power that is thrown at her, the stronger her next attack becomes.

REALLY?!

Molly Hayes is just a little kid, but she can **punch** so hard she once sent Wolverine **flying through a wall.** No wonder they call her **Bruiser,** though she prefers the name **Princess Powerful!**

WHEN GOOD GUYS GO BAD!

EVIL INSIDE
Sentry (Bob Reynolds) is created by an improved version of the Super-Soldier serum that transformed Steve Rogers into Captain America. He has the power of one million exploding suns, but has a dark side named the Void, who destroys the city of Asgard!

THICK-SKINNED HERO
Piotr Rasputin is a **nice guy** with a **hard exterior.** When the going gets tough, he becomes the hero **Colossus**—a member of **the X-Men** with the power to convert his body tissue into **organic steel**

UPGRADED!

Rhino isn't big on brains, but this musclebound Russian science experiment doesn't care. His superpowered suit makes him almost invulnerable—and it's bonded to him for life!

BACK FROM THE DEAD!

Wonder Man is living ionic energy! He's as strong as they come and **can't feel pain**—which is just as well as he has **died several times!**

TOP 4

Reasons Thor Fights Hercules

1 Herc hits on Thor's girlfriend **JANE FOSTER**

2 Herc joins up with the evil god **PLUTO**

3 Herc and Thor argue over a **MAGIC PIG**

4 They both want to **CROSS A BRIDGE FIRST**

1. SHANG-CHI—it takes a lot to break Shang-Chi's state of Zen calm, but if you do, watch out!

2. ELEKTRA—swaps life as a deadly assassin-for-hire to fight crime alongside Daredevil

3. IRON FIST—martial arts master who possesses the ancient power of the Iron Fist

4. KARNAK—a warrior monk who has trained to the point of Inhuman physical perfection

5. DAREDEVIL—trained by the legendary Stick to fight the underworld bosses of Hell's Kitchen, New York City

Power Up!

HARD HITTER
DANIEL RAND (Iron Fist) gains his greatest power in a **SPECIAL RITUAL.** He slays the dragon **SHUO-LAO THE UNDYING** and then plunges his hands into its **MOLTEN HEART**— imbuing them with the hard-hitting mystic power of **IRON FIST!**

FISTS OF FURY

Patience, hard work, and **dedication** can transform body and mind into an **ultimate fighting machine.** These **masters of martial arts** may not all have superpowers, but mess with them and they will **take you down!**

UPGRADED!

Karnak utilizes the **superhuman strength** all **Inhumans** are born with by studying **martial arts.** Instead of gaining more powers through the **Terrigen Mists** like other Inhumans, he trains until he can shatter objects with **a single blow!**

WHEN BAD GUYS GO GOOD!

UNLIKELY ALLIES
Martial arts master Cat (Shen Kuei) believes that Shang-Chi caused his brother's death. When he learns this is not so, Cat teams up with Shang-Chi to take down those actually responsible—Cat's former criminal allies!

MASTER OF KUNG FU
Shang-Chi is the **ultimate martial arts master**. His crime lord father raises him to be a **ruthless assassin**, but the plan backfires. The Kung Fu warrior **swears vengeance**, battling crime as Earth's most **skilful fighter**!

NOOOOOO!! **ELEKTRA** is trained by **STICK**, an enemy of the evil **HAND NINJA**. Stick does not allow Elektra to finish her training—so she **JOINS** the Hand instead!

HEROES FOR HIRE
Iron Fist and **Luke Cage** decide to go into business together as **"Heroes for Hire."** They plan to help people and make money, but the pair often end up doing heroic deeds **for free!**

ALTERNATE UNIVERSE

In the **Mangaverse** (Earth-2301), Peter Parker is not a student and photographer—he's the **last ninja** of the ancient **Spider Clan!** He seeks revenge on **Venom**, the monster who killed his sensei, **Uncle Ben!**

TOP 5

Shang-Chi Versus...

How does the Master of Kung Fu match up against superpowered opponents?

1 **WOLVERINE**—Wolvie is trying to control his rage, but gets angry, fights Shang-Chi, and loses!

2 **SPIDER-MAN**—a misunderstanding leads to a fight, but the pair quickly call a truce.

3 **THING**—Shang-Chi withstands all of the Thing's attacks, then refuses to fight back!

4 **CAPTAIN AMERICA**—both Shang-Chi and Cap land hits, but neither of these tough guys go down!

5 **MAN-THING**—Shang-Chi gets trapped inside the muddy monster!

BACK FROM THE DEAD!
Iron Fist is **murdered** and his crime-fighting partner **Luke Cage** is blamed. However, the victim is actually an **alien double** and the real Iron Fist returns to **clear Luke's name!**

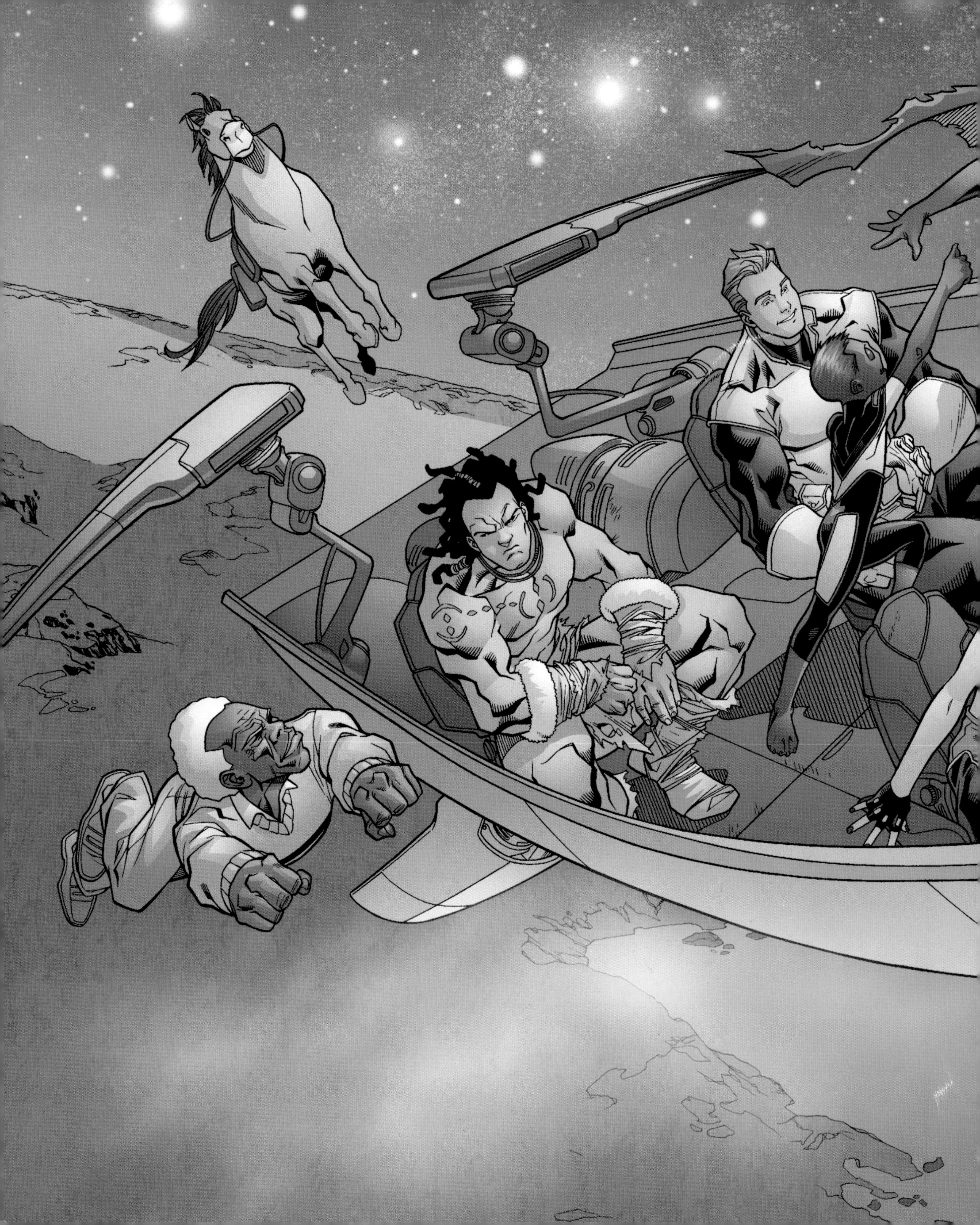

CHAPTER TWO
TEAMS

Wolverine is **MUCH OLDER** than he seems—but what keeps him looking so young?

Who kills **UATU THE WATCHER** and steals his eye?

What turns **MADAME HYDRA** into a humanoid octopus creature?

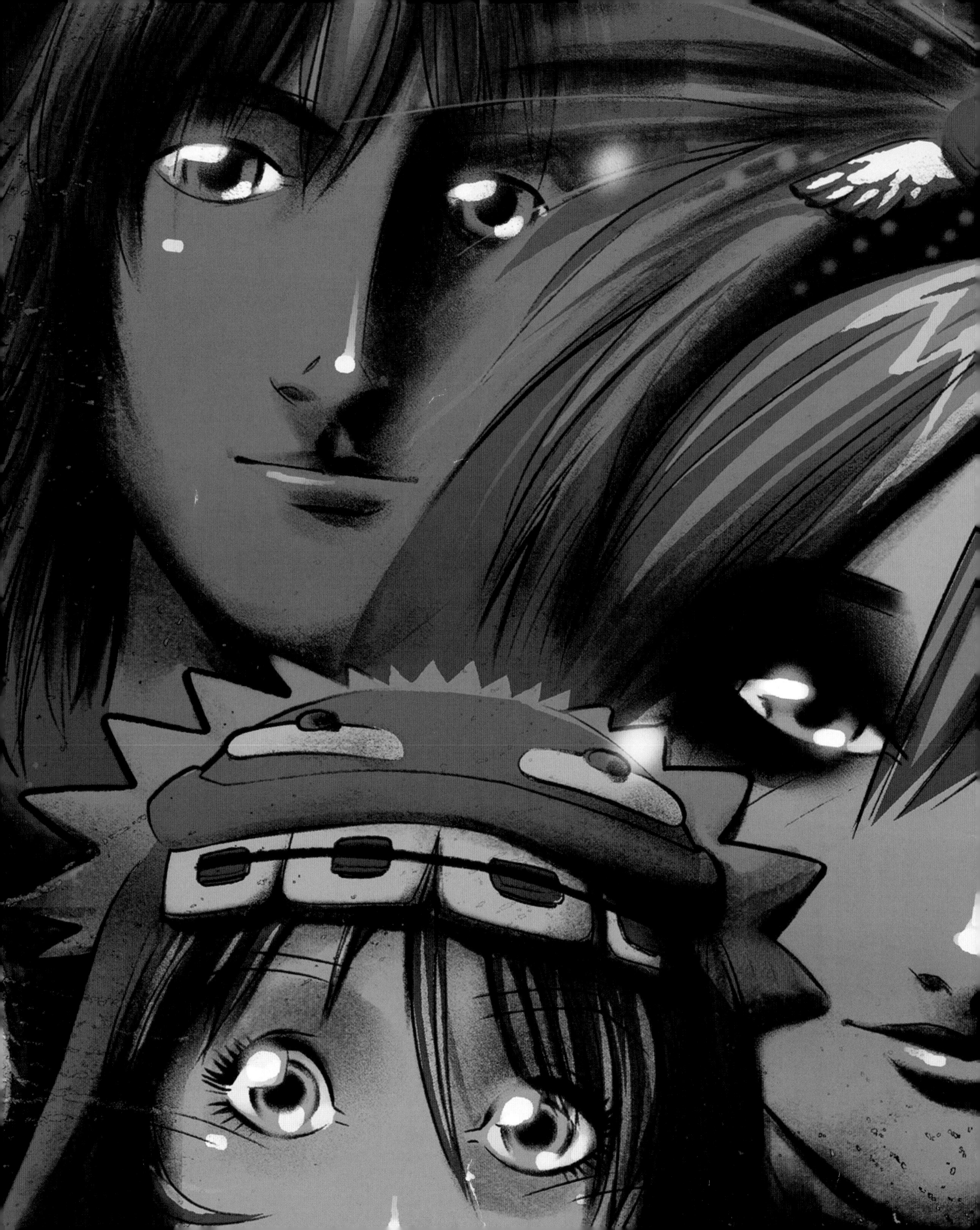

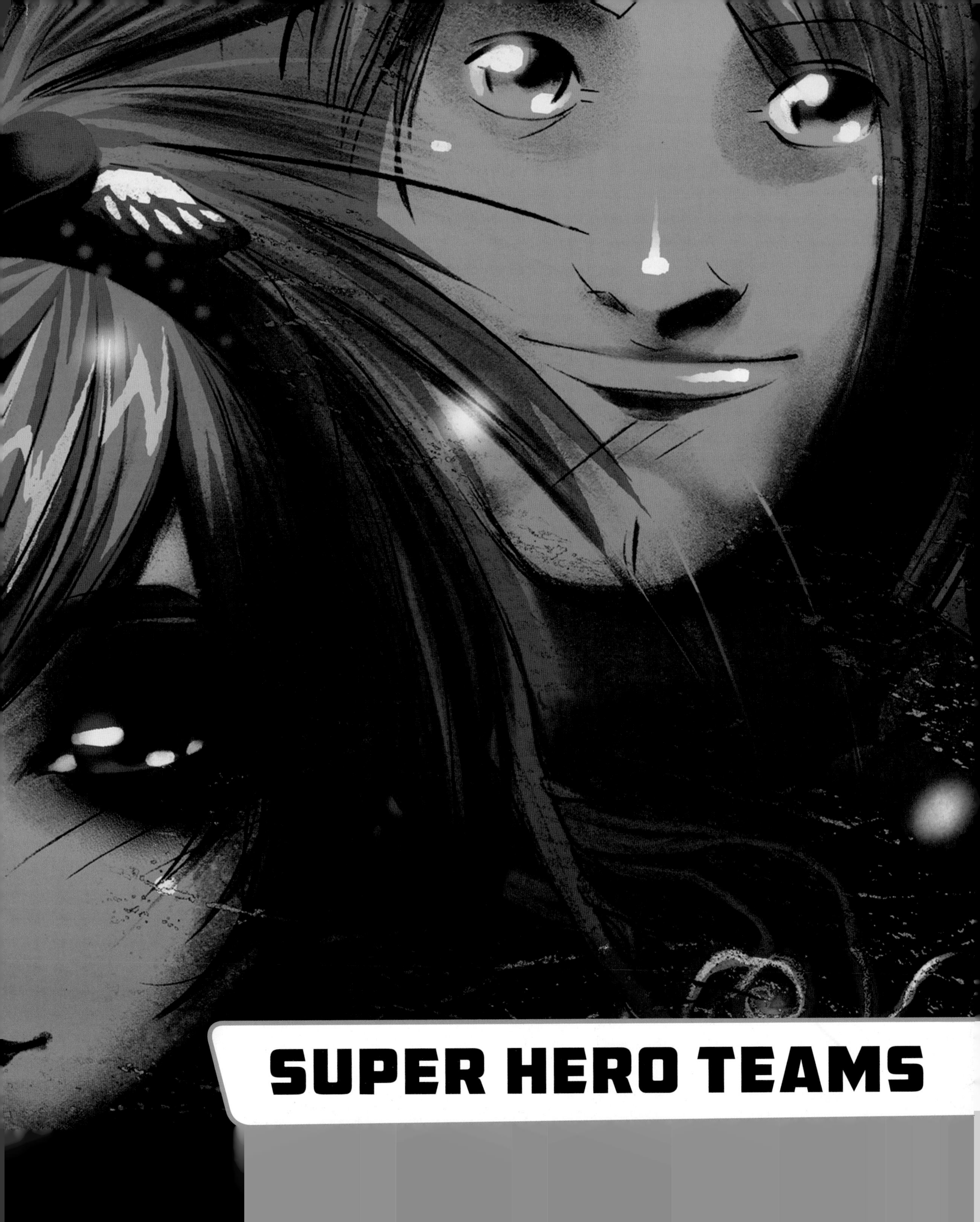

SUPER HERO TEAMS

WOW!

100...

...and counting—past and present Avengers.

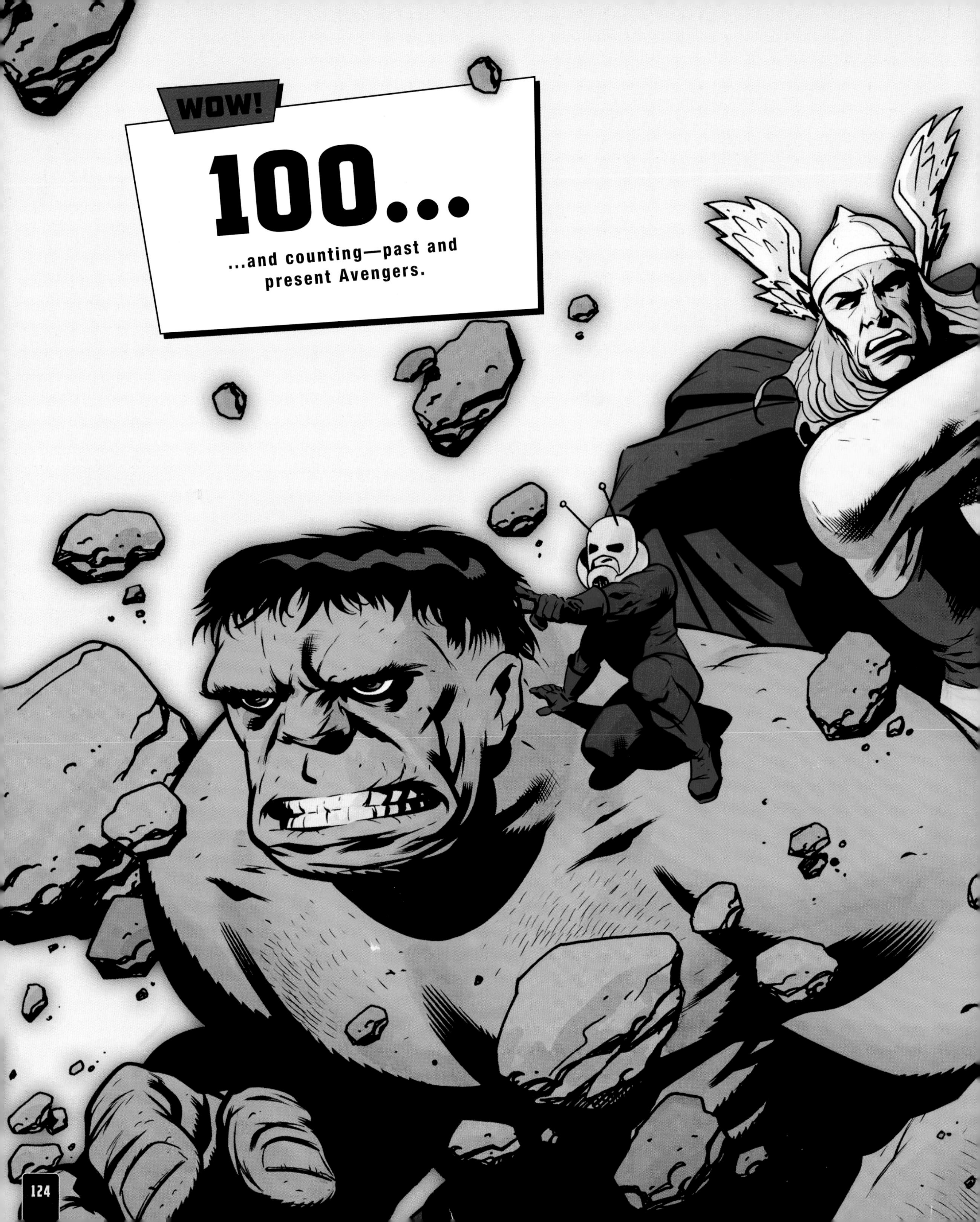

"We need a *name!*
It should be something
colorful and dramatic, like...
THE AVENGERS..."

WASP

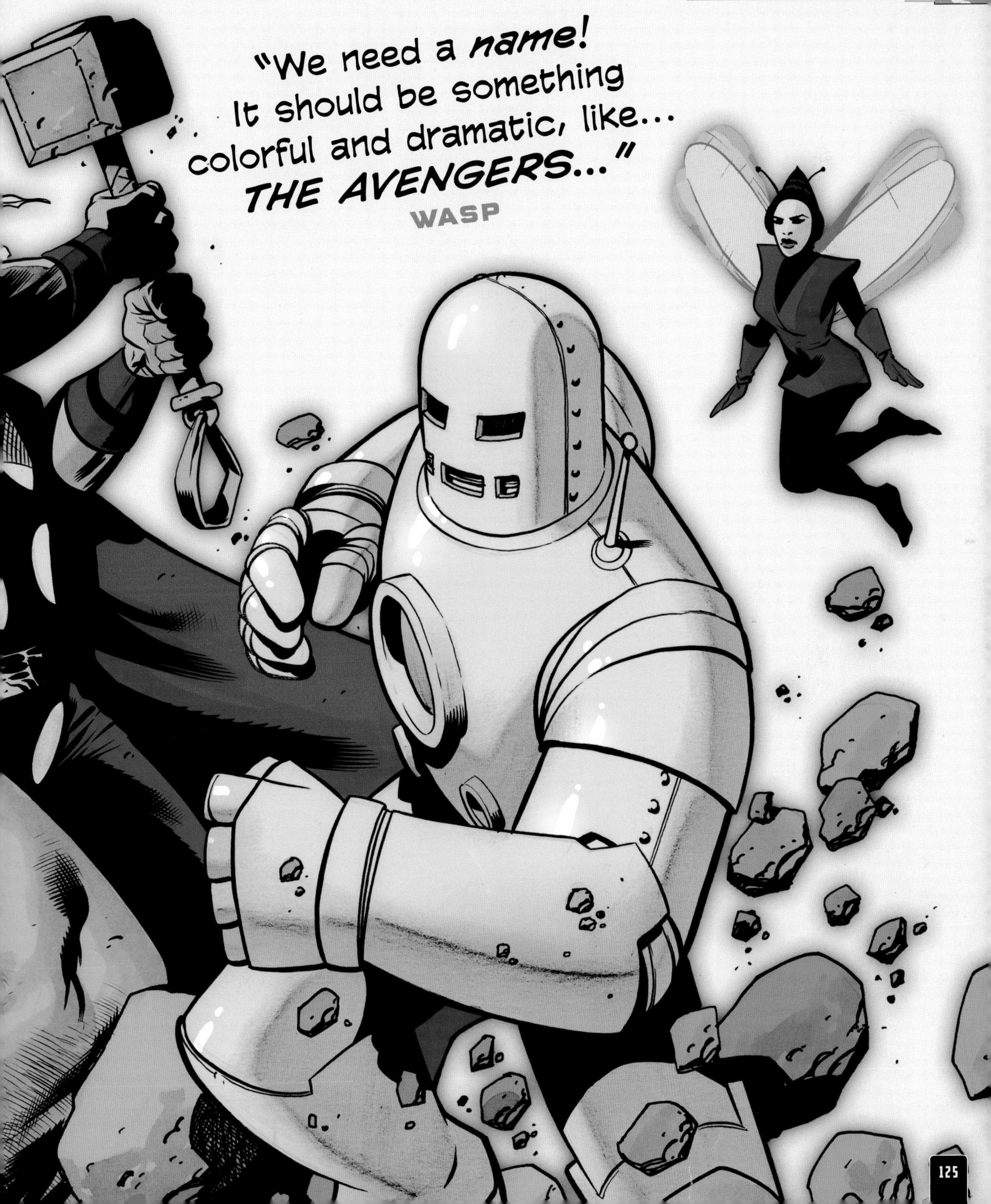

EARTH'S MIGHTIEST!

The Avengers are always facing some **big new problem**! They've been **disassembled, reassembled,** and nearly **obliterated.** They've even **fought** each other. Yet they **regroup** each time a **Super Villain** threatens **the future of humanity!**

Thor

Captain America

Iron Man

"We'll never be beaten! For we are... the *AVENGERS!*"

TOP 8

Times Avengers HQ has been wrecked!

1 THE MASTERS OF EVIL invade Avengers Mansion and TRASH the place!

2 The Avengers move to HYDROBASE, an artificial island off the coast of New Jersey, but attacking robots sink it!

3 The team's rebuilt mansion is TRASHED AGAIN—this time by the extradimensional GATHERERS!

4 SCARLET WITCH, VISION, and JACK OF HEARTS go out of control, and the mansion is wrecked!

5 The team moves into STARK TOWER, but it's wrecked when IRON MAN and HULK clash!

6 An Asgardian-empowered THING wrecks the tower again, battling RED HULK!

7 A new Avengers team moves into a rebuilt AVENGERS MANSION, but it's wrecked yet again when POWER MAN attacks!

8 THE CHILDREN OF TOMORROW from Earth-1610 SMASH a rebuilt Stark Tower!

FAST FACTS

KEY MEMBERS: Iron Man, Thor, Ant-Man (Henry Pym), The Wasp, Hulk, Captain America, Hawkeye, Vision, Scarlet Witch, Quicksilver, Black Panther, Black Widow, Falcon, Winter Soldier, Hercules, Black Knight, She-Hulk, Ant-Man (Scott Lang), Wonder Man, Quasar, Spectrum

ALLIES: Rick Jones, Edwin Jarvis, Nick Fury, Nick Fury Jr., Fantastic Four, S.H.I.E.L.D.

ENEMIES: Ultron, Kang, Masters of Evil, Thanos, Baron Zemo, Loki, and many, many more!

Nova

Spider-Man

Ms. Marvel

Vision

KAPOW!

Ant-Man likes to give Hawkeye's arrows an added punch—by hitching a ride!

BROKEN HEART

Wasp Janet Van Dyne is the **heart** of the Avengers. She **names** the group, **chairs** their first meeting, and **holds** the group together, even when her husband, **Hank Pym,** cracks up.

WHEN GOOD GUYS GO BAD!

ROBO-SPIDEY

When Spider-Man meets the Avengers for the first time, he's an evil webhead —a robot created by Kang the Conqueror sent to destroy them!

Q: What is the Avengers Academy?

A: The Avengers establish the **Avengers Academy** to train super-powered students to become **villains heroes,** rather than the **villains heroes,** they might otherwise become!

LOYAL SERVANT

Edwin Jarvis is the **butler** of **Tony Stark** and the **Avengers.** His loyalty is unwavering—even when he's **beaten senseless** by **Mister Hyde** or replaced by a **Skrull invader!**

BETWEEN...

When the first issue of *Daredevil* was delayed, Stan Lee suggested Marvel release a team-up title. *The Avengers #1* debuted in September 1963, and the rest is history!

...THE PANELS

NOOOOOO!!

She-Hulk doesn't often lose her temper like her cousin Hulk, but when her Avengers teammate Vision is taken over by Ultron and attacks the group, she loses control— and literally tears him apart!

AARRGHH!!

A BASEMENT DOOR in Avengers Mansion turns out to be a PORTAL for Kang the Conqueror to INVADE the world!

When **trouble comes calling**, there's an **Avengers team** ready for action—**any time, any place, anywhere!!**

TOP 5 AVENGERS TEAMS

1 **PET AVENGERS**—a team of super animals

2 **GREAT LAKES AVENGERS**—a collection of America's weirdest heroes

3 **DARK AVENGERS**—Norman Osborn's squad of crooks and murderers

4 **UNCANNY AVENGERS**—a team of mutants and Super Heroes

5 **WEST COAST AVENGERS**—sworn to battle any threat, so long as it's west of the Rockies!

Uncanny Avengers

ALTERNATE UNIVERSE

The main Avengers are reincarnated as **Western heroes** in 1872. Steve Rogers is sheriff of the town of Timely, and Tony Stark is a blacksmith with a drinking problem!

Lockheed

Throg

Redwing

Hairball

Zabu

Ms. Lion

Lockjaw

CREATURE CRUSADERS

The Inhumans' watchdog **Lockjaw** gains telepathy and extra intelligence from the **Mind Gem**. He contacts heroes' pets and forms the **Pet Avengers** team!

PURRRFECT PET AVENGERS

HAIRBALL—Speedball's super-powered feline can bounce off walls!

LOCKJAW—who can resist the big slobbery mug of the Inhumans' teleporting pooch?

THROG—he's a frog AND an honorary God of Thunder!

REDWING—he's just as slick as his human partner Falcon.

MS. LION—Ms. Lion is actually male and a normal, friendly little dog belonging to Peter Parker's Aunt May.

LOCKHEED—Kitty Pryde of the X-Men's super-powered alien dragon.

ZABU—Ka-Zar's faithful Savage Land companion. Who says that saber-toothed tigers are extinct?!

TOP 6
GREAT LAKES AVENGERS

1 **SQUIRREL GIRL**—realizes the lazy team are relying on her, and quits!

2 **MR. IMMORTAL**—able to survive almost any accident

3 **FLATMAN**—super-stretchy, but falls a bit flat

4 **ASHLEY CRAWFORD**—a supermodel who morphs into super-sized, super-strong Big Bertha

5 **DINAH SOAR**—a weird flying creature who loves Mr. Immortal

6 **DOORMAN**—a living portal into the Darkforce

Monkey Joe

BETWEEN...

Great Lakes Avengers writer Dan Slott promised that a team member would die each issue, as a parody of overdone comic book deaths. The first to go: Squirrel Girl's squirrel buddy, Monkey Joe!

...THE PANELS

Squirrel Girl

AAARRGHH!!

HAWKEYE founded the West Coast Avengers alongside Mockingbird, Wonder Man, Tigra, and Jim Rhodes, but they just couldn't get along and were **BROKEN UP** by Captain America.

TELL ME MORE!

The West Coast Avengers disperse, but many years later Hank Pym, Tigra, and Hawkeye return to the team's L.A. headquarters to create Avengers Academy, for teen would-be heroes.

WOW!

50,000

The number of years into the future the Avengers travel to meet the team's final incarnation.

NOOOOO!!

When Norman Osborn becomes U.S. security chief he forms a Dark Avengers team of **SUPER VILLAINS!** Osborn is **IRON PATRIOT,** a devious combination of Iron Man and Captain America.

129

MUTANT MARVELS

The X-Men are a team of **mutants** united by **Professor Charles Xavier's** dream of **peaceful coexistence** with ordinary folks. They protect a world that sometimes **hates and fears** them, while safeguarding the future of the **endangered mutant race!**

Cyclops

THE ORIGINAL X-MEN

The roster soon grows, but the first students to enroll at Professor Xavier's School for Gifted Youngsters are:

- **CYCLOPS** (Scott Summers)—continually shoots force beams from eyes

- **MARVEL GIRL** (Jean Grey)—vast telepathic and telekinetic abilities

- **ANGEL** (Warren Worthington III)—flies like a bird

- **BEAST** (Henry McCoy)—ape-like genius scientist

- **ICEMAN** (Robert Drake)—transforms into ice; can freeze moisture in the air.

Q: WHAT IS A MUTANT?

A: A person born with a **genetic "x-factor"** that gives him or her **abilities** far beyond those of a normal human being. These powers often appear in **sudden and disturbing ways** during the teenage years.

Beast

Nightcrawler

FAST FACTS

KEY MEMBERS:
Professor X, Storm, Jean Grey, Nightcrawler, Colossus, Magik, Iceman, Wolverine, Angel, Beast, Cyclops, Emma Frost, Kitty Pryde

RELATED TEAMS: X-Force, Magneto's Uncanny X-Men

ALLIES: New Mutants, Fantastic Four, Spider-Man

TOP 5

UNFORTUNATE MUTANTS

1. **ROGUE**—absorbs the memories and abilities of anyone she touches, leaving them in a coma!

2. **NIGHTCRAWLER**—a swashbuckling and loyal X-Man, but shunned as a child for his demonic appearance

3. **MAGGOTT**—eats through two slug-like creatures that gobble up food and burrow into his body!

4. **SNOT**—a teenage villain who generates deadly mucus from his oversized nostrils!

5. **BEAST**—Hank McCoy's science experiments have left him with fangs, claws, and thick blue fur

WHOSE SIDE ARE THEY ON?

• **Magneto**—the master of magnetism hates humans, but when all mutants are in danger, he becomes a vital X-Men ally!

• **Gambit**—this master thief is both an X-Man and a criminal!

• **Emma Frost**—this diamond-skinned telepath realizes the X-Men aren't so bad when Sentinel robots attack her people on the mutant haven of Genosha.

• **Jean Grey**—a cosmic force turns her into the world-destroying Dark Phoenix!

Emma Frost

Colossus

AAAARRGHH!!

CYCLOPS cannot control the **FORCE BEAMS** that shoot from his **EYES**. He has to wear a **RUBY-QUARTZ VISOR**, or destroy anything he looks at!

WOW!

100

... and counting

Wolverine's age, but you wouldn't know it, thanks to his amazing healing factor.

TOP 5

X-MEN ENEMIES

1 **APOCALYPSE**—his name says it all. This ancient mutant wants to rule the world, or destroy it!

2 **SABRETOOTH**—big, mean, furry, and full of fury, Sabretooth has only one goal: slay Wolverine!

3 **MR. SINISTER**—genetic manipulator with a cruel streak and an obsession with mutant DNA; a modern-day mad scientist!

4 **MYSTIQUE**—wicked, shape-changing schemer related to Nightcrawler and Rogue

5 **JUGGERNAUT**—nothing stops Xavier's half brother, the super-strong, nigh-invulnerable Juggernaut!

"I'm the best there is at what I do, but what I do best isn't very nice."

Wolverine

FASTBALL SPECIAL

When Wolverine wants to **slice'n'dice** something **far away** he pops his **claws** and gets his big buddy **Colossus** to **chuck him** at the target!

THE THING

FAST FACTS

MEMBERS: Mister Fantastic (Reed Richards), Human Torch (Johnny Storm), Invisible Woman (Susan Richards), The Thing (Ben Grimm).

BASE: Baxter Building, New York City

ALLIES: Agatha Harkness, Alicia Masters, Lyja Storm, Silver Surfer, Wyatt Wingfoot.

FOES: Doctor Doom, Frightful Four, Wizard, Mole Man, Puppet Master, Red Ghost (and his Super Apes), Klaw

Q: How do the Fantastic Four get superhuman powers?

A: Reed Richards, his girlfriend Susan Storm, her brother Johnny, and pilot Ben Grimm make a **test flight** in an **experimental rocket.** The rocket is bombarded by **cosmic radiation** and crashes! The four emerge with amazing **new abilities!**

GOOD DAY

Doctor Doom tries to ruin Reed and Sue's wedding with his **Emotion Changer** machine, but the **Watcher** gives Reed a device to foil Doom's plan, **saving the day!**

YESSS!! The **FRIGHTFUL FOUR** bad guys are fleeing in their spaceship. Mr. Fantastic becomes a giant **SPRING** and he **HURLS** Thing onto the ship for some **CLOBBERIN'!**

MISTER FANTASTIC

WOW!

1,500

Maximum length in feet Mr. Fantastic can extend a body part (457m).

ALTERNATE UNIVERSE

In the **Ultimate Universe** (Earth-1610), Mr. Fantastic **goes insane!** He fakes his death and sends **aliens** to attack his former friends! Battling Nova and Sue Richards, he ends up exiled to the **Negative Zone.**

"Family isn't just who you're related to—It's who cares for you and takes care of you."

INVISIBLE WOMAN

THE HUMAN TORCH

SUPER HERO FAMILY!

Transformed by cosmic rays, the **Fantastic Four** could have become **outcasts**. Instead they see their strange **new powers** as a family bond, and use them for **the good of humanity**! Mister Fantastic is famous for his **scientific genius**, but all four have become **celebrity heroes!**

WHEN GOOD GUYS GO BAD!

THING'S RAMPAGE
A Reed Richards experiment turns the Thing back into Ben Grimm. What's more, Ben can change back whenever he wants. However, Ben's personality changes. He breaks up with his girlfriend, Alicia, quits the FF, and rampages through New York City!

BETWEEN...

The Fantastic Four's November 1961 launch was a turning point for writer/editor Stan Lee, who had considered leaving comics. The FF have gone on to sell more than 150 million comic books.

...THE PANELS

NOOOOO!!
Kristoff Vernard, a child brainwashed to think he's **DOCTOR DOOM**, traps the FF in the Baxter Building, shoots it into outer space and **BLOWS IT UP!**

COSMIC EFFECTS

Mister Fantastic: Reed's body becomes elastic, stretching in amazing ways!

Invisible Woman: Sue's new abilities include projecting force-fields and turning invisible!

Human Torch: Johnny gains the ability to fly, throw fireballs, bathe his body in flames, and the catchphrase, "Flame on!"

The Thing: Ben gains superhuman strength, a rock body, and the catchphrase, "It's clobberin' time!"

UPGRADED!

Super Hero teams need super-fast transportation, so Reed designs the Fantasti-car. He soon upgrades his initial "flying bathtub" design to a machine that can split into four vehicles.

TOP 4
Fantastic Powers

1 THE HUMAN TORCH—can create flaming images of himself; an enemy has to figure out which one is **the real** Johnny Storm!

2 MR. FANTASTIC—his body is so bendy it can even absorb the impacts of **artillery shells.**

3 INVISIBLE WOMAN—can create see-through, but solid, objects with her mind, such as vehicles and weapons.

4 THE THING—can withstand armor-piercing shells, extreme heat and cold, and survive in space and the depths of the ocean.

TERRIGENESIS
Inhumans look just like normal humans, until they are exposed to mutagenic mists from the rare Terrigen crystals—a process known as "terrigenesis." Their bodies mutate inside large green cocoons, before they emerge with unique superhuman powers.

HOME SWEET HOME
The Inhumans' home is the city of **Attilan**. It's been located in **the Himalayas**, the blue area of the Moon, and even **levitating** above New York's **Hudson River**—but it's always home!

BETWEEN...

The Inhumans are no newbies! Medusa debuted in *Fantastic Four* #36, way back in 1965! Her origin story and fellow Inhumans were revealed later that year in *Fantastic Four* #45.

...THE PANELS

HANDLE WITH CARE!

Terrigen crystals create powerful mists that **unlock** Inhuman powers. The mists transform those with Inhuman genes, but can **kill** humans.

AAAARRGHH!!
A **TERRIGEN BOMB** explodes on Earth! Carriers of the Inhuman gene are **FORCED** into Terrigenesis. These new Inhumans become known as **"NUHUMANS."**

TELL ME MORE!

A superpower derived from Terrigenesis can have seriously bad side effects. Any physical change is irreversible, so fingers crossed you get a good one!

Quick Wedding
Not every Inhuman wants to **marry** another Inhuman. Medusa's sister **Crystal** dates the **Human Torch** (Johnny Storm), then marries super-speedster **Quicksilver**!

WHEN GOOD GUYS GO BAD!

...THEN GOOD AGAIN!
Medusa loses her memory, joins up with the Frightful Four, and battles the Fantastic Four! Eventually, she remembers who she is, and joins her former foes in a new team, the Future Foundation!

1 **BLACK BOLT**—king with an earth shattering voice and the ability to manipulate energy

2 **MEDUSA**—queen who can control her long red hair as a whip, to bind people, or lift objects

3 **MAXIMUS THE MAD**—brother of Black Bolt with psionic abilities but questionable sanity

4 **CRYSTAL**—sister of Medusa and ex-wife of Quicksilver; can manipulate earth, air, fire, and water

5 **LOCKJAW**—looks like a dog; can teleport

6 **MS. MARVEL (KAMALA KHAN)**—can morph in size, shape, density, and even appearance

THANE

FAMILY CONNECTIONS

Thane, son of **Thanos** the Mad Titan, is revealed to be of **Inhuman lineage.** After his terrigenesis, the once kind doctor finds he can create **living death** with a touch of his hand—a power he uses to lock his evil father in **suspended animation!**

Power Up!

BLACK BOLT A **WHISPER** from the super-powered voice of **BLACK BOLT**, King of the Inhumans, can level an **ENTIRE CITY.** His terrigenesis took place **EARLIER** than any other Inhuman's, making his powers the **MOST DEVELOPED** of the entire race.

THE SUPER IN HUMANS

The **Inhumans** are a reclusive, genetically enhanced **super race.** Thousands of years ago, the alien **Kree** abducted cavemen and **experimented on them.** They hoped to build **an army,** but instead created an **entire race** of superhumans!

TROUBLESHOOTERS!

When Arthur Douglas' wife is killed by Thanos, he is genetically engineered to become Drax the Destroyer, the ultimate warrior with one aim—to destroy the mad Titan!

Drax the Destroyer

BETWEEN...

When they aren't busy saving the universe, the Guardians like to relax at Starlin's Bar on Knowhere—named for legendary artist and writer Jim Starlin, who worked on many of Marvel's cosmic comics!

...THE PANELS

Q: How did the Guardians of the Galaxy start?

A: When the **Kree homeworld** is attacked by the alien **Phalanx**, the Kree send a team of **expendable troopers** to fight back. Star-Lord leads a bizarre **group of convicts** who save the day. They then decide to stick together as a **cosmic hero team**!

IDENTITY CRISIS?

The team almost name themselves "Rocket Raccoon and his Human Hangers-On" or "Groot and the Branches." Then they meet Vance Astro, formerly in a team named the "Guardians of the Galaxy," and "borrow" that name!

WHEN GOOD GUYS GO BAD!

HARD CHOICES

Magician Adam Warlock is a friend of the Guardians, but while attempting to heal a gap in space-time, his body is taken over by his evil side, the Magus! Magus uses an illusion to make several of the Guardians seem dead, so an angry Star-Lord takes down his old friend.

REALLY?!

The "first" Guardians actually come from the future. Star-Lord and pals come face-to-face with the "originals" (Martinex, Vance Astro, Charlie-27, and Yondu) when they visit in the year 3009!

Gamora

The **Guardians of the Galaxy** are a **motley crew** of adventurers that travel across space, battling alien bad guys, confronting **cosmic threats,** and **blowing things up.** Are they **heroes** or a gang of **troublemakers**? Maybe they're a little of both!

Rocket Raccoon

Groot

S.H.I.E.L.D. DECLASSIFIED

NEW RECRUIT
Tony Stark decides to take a vacation in space, but he is attacked by the alien Badoon. The Guardians come to Iron Man's rescue, and he ends up joining the team for a while.

DOUBLE TROUBLE

TOP 5

Guardians of the Galaxy

1 STAR-LORD (Peter Quill)—a roguish Earthling who can't help being a hero!

2 ROCKET RACCOON—a genetically engineered raccoon with plenty of weapons and even more attitude!

3 DRAX THE DESTROYER—a super-warrior created to take down Thanos.

4 GROOT—a treelike alien from Planet X, and Rocket's best bud!

5 GAMORA—the deadliest woman in the Galaxy! Trained by Thanos as an assassin, but soon sees the error of her ways.

BACK FROM THE DEAD!

Thanos plans to destroy the universe, and, when **Gamora** he tries to stop him, he kills her. **Adam Warlock** uses the Time Gem to project her spirit into a **new body!**

ROCKET & GROOT

Alien TV exec **Mojo** kidnaps **Rocket and Groot** and pits them against bizarre enemies as part of a **reality-TV show** on **Mojoworld**. The show is a hit, and Mojo makes **big money** selling Rocket and Groot **action figures!**

DADDY ISSUES

Star-Lord (Peter Quill) has a human mother, but his father J'son, alias **Jason of Spartax**, is the ruthless leader of the **Spartoi Empire!** He wants Peter to rule by his side, but Peter can't stand his dastardly dad!

JUST ADD WATER

Groot can regrow from just a **twig**, which is handy, as he tends to **get blown up a lot!** Rocket just collects a cutting and grows a **"new"** Groot in a pot.

Star-Lord

FURRY ENCOUNTER

Rocket Raccoon first meets a Super Hero when he is stranded on the bizarre planet of Halfworld—with the Hulk! The two team up to take down the evil mole Judson Jakes!

"NEVER doubt a raccoon."

REALLY?!

A **transporter glitch** sends the Defenders to a universe called **"Here,"** where cute fuzzy animals **talk in rhyme**. To get back home, **Namor** straps on **ruby red slippers** and they all hold hands and say, "There's **no place** like the place I came from before I came **Here!**"

Luke Cage

FAST FACTS

FOUNDING MEMBERS: Dr. Strange, Hulk, Namor, Silver Surfer

KEY MEMBERS: Luke Cage, Iron Fist, Red She-Hulk, Ant-Man (Scott Lang), Black Cat, Valkyrie, Nighthawk, Moondragon

FOES: Egghead's Emissaries of Evil, Satan, Yandroth, Headmen, Nul, Nebulon, Wrecking Crew

Iron Fist

Red She-Hulk

Doctor Strange

WOW!

77

The number of past and present Defenders

FUTURE HEROES

In an alternate year 2510, **Earth is dying.** Reed and Sue Richards create a new team of **Defenders** and save all of the planet's six billion inhabitants—by sending them **back in time!**

The Defenders are formed when Doctor Strange enlists Namor the Sub-Mariner, the Hulk, and the Silver Surfer to stop the evil Yandroth and his Omegatron from detonating every nuclear weapon on Earth.

LAST LINE OF DEFENSE

The Defenders are there when you need them—especially if you're facing a **magical threat!** Often led by **Doctor Strange,** this team of Super Heroes bands together out of necessity—when **defense** is the best form of **attack!**

BEST KNOWN FOR

COMING TOGETHER IN THE NICK OF TIME

ALTERNATE UNIVERSE

On (Earth-1610), the Defenders aren't that nice. The team have **no superpowers** and are far more interested in **fame** than being heroes. Desperate for power, they even **team up with Loki!**

AAARRGHH!!

SATAN pulls the Defenders **INTO HELL** where he forces them to face a series of **DIRE CHALLENGES.** If they fail, he will take over the Earth for **A THOUSAND YEARS!**

TOP 4

Defenders Lineups

1 **THE NEW DEFENDERS**—assembled by Beast; includes Angel, Valkyrie, Gargoyle, Iceman, and Moondragon

2 **THE SECRET DEFENDERS**—to battle magical foes, Doctor Strange recruits the Hulk, Ghost Rider, and the Silver Surfer

3 **THE LAST DEFENDERS**—Nighthawk, She-Hulk, Colossus, and Blazing Skull protect New Jersey as part of the Fifty-State Initiative

4 **THE FEARLESS DEFENDERS**—an all-female team led by Misty Knight, Valkyrie, and Dr. Annabelle Riggs to face off against the villainous Caroline le Fay

HUSH-HUSH!

MI-13 is the British government's **first line of defense** against **super-powered** and **paranormal threats**. Overseen by secret agent **Pete Wisdom** and led by patriotic hero **Captain Britain**, MI-13 works behind the scenes to **keep the U.K. safe**!

"Just you and me, children. Saving the world. From itself."

TOP 3
International Recruits

MI-13 is a British intelligence agency, but notable heroes from around the globe have joined its ranks.

1 **BLADE**—the legendary vampire hunter signs on when the agency clashes with Dracula and his vampire hordes. Hunts vampires along with Spitfire.

2 **BLACK KNIGHT**—former Avenger Dane Whitman, wielder of the Ebony Blade, joins to repel an alien invasion. In love with Faiza Hussain.

3 **SHANG-CHI**—Pete Wisdom calls on the Chinese Master of Kung Fu to defeat the Welsh Dragon, an ancient beast who finds a new calling as a crime lord.

S.H.I.E.L.D. DECLASSIFIED

JOINING THE DOTS
MI-13 is the latest British agency tasked with monitoring the unknown. Previous ones include S.T.R.I.K.E. (Special Tactical Reserve for International Key Emergencies), W.H.O. (Weird Happenings Organization), and Black Air.

Blade

Pete Wisdom

Faiza Hussain

STEWARD OF THE SWORD
Doctor Faiza Hussain is struck by an alien weapon and given near-complete control over biological organisms, allowing her to alter matter at a **subatomic** level. While serving with MI-13, she inherits **Excalibur**, the legendary sword of **King Arthur**!

ALTERNATE UNIVERSE

The Captain Britain of **Earth-833** is a British version of **Spider-Man**!

TELL ME MORE!

Captain Britain's superhuman strength, speed, durability, and flight are tied to his emotions. When he feels confident, he's nearly invincible. If he feels doubt, his powers weaken dramatically.

YESSS!! **DRACULA** stages an invasion, believing the U.K.'s magical **ANTI-VAMPIRE** barriers have fallen. MI-13 has tricked the vampire lord, and most of his forces are **WIPED OUT** when they enter British airspace!

FAST FACTS

OTHER NAMES:
E.I.S. (Extraordinary
Intelligence Service),
"The Department"

LEADERS: Pete Wisdom,
Captain Britain

TOP AGENTS: Alistaire
Stewart (scientific advisor),
Spitfire, Union Jack,
Excalibur, Lionheart

BASES: Whitehall, The
Shard (London, U.K.)

ALLIES: Meggan, Avengers,
X-Men

FOES: Dracula, Mys-Tech,
Oberon of Otherworld,
Killpower, Plokta

Captain Britain

UPGRADED!

Lady Jacqueline Falsworth
Crichton, alias **Spitfire**, is the
daughter of the hero **Union Jack**.
She was bitten by **Baron Blood**
during World War II and turned into
a **vampire**—but a good one!
As well as vampire powers,
she has **superhuman
speed.**

Power Up!

HOT KNIVES!
PETE WISDOM has the
mutant ability to absorb
heat and release it as
"HOT KNIVES." He can
use his "hot knives"
in various ways, such
as **FIRING THEM** at
opponents, using them
as **CLAWS,** or even
creating a protective
FORCE FIELD.

Q: Who is Captain Britain?

A: **Brian Braddock** is Earth's
representative of the **Captain
Britain Corps**, an **inter-
dimensional league** of heroes
granted powers by the magician
Merlin. He is married to mutant
empath **Meggan**, a Romany with
shape-shifting powers.

Spitfire

Black Knight

WOW!

770

The speed that Captain Britain can
fly in miles per hour (1,239 kmh)—
faster than the speed of sound.

COMPULSORY HELP
By order of the British prime
minister, any Super Hero
operating in the U.K. may be
called on to assist MI-13—
whether they want to or not!

TOP 5

Strangest MI-13 Agents

1 **CAPTAIN MIDLANDS**—
a senior citizen
super-soldier!

2 **TINK**—a fairy from the
Otherworld of Avalon!

3 **DIGITEK**—a living
Protosilicon computer!

4 **TANGERINE**—an emotional
vibe reader!

5 **MOTORMOUTH**—a foul-
mouthed woman with
a sonic scream !

YESSS!! NICO and CHASE are kidnapped and forced to fight in wicked assassin Arcade's **BOOBY-TRAPPED** island arena. They survive and go undercover to infiltrate the Super Villain nation of **BAGALIA!**

VICTOR MANCHA

CHASE STEIN

BEST KNOWN FOR PREVENTING THEIR MOMS AND DADS FROM TAKING OVER THE WORLD!

Power Up!

TIME FOR A SNOOZE
Molly Hayes, the youngest original Runaway, possesses immense **STRENGTH** and is nearly **INVULNERABLE.** However, using her powers makes her really **SLEEPY.** Even heroes need **NAPS!**

A BUMPY RIDE! Chase pilots the group's **ship,** the **Leapfrog.** This frog-shaped vehicle—stolen from Chase's evil inventor parents—doesn't actually fly—it **jumps!**

RUNNING OUT OF TIME
The Runaways are **thrown back in time** to the year 1907 when a mission goes wrong! They get involved in a **super-powered turf war** and rescue young **plant-manipulating mutant Klara Prast,** who returns with them to the present.

Q: So what *is* the Pride?!
A: The Pride is a wealthy, powerful **gang of Super Villains,** formed of six couples. They are sworn to serve the **Gibborim** —a **race of giants** who want to **wipe out** humanity.

WHEN GOOD GUYS GO BAD!

TREACHERY!
Alex Wilder, original leader of the Runaways, betrays the team to gain his evil parents' approval.

FUGITIVES!

What would **you** do if you found out your parents were secretly members of Super Villain clan, the **Pride?!?** If you were the **Runaways,** you'd steal a **magical staff,** a pair of **fire-shooting gauntlets,** and a telepathically linked **dinosaur**—and **hit the road!**

S.H.I.E.L.D. DECLASSIFIED

LIKE FATHER, LIKE SON?
Victor Mancha is a cyborg, built by Ultron using cloned DNA and advanced nanotechnology. Ultron hopes to plant his "son" among the Avengers as a double agent, but Victor rejects his programming and becomes a true hero.

"Lots of kids think their parents are evil. Mine really were. Honestly."

UPGRADED!
The Leapfrog is **destroyed** when **missiles** tear apart the team's Malibu hideout. Luckily, Victor **salvages** the ship's computer and installs it in a new, upgraded Leapfrog that can **fly**!

KLARA PRAST

FAST FACTS

KEY MEMBERS:
Nico, Chase, Gertrude, Karolina, Molly, Old Lace, Victor, Klara, Xavin

FRIENDS: Young Avengers, Avengers Academy, Cloak & Dagger

FOES: The Pride, Majesdanian Light Brigade, Arcade

BASE: Malibu, California (formerly beneath La Brea Tar Pits)

NICO MINORU

HANDLE WITH CARE!
Nico channels her magic through the **Staff of One.** This hugely powerful artifact has just two **drawbacks:**
1. Nico may only use a spell **once,** or the staff will backfire.
2. The staff **cannot** bring the dead back to life.

WHAT?!
Old Lace is a **genetically engineered dinosaur** from the **87th century** who shares a **telepathic bond** with Gertrude! ▶

IDENTITY CRISIS?
Karolina Dean is raised as a human, but one day she discovers that both she and her parents are secretly solar-powered aliens from another world, Majesdane!

MOLLY HAYES

SQUABBLES & SUPERPOWERS

Think your siblings are **annoying?** Try dealing with a little brother who can turn into a **cloud**—or a baby sister able to **disintegrate matter!** When they aren't fighting crime, the young heroes of **Power Pack** are usually **fighting one another!**

FAST FACTS

ABILITIES:
Gravity control–Alex (Gee) • Energy absorption/disintegration –Katie (Energizer) • **Density manipulation**–Jack (Mass Master) • **High-speed flight**– Julie (Lightspeed)

NOT-SO-FRIENDLY FOES:
Snarks, Kurse, Bogeyman

PARENTS: Dr. James Power, Margaret Power

IDENTITY CRISIS!

"Let's see... you got my power and I got Jack's power and Jack got Alex's power and Alex got your power! What a mess!" —Julie

TELL ME MORE!

TELL ME MORE!

Horse-headed Kymellian scientist Aelfyre Whitemane is wounded by alien Snarks while defending physicist Dr. Power's new invention. Before Whitemane dies, he bestows his powers onto Dr. Power's children, along with his spaceship!

UPGRADED!

The team's powers often swap around, so they find new ways to use their gifts. Jack works out how to use Alex's powers to throw a gravity-powered "Super-G" punch.

GOOD DAY

Alex Power is a **teen genius**, so Reed Richards drafts him into the **Future Foundation**, made up of the most **brilliant young minds** on the planet.

JULIE

ALEX

"I'll take a crazy villain over a mad little sister any day..."
JACK

JACK

Power Up!

SOAR
Julie takes a while to master her flying abilities. At first, she can only stay aloft while **ACCELERATING**—and slow down by running **INTO** something!

SHAPE-SHIFT
Boisterous Jack can transform into a **GAS**, or become solid and drop onto enemies as a **"JACK HAMMER."**

KATIE

REALLY?!
"Snark" is just a nickname for the evil alien **Z'nrx** race, as their real name is **unpronounceable** by human tongues!

Top 4 Goofiest Codenames
1. Mistress of Density—Julie
2. Molecula—Julie
3. Counterweight—Katie
4. Powerpax—Alex

FAMILY CONNECTIONS
Space vessel **Smartship Friday** is the Power Pack's main mode of transportation. The computer **A.I.** that runs the ship is genderless, but the kids think of Friday as a **surrogate space mother.**

QUEST FOR REVENGE!
Dr. Power's greedy ex-boss, **Douglas Carmody,** blames Power Pack for his **financial ruin.** His vengeful **obsession** leads him to Limbo, where he is transformed into the **grotesque Bogeyman!**

Power Up!

CRUMBLE
Katie is just **FIVE** when she obtains her disintegration powers. When Norse monster Kurse attacks, she **TOPPLES** a building onto him—and then **FEELS BAD** about it!

MANIPULATE
Alex's control over gravity lets him make objects **WEIGHTLESS,** or increase the **PRESSURE** on bad guys. He can even **FLY** with homemade wings!

145

Shaman

WHAT?!

Physicist Dr. Walter Langkowski accidentally opens a **portal** to the magical **Realm of Great Beasts**, allowing the monster **Tanaraq** to possess him. Now Walter can transform into the massively strong and hairy **Sasquatch**!

Sasquatch

Aurora

Guardian

FAMILY CONNECTIONS

Originally, twins **Northstar** and **Aurora** could only access their full powers when they were in **direct contact.** Now, both mutant heroes can independently summon massive bursts of **devastating light,** which can take the form of **concussive blasts!**

Snowbird

FROM THE SEA

Marrina is a member of the highly adaptive **Plodex alien race.** Marrina's egg pod lands in the depths of the ocean and she later acquires **unique amphibious abilities**— which she puts to use as Alpha Flight's most **hotheaded member!**

Northstar

Marrina

TELL ME MORE!

As Alpha Flight's former leader, Guardian (inventor James "Mac" Hudson) wears a suit that gives him flight, body armor, and the ability to fire powerful bursts of energy.

Puck

DEPT. H DECLASSIFIED

FROM GAMMA TO ALPHA

Overseen by Department H, Alpha Flight isn't known as "Canada's Premier Super Team" for nothing! The department trains would-be heroes as Gamma Flight. When they're ready, they take to the field as Beta Flight. Only the best of the best graduate to Alpha Flight status!

INTO ORBIT
Based on a space station, **Alpha Flight (Space Program)** gets a new commander—**Carol Danvers**, alias **Captain Marvel!** Dealing with threats to the galaxy, the elite team comprises **Puck, Aurora, Sasquatch,** and science officer **Wendy Kawasaki**.

CANADA'S CHAMPIONS

Whenever **Canada** is threatened by **mythical marauders** or **super-powered menaces**, the government doesn't make an international call to **Avengers Tower.** It contacts its very own Super Hero team—**Alpha Flight!**

HANDLE WITH CARE!

First Nations member Dr. Michael Twoyoungmen, also known as **Shaman**, can draw all sorts of **potions** and **artifacts** from his **enchanted medicine bag**. It takes years of training just to **look in it!**

BACK FROM THE DEAD!

When Guardian **seemingly dies,** an alien, fishlike race named the **Qwrlln** fuse his Guardian suit to his body. The result? They turn him into a **cyborg**, but they save his life!

Power Up!

ANIMAL MAGIC

SNOWBIRD is the half-human daughter of the Inuit goddess **NELVANNA**. She can transform into an albino version of any northern animal, such as a **SHARP-EYED OWL**—or a **SHARP-CLAWED POLAR BEAR!**

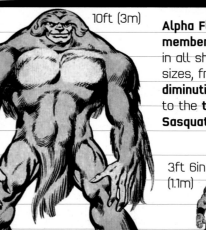

10ft (3m)

Alpha Flight members come in all shapes and sizes, from the **diminutive Puck** to the **towering Sasquatch!**

3ft 6in (1.1m)

LOOKS AREN'T EVERYTHING!

The Avengers **fly high** above sunny streets, but other champions **lurk deep underground**. The **Legion of Monsters** are **shunned** for their horrific appearance, but they **protect** their fellow creatures of the night from **monster hunters** and **hateful humans!**

The curse of **lycanthropy** has blighted generations of Jacob "Jack" Russell's family. Jack usually keeps his **werewolf side** under control, but sometimes he gives into his rage. The result? Clashes with **Moon Knight** and **Dr. Strange!**

WHEN BAD GUYS GO GOOD!

CLUED UP
Satana is drafted into Luke Cage's **Thunderbolts** to **beef up** the team's magical defenses. Her first-hand knowledge of **demons** comes in handy when the Asgardian, Kuurth, possesses the body of fellow team member Juggernaut!

YECCH!

The Legion of Monsters guards **Monster Metropolis**, located deep below New York City in the filthy, smelly sewers! It's a safe haven for others of their kind.

UPGRADED!

3,000 years ago, warrior N'Kantu was **magically embalmed** by an evil priest and kept in a tomb for millennia—**awake, but paralyzed!** Now he's free, the **mystical fluids** that flow in him grant amazing strength.

FAMILY CONNECTIONS
Satana isn't known as the **Devil's Daughter** for nothing: She inherits vastly powerful **dark magicks** from her demonic father—making her one of the most powerful **witches** on Earth.

AAARRGHH!!
N'Kantu is imprisoned during the superhuman civil war. How? Iron Man designs a **CAGE** of **ROARING FLAMES** to contain the mystical mummy!

WEREWOLF BY NIGHT

TELL ME MORE!
Man-Thing guards the Nexus of All Realities—a gateway between different dimensions—through which he can teleport himself and his teammates.

REALLY?!
Frank Castle, the **Punisher,** is **chopped** to **pieces** by the assassin Daken. Morbius **stitches** him back together into a **patchwork "FrankenCastle!"**

MAN-THING

"I'm the primary caregiver to all manner of creepy crawlies."

MORBIUS

Legendary **monster hunter Elsa Bloodstone** is actually an **ally** of the Legion and the peaceful inhabitants of Monster Metropolis: These beasts **police themselves** and pose **little threat** to humans!

ELSA BLOODSTONE

One of **Peter Parker's** Horizon Labs colleagues works behind closed doors in a **hazmat containment suit.** Peter discovers it's none other than **Dr. Michael Morbius—** searching for a **cure** for his vampirism!

WHAT ARE YOU LOOKING AT?

WIDE, WEBBED FACE GILLS—allow Manphibian to breathe underwater.

SHARP CLAWS—for attacking and defending.

TOUGH, ARMOR-LIKE SKIN—can even withstand missile attacks!

FAST FACTS

MEMBERS: Werewolf by Night, Man-Thing, Morbius the Living Vampire, Satana, N'Kantu the Living Mummy, Manphibian

BASE: Monster Metropolis

ALLIES: Punisher, Elsa Bloodstone, Ghost Rider

FOES: Hunter of Monster Special Forces, Robert Hellsgaard

Q: What's a "Living Vampire?"

A: **Unlike** most bloodsuckers, Morbius's need for blood stems from a scientific **accident,** not a supernatural curse. He's vulnerable to sunlight but is **not truly undead,** and he's **immune** to holy water, garlic, and crucifixes.

MANPHIBIAN

"Thisss is jussst how we look."

149

WHAT?!

To gain **knowledge of the future**, Odin tears out his own eye and throws it into the **Well of Wisdom**. The eye grows and takes on **a life of its own**, traveling the universe and giving enigmatic advice to Thor.

TOP 5
No-Good Gods

1 **AMATSU-MIKABOSHI**— Japanese God of Evil; kills Zeus and launches the Chaos War to wipe out all of existence

2 **LOKI**—Asgardian God of Mischief obsessed with power and getting one over on his brother Thor

3 **SETH**—Egyptian God of the Dead; imprisons other Egyptian gods and inspires Apocalypse to conquer the world

4 **PLUTO**—Greek God of Death; plots to conquer Olympus and the world, but is defeated by Earth's Super Heroes

5 **HELA**—Queen of the Dead; wants to bring all mortals and the gods of Asgard into Hel

HANDLE WITH CARE!

Odin has a powerful weapon— **Gungnir, the Spear of Heaven!** It's made of Uru metal and can **channel the Odinforce.** Unlike Thor's hammer, Mjolnir, you don't have to be worthy to wield it.

Q: Why do the gods of Earth no longer interact with mortals?

A: 1,000 years ago the **Celestials** made them promise **not to interfere** with humanity! That's why Zeus and Odin get so angry when Hercules and Thor keep going to Earth and **playing the hero!**

GODS AMONG US

YESSS!! To protect Earth, Odin builds a **MIGHTY WEAPON**: a massive suit of armor named the **DESTROYER**. It contains the life-forces of **EVERY ASGARDIAN!**

REALLY?!

Even gods fear **Atum the God Eater,** also known as the Demogorge. He **lives in the sun** and devours deities that turn against humanity. He suffers a **fatal case of indigestion** when he swallows the Skrull god Sl'gur't!

TELL ME MORE!

The Asgardians and Olympians get most of the attention thanks to Thor and Hercules, but Earth is home to many families of gods. They include the Gods of Heliopolis (Egyptian), the Vodu (African), the Amatsu-Kami (Japanese), the Xian (Chinese), and the Manidoog (Native American). The gods of Earth meet at the Council of Godheads to decide matters of heavenly importance.

WOW!

25,000

The height in feet (7,620m) of the massive Godkiller armor, built by the Aspirants to kill the Celestials.

TEAM PLAYER

When the Skrulls launch their **Secret Invasion,** Hercules leads a **God Squad** to defend Earth. It includes Amadeus Cho, Atum, Snowbird, Ajak of the Eternals, and Amatsu-Mikaboshi. Amatsu **betrays Herc** and unleashes the devastating **Chaos War!**

The Multiverse is home to **many gods.** They usually **stay out** of mortal affairs—but when they do get involved, the results can be **Earth-shattering!**

S.H.I.E.L.D.

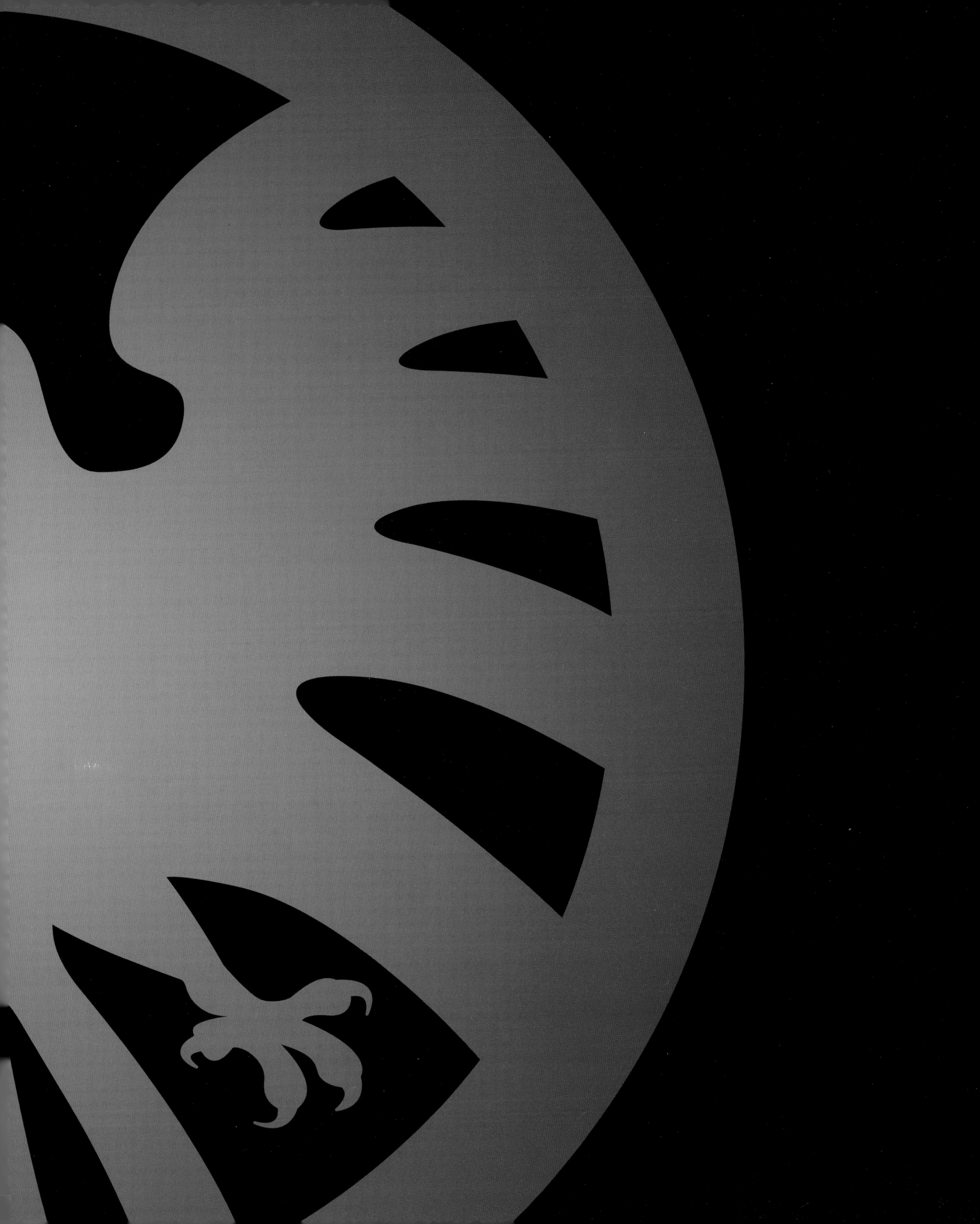

FAST FACTS

FULL NAME:
Strategic Hazard Intervention, Espionage, and Logistics Directorate

ORIGIN: Founded by the U.S. government with the help of Tony Stark

HEADQUARTERS:
S.H.I.E.L.D. Helicarrier

ABILITIES: Advanced weaponry, technology, surveillance, intelligence, massive manpower

ALLIES: Avengers, S.W.O.R.D., Secret Avengers

FOES: Hydra, A.I.M., Masters of Evil

S.H.I.E.L.D. DECLASSIFIED

THE HELICARRIER
S.H.I.E.L.D.'s primary vehicle and HQ is a flying aircraft carrier designed by Tony Stark and built by Stark Industries. There have been several versions—and a number of spectacular crashes!

S.H.I.E.L.D. DECLASSIFIED

S.H.I.E.L.D.'S FLYING CARS
Stark Industries manufactures a wide range of flying cars for S.H.I.E.L.D. These armored sports cars not only fly at high speeds and altitudes, they can also travel underwater as submarines.

NUMBER CRUNCH!

3000
Active S.H.I.E.L.D. agents prior to the superhuman civil war

550 miles (885km)
Maximum distance flown by a S.H.I.E.L.D. flying car

10 hours
Maximum oxygen supply inside a flying car

Mach 2.1
Quinjet max speed

S.H.I.E.L.D. DECLASSIFIED

ROBOT REPLACEMENTS
Life Model Decoys (LMDs) are androids developed by S.H.I.E.L.D. to impersonate people. Externally, these robots are indistinguishable from living humans. They are controlled remotely and have superhuman strength.

S.H.I.E.L.D. DECLASSIFIED

THE QUINJET
Quinjets are originally created by Black Panther's Wakanda Design Group. They are often stowed aboard S.H.I.E.L.D. Helicarriers, ready to transport agents for dangerous missions—even in space! Quinjets are capable of vertical take-off and landings.

UPGRADED!
Tony Stark wins the superhuman civil war and becomes director of S.H.I.E.L.D. after Maria Hill resigns. He designs a new red-and-gold Helicarrier, makes improvements, and raises morale.

NOOOOO!! Nick Fury has an **AUTONOMOUS** Life Model Decoy known as Max Fury. It becomes **SO DANGEROUS** that Nick tries to destroy it —but the LMD **GETS AWAY!**

TOP 4
Directors of S.H.I.E.L.D.

1 **RICK STONER**—the first director; assassinated by Hydra terrorists

2 **NICK FURY, SR.**—ageless director for 40 years; still active in team

3 **TONY STARK (IRON MAN)**—director after the superhuman civil war; sacked for failing to anticipate Skrull invasion

4 **MARIA HILL**—the strongest leader since Nick Fury; has had more than one spell as director

WHEN BAD GUYS GO GOOD!

DARK REIGN
Norman Osborn replaces Tony Stark (Iron Man) as director of S.H.I.E.L.D. after Stark fails to prevent the Skrulls' Secret Invasion. Osborn renames the organization H.A.M.M.E.R.

WORLD SAVED!

S.H.I.E.L.D. is Earth's **front line** of defense, combating **global threats** from Super Villains, supernatural menaces, alien invaders, and terrorist groups. **S.H.I.E.L.D.** is equipped with **cutting-edge technology** and commands a force of **superbly trained agents.**

FAST AND FURIOUS!

They are **father and son**. They share the name **Nick Fury** and a **common cause**: safeguarding the U.S.—and the world—from **all manner** of threats as the **main men of S.H.I.E.L.D.!**

⬡ **S.H.I.E.L.D.** DECLASSIFIED

SECRET OF A LONG LIFE
When Nick Fury is wounded in France during World War II, he is saved by Professor Sternberg's Infinity formula. The formula also maintains Fury's youth, but he must receive regular doses to prevent dramatic aging.

FAST FACTS

FULL NAME: Nicholas Joseph Fury

STRENGTHS: Expert strategist, vast combat experience, fast healing

WEAKNESSES: Blind in left eye, disregard for rules and ethics

ALLIES: Dum Dum Dugan, Daisy Johnson, Spider-Man, Avengers, S.H.I.E.L.D., Secret Warriors, Howling Commandos

FOES: Axis, Red Skull, Hydra, Doctor Doom, Taskmaster

Q: Who are the Howling Commandos?

A: They are a bunch of misfit but brave World War II soldiers. **Sergeant Nick Fury** leads them against Axis villains such as **Red Skull** and **Baron von Strucker**.

BEST KNOWN FOR
BEING A RUTHLESS S.H.I.E.L.D. DIRECTOR

DASTARDLY DEED!

Nick Fury launches an investigation to discover who murdered Uatu the Watcher and stole one of his all-seeing eyes. He omits to mention that he did it himself!

"Nick Fury ain't watchin' the end o' the *WORLD* in bed, Mister!"

FULL NAME:
Nicholas Joseph Fury (formerly Marcus Johnson)

STRENGTHS: Expert combatant, infinity formula in blood gives even greater healing and anti-aging powers than Nick Sr.

WEAKNESSES: Blind in left eye

ALLIES: Avengers, Secret Avengers, Phillip Coulson, Wolverine, Nick Fury Sr., S.H.I.E.L.D., U.S. Army Rangers

FOES: Orion, Taskmaster, Leviathan

BEST KNOWN FOR
BEING NOT QUITE AS RUTHLESS AS HIS DAD

Q: How does Nick Fury Jr. lose his eye?

A: Fury Sr.'s enemy **Orion** wants to extract **the Infinity Formula** in the veins of Fury's son. Father and son stop Orion, but the villain takes Nick Jr.'s eye—a **spiteful act** to make him look **more like his father.**

TOP 6
Howling Commandos

1 **DUM DUM DUGAN**—circus strongman

2 **IZZY COHEN**—car mechanic

3 **GABE JONES**—jazz trumpeter

4 **JONATHAN JUNIPER**—eager beaver, Ivy League college graduate

5 **DINO MANELLI**—dashing actor with matinee idol looks

6 **REBEL RALSTON**—skilled horseback rider

SCORPIO

FAMILY DISCONNECTIONS

Nick Jr. follows in his father's footsteps, but not all the Furys are on the same side. Fury Sr.'s brother, Jake, becomes the **villain Scorpio** and joins Hydra. Nick Jr.'s brother, Mikal, **tries to kill his father!**

TELL ME MORE!

Fury (Sr.) tricks a team of heroes into joining him on an **illegal mission** to overthrow villainous Latvarian prime minister, Lucia von Bardas. When it's over he **wipes the team's memories!**

AAARRGHH!!
Fury's dark deeds are **PUNISHED** when the Watchers force him to take dead Uatu's place, **HELPLESSLY** watching events on Earth as **"THE UNSEEN."**

ALTERNATE UNIVERSE

On Earth-1610, Nick Fury is a test subject in **Project Rebirth**, and given an **super-strength** injection. He loses his eye in the Gulf War. As S.H.I.E.L.D. director, he forms an Avengers taskforce called "the Ultimates."

BETWEEN...

The first issue of *Sgt. Fury and His Howling Commandos* appeared in May 1963. Stan Lee and Jack Kirby were confident of success despite the comic book's rather unwieldy title.

...THE PANELS

PY SOLDIERS

S.H.I.E.L.D. agents undergo rigorous **spy school training,** learning fighting techniques, how to use the latest technology, and much more. Most operatives are **unswervingly loyal**—and some even carry on serving **after they're dead!**

BEST KNOWN FOR
KEEPING SECRETS AND COOL UNIFORMS

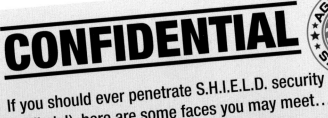

CONFIDENTIAL

AGENTS OF S.H.I.E.L.D

If you should ever penetrate S.H.I.E.L.D. security (unlikely!), here are some faces you may meet…

- **NICK FURY JR.**—the secret son of C.I.A. agent Nia Jones and Nick Fury Sr. Heads up the Secret Avengers Initiative with Phil Coulson.

- **DEATHLOK** (Henry Hayes)—every covert team should have it's own cyborg assassin!

CONFIDENTIAL

- **MELINDA MAY** (Cavalry)—one of S.H.I.E.L.D.'s top agents with amazing fighting skills

- **JEMMA SIMMONS**—may only have a short time to live after being infected by an A.I.M. DNA bomb!

- **LEO FITZ**—British agent who has been on dangerous missions involving magic and demons

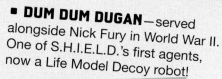

- **DUM DUM DUGAN**—served alongside Nick Fury in World War II. One of S.H.I.E.L.D.'s first agents, now a Life Model Decoy robot!

CONFIDENTIAL

- **MOCKINGBIRD**—Barbara "Bobbi" Morse (Agent 19), a baton-wielding bio-chemist and high- level agent. Has also served with the West Coast Avengers.

- **QUAKE** (Daisy Johnson)—can create seismic disturbances with her hands. Causes such a shake-up in Nick Fury Sr.'s Secret Warriors team that she briefly ends up as director of S.H.I.E.L.D.

- **AGENT 13** (Sharon Carter)—Peggy Carter's niece, and longtime girlfriend of Steve Rogers. The first leader of Femme Force, a team of female agents.

- **PHIL "CHEESE" COULSON**—a high-ranking member, often helming his own elite Secret Avengers team, sometimes with best friend Nick Fury Jr. Phil is a big Super Hero fan!

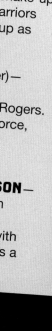

"I'm a guy with a *PLAN*."
PHIL COULSON

WHEN GOOD GIRLS GO BAD!

MADAME HYDRA
The Contessa Valentina Allegra de Fontaine is a loyal S.H.I.E.L.D. agent and Nick Fury's love interest for decades. Then she joins terror group Hydra as the ruthless Madame Hydra!

REALLY?!

Mechanical menace **M.O.D.O.K.** has a secret agenda when he teams up with S.H.I.E.L.D. He plans to **kill** Director Maria Hill, but ends up **crying tears** of love!

LOVE PUNCH

The first time Nick Fury meets the Contessa he totally underestimates her combat skills. His embarrassment soon turns to love!

S.H.I.E.L.D. DECLASSIFIED

THE GIFT OF ETERNAL LIFE
The amazing robot technology showcased in Life Model Decoys dates back to Leonardo da Vinci's time! Some LMDs are so advanced that a human consciousness can be uploaded into them. This enables a person to, in effect, live on forever!

NOooooo!!

Even after **DEATH**, Dum Dum Dugan carries on working for S.H.I.E.L.D.—as a **LIFE MODEL DECOY**. Dugan doesn't know he's a **ROBOT**—and is dismayed when he finds out!

BACK FROM THE DEAD!

Top agent Jasper Sitwell is **shot dead** by a brainwashed **Black Widow**. He returns as a **zombie** and joins S.H.I.E.L.D.'s Howling Commandos!

S.H.I.E.L.D. OPERATIONS

Battling **terror groups**, facing down **Super Villains**, and dealing with **sneaky extraterrestrial invasions** is no easy task. Throw in sudden outbreaks of **treachery** and **betrayal** from within and it's a wonder that **S.H.I.E.L.D.** is still going strong!

TOP 6

Most Wanted Foes

1 **BARON VON STRUCKER**—death-dealing terrorist leader!

2 **RED SKULL**—death-dealing terrorist leader!

3 **BARON ZEMO**—death-dealing terrorist leader and scientist!

4 **MADAME HYDRA**—death-dealing terrorist leader!

5 **ARNIM ZOLA**—death-dealing scientist!

6 **SCORPIO**—death-dealing terrorist!

S.H.I.E.L.D. DECLASSIFIED

SECRET WARRIORS

When Nick Fury Sr. (former Director of S.H.I.E.L.D.) uncovers a secret invasion of Skrulls, he knows nowhere is safe. He assembles the Secret Warriors—a young, super-secret squad, some of whom have super-powered parents.

REALLY?!

If a mission is **too strange** even for S.H.I.E.L.D., they send in the **Howling Commandos**—led by a Life Model Decoy (LMD) of **Dum Dum Dugan**, with the help of **Man-Thing, Hit Monkey, Vampire by Night, Teen Abomination, Warwolf,** and more. From Plant Zombies and dark magic to the **strangest monstrosities**, these guys have it covered!

AAAARRGHH!!

Iron Man's shortlived role as **DIRECTOR** of S.H.I.E.L.D. ends when his armor goes **BERSERK** with an alien **COMPUTER VIRUS**. He ends up being **FIRED** by the **U.S. PRESIDENT** himself!

Artist Leonardo Da Vinci, physicist Isaac Newton, and astronomer Galileo Galilei were once members of the Brotherhood of the Shield! Long before the days of Nick Fury or the Avengers, these heroes were the first to defeat Galactus, the Brood, and the Celestials.

YESSS!!
Former agent **MENTALLO** tries to conquer S.H.I.E.L.D. and control Nick Fury's mind. Luckily, Fury is able to **TIP OFF** the S.H.I.E.L.D. ESP team, cueing Tony Stark to neutralize an **H-BOMB**—and win the day!

TEAM PLAYER
Captain America is a key player in many S.H.I.E.L.D. operations. His **link** with Nick Fury dates back to **World War II.** Cap has also had a **close relationship** with high-ranking operative **Sharon Carter.**

"Our **TARGET** is in possession of the Cosmic Cube. So surprise is **VITAL.**"

DASTARDLY DEED!

Hydra has been trying to **topple** S.H.I.E.L.D. since World War II. Hydra's science division, Advanced Idea Mechanics, **infiltrates** S.H.I.E.L.D. with **LMDs,** and also tries to ruin Mr. Fantastic's **wedding** with a Vortex bomb!

ALTERNATE UNIVERSE

On planet Battleworld, the **Shield** is a **fortified, giant wall** that stands between Battleworld's **inhabitants** and a mixture of **zombies, Ultron's hordes,** and villainous **monsters!**

SUPER VILLAIN TEAMS

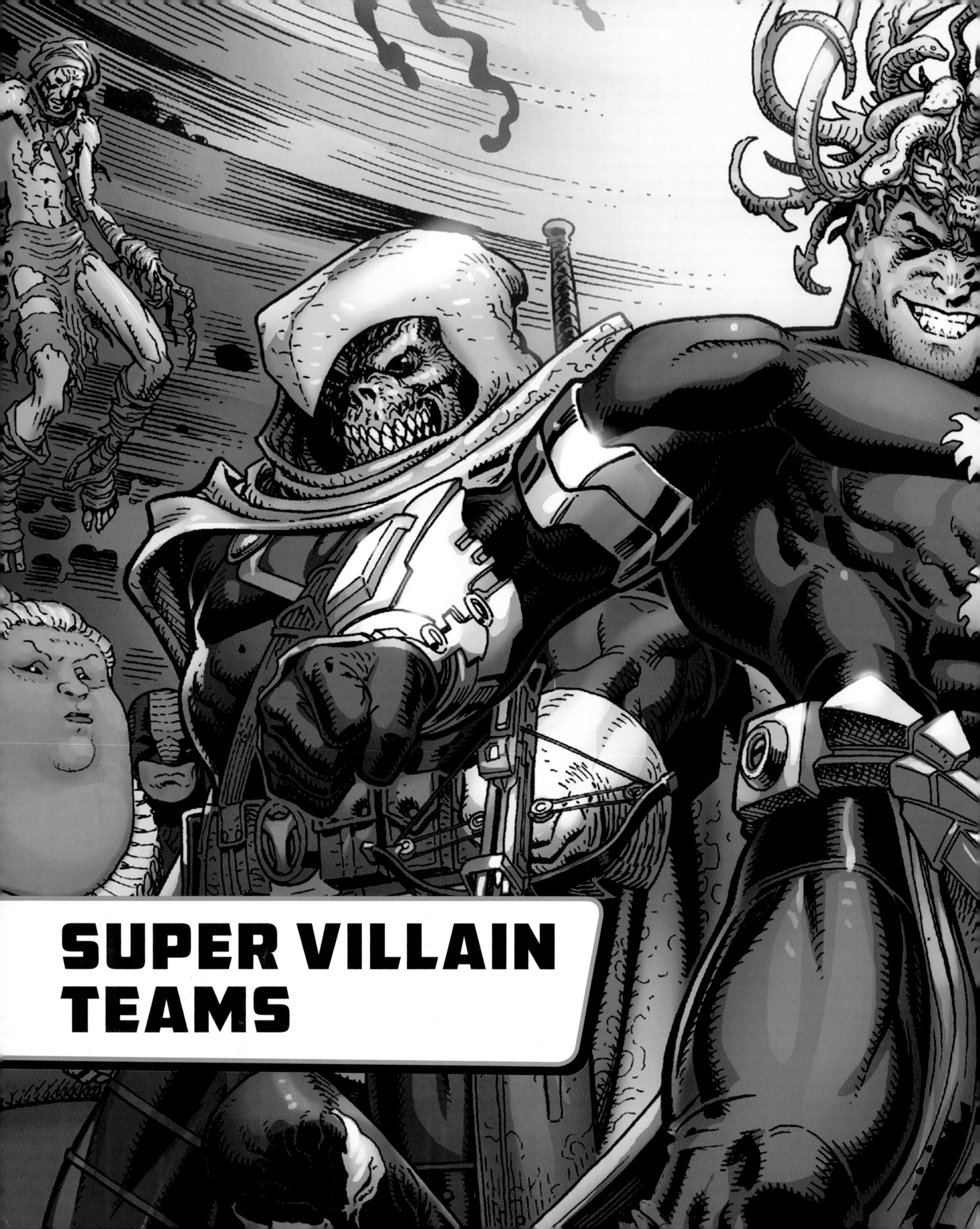

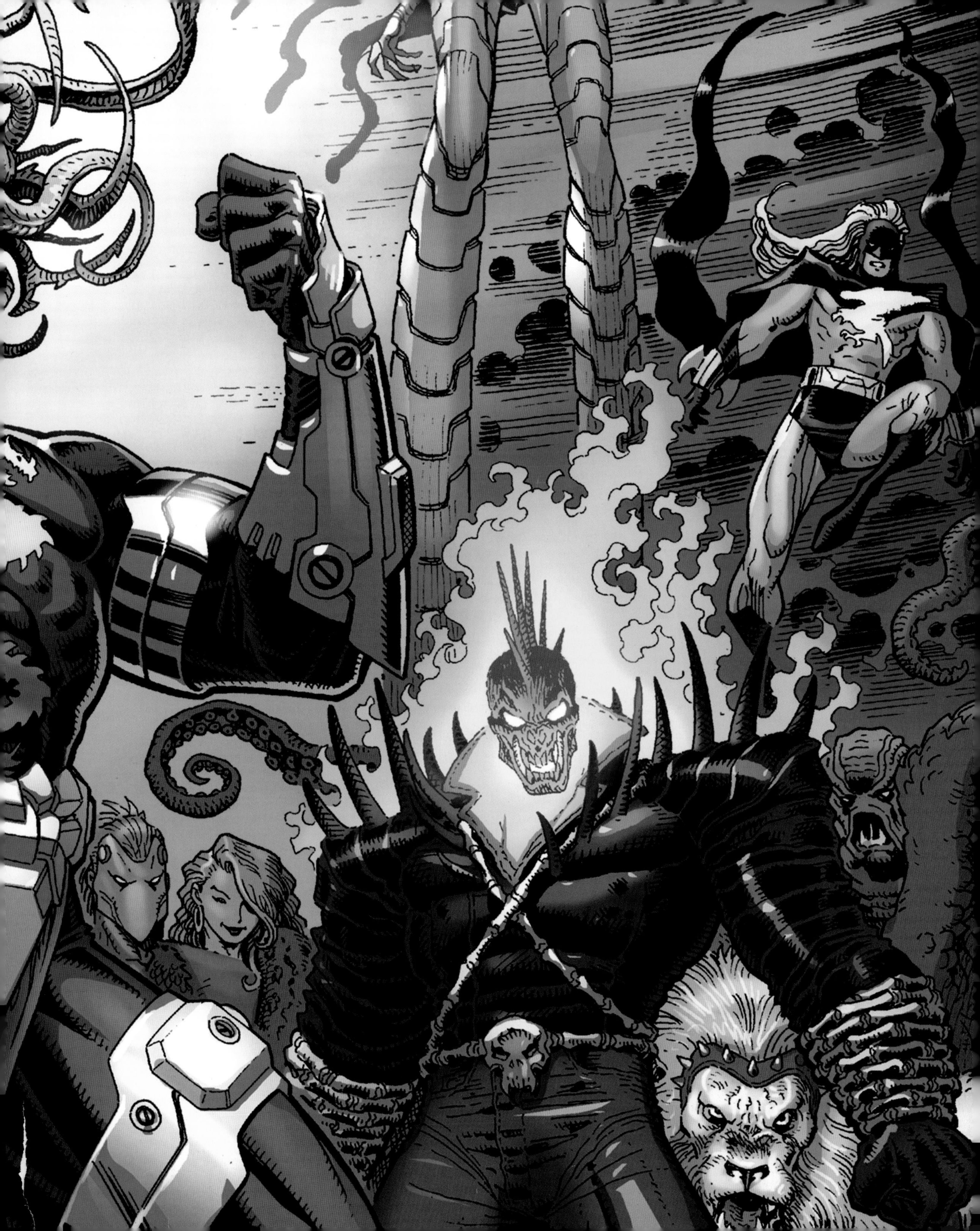

MANY-HEADED MENACE

Cut off a head, and two more shall take its place! Named for the monster of Greek Myth, **Hydra** is the **most dangerous** and widespread **villainous organization** on Earth. This **team of terror** spreads **corruption and violence** in a bid for **global domination!**

LEADERSHIP:
A secret council variously including key members Baron von Strucker, Baron Zemo, Madame Hydra (alias Viper), Gorgon, Kraken, and many more!

FOES: S.H.I.E.L.D., Avengers, Fantastic Four, right-thinking people everywhere!

"HAIL HYDRA!"

FAILURE IS NOT AN OPTION!
Hydra does not accept **failure!** Unsuccessful agents are **executed**— or forced to fight for their lives in **duels to the death!**

S.H.I.E.L.D. DECLASSIFIED

ORIGINS UNKNOWN
The roots of Hydra may lie in ancient Egypt or medieval Japan, but the modern organization was established by Nazi fanatic Baron von Strucker after World War II.

YESSS!!
Hydra unleashes a vast vehicle called the **TERROR-CARRIER** (similar to S.H.I.E.L.D.'s Helicarrier) to capture the **U.S. PRESIDENT.** A giant Yellowjacket (Hank Pym) rides it to destruction!

WHAT?!

After years of planning, **Hydra agents** infiltrate S.H.I.E.L.D. and **take it over!** Baron von Strucker believes he has defeated his old enemies, but then S.H.I.E.L.D. chief **Nick Fury** reveals that he's been **controlling Hydra** all along!

HANDLE WITH CARE!

Hydra's **Death Spore bomb** is set to wipe out **everyone on Earth**—except the Hydra agents in Baron von Strucker's island base! **Nick Fury** has other ideas and blows up von Strucker and his HQ instead!

BACK FROM THE DEAD!

Baron von Strucker is killed on **Hydra Island,** but his faithful agents find the Baron's remains—and **sacrifice** themselves to return him to life!

BACK FROM THE DEAD!

When Hydra leader **Viper** is shot dead, she is brought back to life by a horrible Hydra labs creation—**Hive parasites**. As a result, she looks like a **humanoid octopus!**

Power Up!

SATAN CLAW

This mechanical glove unleashes **ELECTRIC SHOCKS** and gives Baron von Strucker enhanced **STRENGTH**— so that he can battle Nick Fury toe to toe! It's been upgraded with a **GATLING GUN**, a **TELEPORTER**, and a **NUCLEAR REACTOR!**

Baron von Strucker

TOP 3

Hydra Splinter Groups

THESE GROUPS WERE ONCE PART OF HYDRA—BUT ARE NOW ITS ENEMIES!

1 **A.I.M.**—Advanced Idea Mechanics is Hydra's hi-tech research branch, until it goes independent after Baron von Strucker is killed on Hydra Island.

2 **SECRET EMPIRE**—Hydra creates the Secret Empire to cause trouble and draw attention away from Hydra itself. It specializes in political corruption and destroying heroes' reputations!

3 **THE HAND**—this clan of evil ninja helped to found the modern Hydra, but it has also fiercely opposed it at times.

BETWEEN...

Movies, books, and TV series about spies were all the rage in 1965, so Marvel's Stan Lee and Jack Kirby introduced Hydra in *Strange Tales* #135 as the evil equivalent of S.H.I.E.L.D.

...THE PANELS

UNDERCOVER

Jake Fury steals the **identity** of **Kraken**—one of Hydra's most **ruthless assassins**— and helps his long-lost brother Nick start a **civil war** within Hydra, and **kill** Baron von Strucker!

AAARRGHH!! The mysterious **SHADOW COUNCIL** sets up its own nation of **BAGALIA**. Don't go there—a Masters of Evil team made up of **HUNDREDS** of members serves as the **POLICE FORCE!**

Moonstone

Goliath

TROUBLEMAKERS!

ALTERNATE UNIVERSE

In the **Heroes Reborn** universe, **Black Knight** has grand plans to reshape the world with his Masters of Evil. Unfortunately, one of Dr. Doom's **Doombots** blows his head off, before **eliminating** all but one of the Masters!!

Wrecker

Q: How was the first Masters of Evil team created?

A: **Baron Heinrich Zemo** discovers that his supposedly dead foe, Captain America, is alive and a member of the **Avengers**—so he forms the **Masters of Evil** to **destroy** them all! Zemo **handpicks** each Super Villain member to match the powers of each Avenger.

The first **Masters of Evil** was founded by a mad scientist, but **many other teams** have since taken the name. They all have three things in common: loads of **B-list bad guys, wacky plans** to defeat Super Heroes, and a love for **wreaking havoc!**

Mister Hyde

REALLY?!

On their first mission, **Heinrich Zemo's** Masters of Evil stop the Avengers in their tracks by spraying them with **super-sticky Adhesive X glue.** Luckily, Earth's Mightiest Heroes use a cylinder of **Super-Dissolver** to melt the glue and **break free!**

HANDLE WITH CARE!

Egghead and his Masters of Evil kidnap **Hank Pym** to help Egghead build a **longevity machine**. Instead, Hank builds a weapons system with **force fields, cadmium tentacles,** and a **disruption stunner** to take down the Masters **single-handed!**

Bulldozer

Thunderball

WHEN GOOD GUYS GO BAD!

TRIPLE BLUFF!
The mysterious Crimson Cowl assembles a new Masters of Evil team. The Avengers get a shock when they discover that the Cowl is none other than their beloved butler, Jarvis! Or is he...?!

Titania

Piledriver

Yellowjacket

DASTARDLY DEED!

Absorbing Man

Helmut Zemo

Tiger Shark

Baron Helmut Zemo decides that the **best way** to beat the Avengers is by **swamping them with enemies!** He recruits an **18-strong** Masters of Evil team including Goliath and Bulldozer, which trashes **Avengers Mansion** —and the Avengers!

FAST FACTS

TEAM LEADERS: Baron Helmut Zemo, Shadow Council, Ultron 5 (as Crimson Cowl), Egghead, Baron Heinrich Zemo, Doctor Octopus, Black Knight, Lightmaster

LAIR: Inaccessible (underground or mountaintops)

MAIN FOES: Avengers, Guardians of the Galaxy

CLAIM TO FAME: Capturing Avengers Mansion

WHEN BAD GUYS GO GOOD!

NOT WHAT HE EXPECTED
Baron Helmut Zemo has a cunning plan: His second Masters of Evil lineup pretends to be a team of heroes, the Thunderbolts! Zemo is thwarted when all the villains— except for him—decide that they like being liked and become heroes for real!

FEELING SINISTER?

Just one thing unites **the Sinister Six:** They all **hate Spider-Man!** Six against one may not seem like a fair fight, but these bad guys spend as much time **fighting each other** as they do battling Spidey!

TELL ME MORE!

The first Sinister Six—Doc Ock, Kraven, Electro, Mysterio, Vulture, and Sandman—all want a solo victory over Spider-Man. They attack him one at a time, but Spidey easily knocks them out!

AAARGHH!!

The **FUTURE FOUNDATION** explores a Caribbean island and is attacked by **ZOMBIE PIRATES!** However, the zombies turn out to be fakes—controlled by an **ALL-NEW SINISTER SIX.**

Sandman

HANDLE WITH CARE!

Just in case the untrustworthy Sandman betrays the team, Doc Ock always keeps a **melter-ray** handy—to heat him into solid glass.

Doctor Octopus

REALLY?!

When Doctor Octopus **holds the world ransom,** Spider-Man tracks him down and is forced to battle a new Sinister Six team—made up of mind-controlled Avengers!

DASTARDLY DEED!

Vulture, Mysterio, Hobgoblin, and Electro create a "Sinister Five" to get **revenge** on Doc Ock. To make Sandman join, they bomb the home of a family he's staying with—and **blame Doc Ock!**

DOUBLE TROUBLE!

The Green Goblin blackmails Spider-Man into busting him out of jail, then sends a double-size team, the Sinister Twelve, to squash the wall-crawler.

Chameleon

CRIME ON THE WING
Vulture (Adrian Toomes) is a founding member of the Sinister Six and one of Spidey's oldest enemies. His electromagnetic flying harness is great for aerial attacks and **smash and grab** raids!

WOW!

66

Alien TV boss Mojo assembles the "Sinister Sixty-Six" to fight Spider-Man.

Rhino

Power Up!

TECH SUPPORT
The Sinister Six needs more firepower, so they take an **INTER-DIMENSIONAL TRIP** to steal hi-tech weapons! Armed with a new **FUTURISTIC ARSENAL**, the Six quickly knock Spidey out of action!

Mysterio

Electro

TOP 4

Worst Teammates

1 DOCTOR OCTOPUS—mean and manipulative, Doc Ock blackmails, betrays, and even mind-controls to get his way

2 SANDMAN—not such a bad guy, which is why he switches sides and fights for the good guys more than once

3 MYSTERIO—Spidey persuades him to sell out his boss when Doc Ock threatens to roast the world

4 CHAMELEON—this master of disguise can fool almost anyone—even other villains

GOOD DAY
The Sinister Six don't **always lose!** In one battle, they manage to beat up both Spidey and the **Incredible Hulk!**

ALTERNATE UNIVERSE
On Earth-803, New York is terrorized by techno-freaks known as the **Six Men of Sinestry.** Fortunately, they are **no match for the** costumed heroine **Lady Spider.**

LOOK OUT!
Criminal thug Aleksei Sytsevich gets permanently bonded to a super-tough exoskeleton. He becomes an enforcer for Super Villains as the **rampaging Rhino!**

ARGUING AMONG THEMSELVES AND BEING DEFEATED

FAST FACTS

NAME: Lethal Legion

LEADERS: Grim Reaper, Count Nefaria

KEY MEMBERS: Living Laser, Man-Ape, Swordsman, Whirlwind, Black Talon

OBJECTIVE: Destroy the Avengers by any means possible!

HANDLE WITH CARE!

Grim Reaper has a **high-tech scythe** instead of a right hand. The scythe has a built-in knockout ray, electroshock circuit, and energy blaster. It can also **spin** like a **buzzsaw**, become a **shield**, and rotate **fast enough** for him **to fly!**

GOOD DAY

The Lethal Legion **almost defeat** the Avengers at the **first attempt!** They trap half the Avengers in a **giant hourglass** filled with poison gas—until the Vision **tricks Grim Reaper** into **breaking the glass!**

TOP 6

Not-So-Lethal Legionnaires

SWORDSMAN—handy with a sword, but not much else

MAN-APE—stronger than a gorilla, but dumb

TRAPSTER—great at squirting superglue!

PORCUPINE—invents a spiny suit with lasers, but sells it to avoid arrest

BATROC—acrobat with a great moustache, but looks alone can't defeat heroes!

WHIRLWIND—can spin like a deadly whirlwind, but only in a straight line

WHEN BAD GUYS GO GOOD!

BROTHERS IN BADNESS!

When Norman Osborn becomes Director of S.H.I.E.L.D. and renames it H.A.M.M.E.R., Grim Reaper recruits a new Lethal Legion—and gets his brother Wonder Man to join! For once, the Williams brothers are fighting on the same side!

YESSS!!

Not all the Lethal Legion's missions are DISASTERS. With help from ULTRON they storm the West Coast Avengers' base, free teammate Goliath, then KIDNAP WONDER MAN and HANK PYM!

BAD DAY

Crime boss **Count Nefaria** gives the Living Laser, Power Man (Erik Josten), and Whirlwind a job in a **new Lethal Legion team.** He offers to **boost their powers,** then betrays them. The shifty Count **steals their powers** so he can take on **the Avengers!**

LETHAL LOSERS

The **Lethal Legion** aren't the greatest villains. Their founder, **Grim Reaper,** wants a Super Villain team to **take down** Earth's Mightiest Heroes, but just **can't find the right teammates!**

FAMILY CONNECTIONS

Lethal Legion boss **Grim Reaper** (Eric Williams) is **jealous** of his brother Simon (Wonder Man), his parents' favorite. Simon grows up to be a **Super Hero,** but Eric becomes a **Super Villain!**

TELL ME MORE!

Grim Reaper starts the Lethal Legion because he blames the Avengers for the apparent death of his brother, Wonder Man. However, his loyalties become confused when he finds out that Wonder Man's brain patterns were used to program Vision!

BACK FROM THE DEAD!

Vampiric mutant Nekra loves the Grim Reaper. When he dies she brings him back to life—**as a zombie!** To stay living, he is forced to absorb one life every 24 hours—and he starts with **Nekra!**

THEY COME FROM OUTER SPACE

If you think the **heroes** and **villains** of Earth are **extraordinary**, wait until you get **an eyeful** of these extraterrestrials! **Unfortunately**, most of them are **not big fans** of the human race!

YECCH!

The **toothy, cruel Brood** reproduce by laying their eggs in living hosts!

BEST KNOWN FOR

WANTING TO CONQUER OR DESTROY EARTH!

WOW!

192

The number of different words the Chitauri have for "hate!"

"What we want...is to destroy a world. EARTH."

WHEN BAD GUYS GO GOOD!

BACK TO SCHOOL
The Brood are infamously ruthless—but there are exceptions! Broo, a young Broodling, has extreme intelligence and no aggression. He leaves the Brood hivemind to join the X-Men at the Jean Grey School of Higher Learning.

S.H.I.E.L.D. DECLASSIFIED

SKRULL INVADERS OF EARTH
The shape-changing Skrulls place sleeper agents in the human population, even replacing Super Heroes such as Spider-Woman. S.H.I.E.L.D. and the Avengers beat back the invasion, but they lose the public's trust in the process.

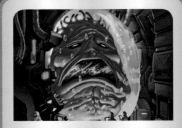

HEAD OF THE CLASS

The Kree are led by the **Supreme Intelligence,** an artificial intelligence composed of **the brains** of their **greatest thinkers,** but he has one **big weakness.** Because the Supreme Intelligence is **a giant head in a tank,** if the tank is smashed, he will **perish!**

TELL ME MORE!

The super-clever Inhumans of Earth are the result of genetic manipulation by the Kree. They later try to wipe out the Inhumans to prevent them from growing too powerful.

TOP 6
Alien Races

1 **KREE**—blue-skinned, warlike, advanced technology

2 **TROYJANS**—ruthless intergalactic invaders firing powerful cosmic energy blasts

3 **BADOON**—reptilian-humanoid conquerors (males) or pacifists (females)

4 **BUILDERS**—roam the galaxy destroying races that don't meet their high standards.

5 **RIGELLIANS**—would-be Earth conquerors with creepy mind-controlling abilities

6 **KYMELLIANS**—superpowered, peaceful, horse-headed humanoids

YESSS!!

Troyjan Arm'Chedon tries to resurrect his violent son Trauma. Hulk tricks Arm'Chedon into overloading his reanimation machine, vaporizing Trauma.

REALLY!?

The Fantastic Four trick **Skrull shape-shifters** into becoming cows—and then **hypnotize** them into thinking they've **always been cows!**

TOUGH BUGS

The Brood are a race of insectoid parasites, considered **evil** in almost every corner of the galaxy. One Brood, however, proves herself **an exception** as one of Hulk's devoted **Warbound**—joining him in his war against the Illuminati.

DASTARDLY DEED!

GALACTIC STORM

The Kree race is all but **destroyed** by a Shi'ar **Nega-Bomb,** ending the Kree-Shi'ar war. It turns out that both the war and the bomb are part of the Supreme Intelligence's **ruthless plan** to create **genetically improved Kree** from the few survivors!

NOOOOO!!

Space Phantoms can **STEAL** people's identities. When this happens the real person is **SHUNTED INTO LIMBO** until the Space Phantom chooses a new form!

ALTERNATE UNIVERSE

In the Ultimate Universe (Earth-1610), the **shape-shifting Chitauri** take over S.H.I.E.L.D., wipe out **20,000** S.H.I.E.L.D. officers, and try to **blow up** the whole world!

1 **THE HELLFIRE CLUB** — dedicated to political plots, skullduggery, and fancy parties!

2 **THE HAND** — ancient clan of demon-worshipping ninja with mystic powers.

3 **ZODIAC GROUP** — astrology-themed villains who take horoscopes very seriously.

4 **ATLAS FOUNDATION** — once a huge criminal organization, now seeking world stability through bizarre Super Hero team, Agents of Atlas.

5 **SONS OF SATANNISH** — sorcerers who serve the infamous demon lord.

Codename: *Black King*
Mutant who absorbs energy and turns it into physical power • The more you hit him, the stronger he gets

Shinobi Shaw
CODENAME: *Black King*
Sebastian's son • Evil mastermind • Uses density-changing powers to reach into people's chests and stop their hearts

Q: Who are the ringleaders of the Hellfire Club?

A: It is controlled by the secret **Inner Circle,** with members given codenames based on **chess pieces.** However, frequent **backstabbing** means that members of the Inner Circle don't often **stay in power** for long.

HANDLE WITH CARE!

The Sons of Satannish use the blue **Crystal of Conquest** to **teleport beings,** and to access the **magical powers** of **every member** in the group.

Nooooo!!

The Sons of Satannish **BANISH** Dr. Strange to an **ALIEN DIMENSION** and **STEAL HIS TREASURED ARTIFACTS!**

IN THE SHADOWS

In the **dark corners** of the universe, **secret organizations** meet to plot and scheme. These mysterious clans of **mystics, martial artists, and masterminds** use **blackmail, assassination, and treachery** to control the world from the shadows...

REALLY?!

The Hellfire Club starts its own school to teach **young mutants** how to be villains! Classes include **Introduction to Evil** and **Subjugation Through Science.** The punishment for flunking is **death!**

Selene

CODENAME: *Black Queen*
Sorceress • Mutant "psychic vampire" • Absorbs the life-force of others • Has survived for more than 17,000 years

Emma Frost
CODENAME: *White Queen*
Omega-class psychic • Can transform body into near-invulnerable diamond form (though this stops her from using her mental powers)

Blackheart
CODENAME: *Black King*
Sorcerous demon • Supernaturally strong • Spawn of the evil ruler Mephisto • Teleportation powers • Really puts the "hell" into Hellfire Club!

Kade Kilgore

Codename: *Black King*
Twelve-year-old genius • Master of bribery and blackmail • Has array of amazing high-tech weapons • Ruthless personality

YECCH!
Agents of Atlas's Marvel Boy is human, but his body is modified by Uranians. When he eats, a gross tentacle-like appendage extends from his mouth to devour his food!

THE STRANGE AGENTS OF ATLAS
This misfit group contains some of the weirdest "heroes" ever...

MARVEL BOY/URANIAN
A headband gives him telepathic powers and lets him control a flying saucer.

GORILLA-MAN
A human trapped in a gorilla's body by an enchantment. He has an amazing sense of smell!

VENUS
Not the goddess, but a siren with the power to control humans' moods with her voice.

M-11 THE HUMAN ROBOT
A mechanical being built in the 1950s, with a death-ray eye beam and the ability to hack computers from afar.

WOW!
800
The number of years the Atlas Foundation has existed. It was founded by followers of the warlord Genghis Khan!

The Hand's members usually wear masks to hide their identity. Even if they are killed, you won't find out who they are—their bodies turn to dust by magic!

DASTARDLY DEED!
The Serpent Society comes up with a **particularly evil plan** to attack Washington D.C. It slips a **snake mutagen** into the water supply, which turns citizens—even the **U.S. president**—into **scaly snake-things**.

BACK FROM THE DEAD!
The Hand clan recruits members by using **mystic rites** to bring the dead **back to life**. It then **brainwashes** them to create **blindly obedient** warriors.

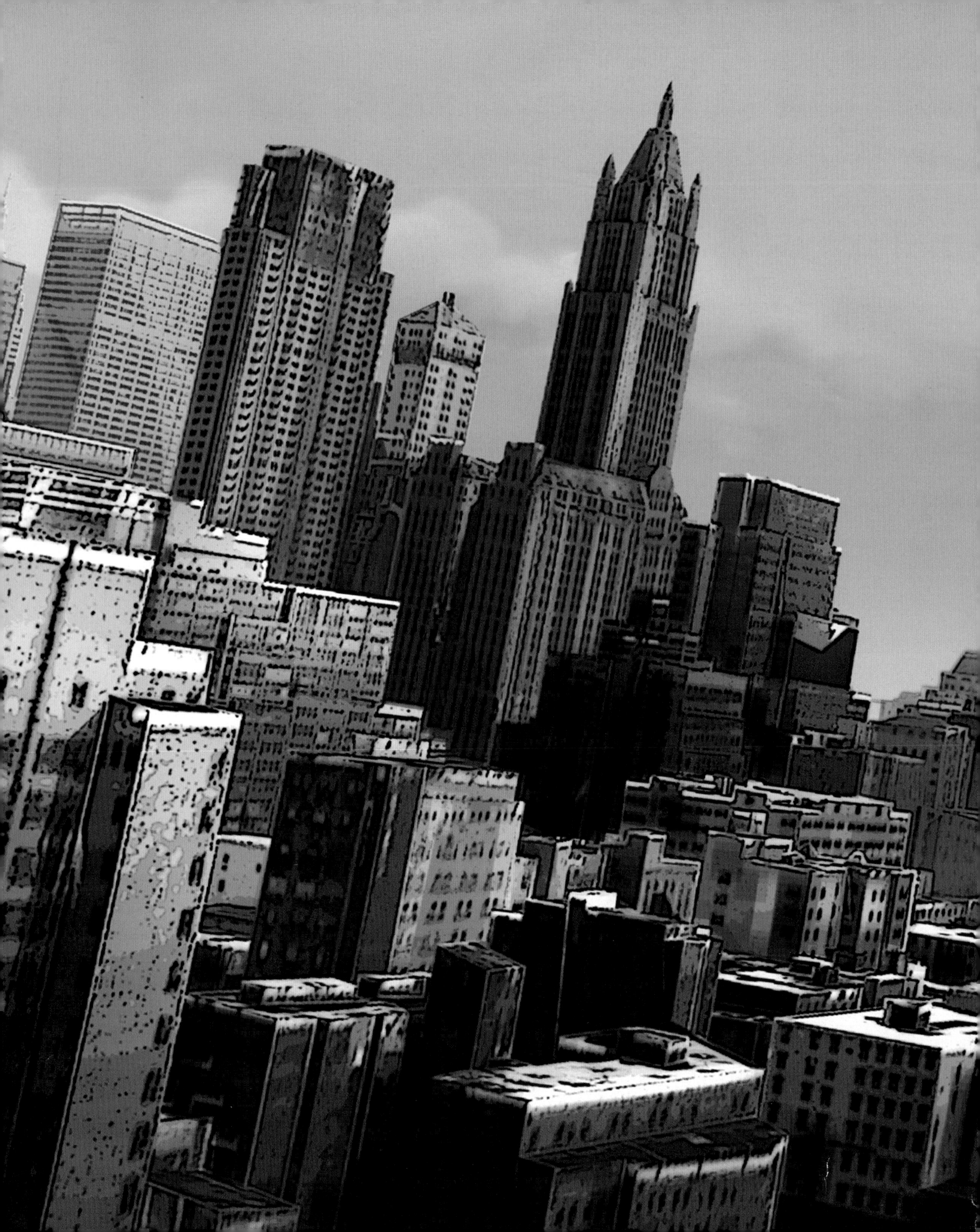

CHAPTER THREE
LOCATIONS

Who or what **HAS A SON** named Id the Selfish Moon?

What is home, sweet home to Surtur the **FIRE-DEMON**?

Where on Earth can you find **LIVING DINOSAURS**?

99.999%

The chance of death for convicts in the Kyln, a massive orbital prison for the universe's worst villains!

TOP 5
Weirdest Planets

1 **EGO THE LIVING PLANET**— an actual living world! Ego is very powerful – and completely crazy!

2 **HALFWORLD**—the universe's largest asylum for the criminally insane and the former home of Rocket Raccoon!

3 **POPPUP**—its inhabitants can change into anything they can think of! Home to the Impossible Man.

4 **WRAITHWORLD**—home of the Dire Wraiths, who draw their power from the planet's Black Sun!

5 **COUNTER-EARTH**—Earth's secret twin orbits on the far side of the Sun and is ruled by the High Evolutionary!

YECCH!

In one of his wackiest pranks, the Impossible Man tricks Galactus into devouring his homeworld, Poppup. Poppup gives Galactus a bad case of cosmic indigestion, and he turns into a helpless ball of energy!

FAMILY CONNECTIONS

Ego the Living Planet has a son: **Id the Selfish Moon!** This mad planetoid enjoys destroying worlds and breathing in their dust – but is destroyed when Deadpool tricks it into inhaling a **powerful bomb!**

Q: What's the biggest planet in the universe?

A: **Gigantus**, which was larger than entire galaxies! Unfortunately, the warlike **Eternals of Eyung** declared war on the peaceful Gigantians, and destroyed Gigantus. The Gigantians then retaliated and destroyed **Eyung!**

ALTERNATE UNIVERSE

Ego the Living Planet is bad news, but he's a pushover compared to Earth-TRN157's **Doom the Living Planet!** This metal-masked menace is as powerful as Ego and as evil as Doom—literally **the worst** of both worlds!

Power Up!

EGO'S ENGINE!
When Ego the Living Planet's sun is about to **GO NOVA** and destroy him, Galactus attaches a **SIDEREAL PROPULSION UNIT** to Ego's South Pole. This massive engine propels the Living Planet **OUT OF HARM'S WAY** at faster-than-light speeds!

NOOOOO!!
The planet Hala is the **CENTER** of the Kree Empire—but a barrage from **MISTER KNIFE** and the Slaughterlords' flying fortress destroys the planet!

S.H.I.E.L.D. DECLASSIFIED

THE WORLD
The barren planet known only as the World is the location of the M'kraan Crystal. This gem is the Nexus of All Realities, the point at which all realities meet. It is sacred to both the Shi'ar and Sc'yar Tal races, who have fought brutal wars to possess it!

BEYOND THE STARS

The **Marvel Universe** is full of wonders, from **bizarre planets** and **strange moons** to **mighty** alien empires! Prepare yourself for an intergalactic voyage of discovery and adventure!

WHEN GOOD GUYS GO BAD!

ISAAC OF TITAN
A group of Eternals builds a secret, high-tech paradise on Saturn's moon Titan. This paradise's ecology is controlled by a computer network named ISAAC. When the mad Titan Thanos takes control of Titan, he reprograms ISAAC to create deadly superhumans for his army!

Greetings From ASGARD!

Top Tourist Spots

Bored by the magnificent sights of the Golden Realm? The Golden City of Asgard is linked to other magical worlds—and you can travel between them, if you know how!

Escape the winter chill and top up your tan with a trip to **SUNNY MUSPELHEIM!** (Warning: Home to the evil Fire Demon Surtur.)

If you're searching for the ultimate paradise, visit the enchanting realm of **HEL!** (Warning: Only the dead may enter.)

Fancy some country air? Take a leisurely stroll through the beautiful mountains of **NIDAVELLIR!** (Warning: Mountains may contain heavily armed Dwarves.)

The winter wonderland of **JOTUNHEIM** is great for skiing, sledding, or throwing snowballs at your friends! (Warning: Beware of Frost Giants.)

Q: What is Yggdrasil?

A: Yggdrasil is the cosmic World Tree that joins Asgard to the other Nine Realms. At its roots is **Mimir's Well**, which both Odin and Thor drink from to gain wisdom.

REALLY?!

The Dwarves of Nidavellir create **mighty weapons,** including Thor's hammer, Mjolnir. It is forged in the **heart of a sun,** and the energy released causes fire to **rain from the skies** across the Nine Realms. Allegedly, this rain of fire wipes out **the dinosaurs** of Midgard (Earth)!

FAST FACTS

RULER: Odin the All-Father

NOTABLE INHABITANTS: Thor, Loki, the Warriors Three, Heimdall, Lady Sif

FOES: Dark Elves, Frost Giants, Surtur, Fenris Wolf

BEWARE OF: Ragnarok— the end of everything!

TOP 6 Asgard's Worst Foes

1 **SURTUR**—this towering Fire Demon burns with a hatred for Asgard and is destined to destroy it at Ragnarok!

2 **FENRIS**—the wolf-like spawn of Loki; during Ragnarok, Fenris will devour the sun!

3 **THE ENCHANTRESS**— Amora is a powerful sorceress who wants to make Thor her husband!

4 **HELA**—Loki's daughter and ruler of Hel, land of the dead.

5 **THE EXECUTIONER**— Skurge fights Thor to prove his love for Amora, but ultimately sacrifices his life to save Asgard!

6 **FAFNIR**—one-time king of the fire-breathing dragons of Nostrond!

TELL ME MORE!

Every now and again Odin has to recharge his magical Odinforce. He does this by falling into the Odinsleep, a deep sleep that can last for days. At these times, he is as vulnerable as a normal person.

180

ANGELA

THE REALM ETERNAL

In a **distant dimension** lies **Asgard**, home of the **Norse gods**. It's a place of **wonders and terrors** where Odin, Thor, and the Asgardians battle against **monstrous mythological** foes—as well as **each other!**

ODINFORCE

When Odin's brothers **Vili** and **Ve** die, he inherits their powers. Added to his own, this power becomes the mighty **Odinforce.**

HANDLE WITH CARE!

The Bifrost—a Rainbow Bridge between Asgard and Midgard (Earth)—is guarded by the all-seeing, all-hearing god **Heimdall.** If he accidentally leaves it open, it will destroy **every realm!**

FAMILY CONNECTIONS

Odin believes the **Queen of Angels** has **killed** his daughter, **Aldrif.** In fact, she has been kidnapped and raised in Heven as an **Angel** named **Angela!** However, this isn't the chance for Thor to finally have a **healthy** sibling relationship—the first time they meet, Angela **defeats** her little brother in battle!

ASGARD'S UPS AND DOWNS

DOWN

RAGNAROK'N'ROLL!
The evil Fire Demon Surtur attacks Asgard, and the Realm Eternal is destroyed!

UP

ASGARD, OK!
Thor uses the power of his hammer Mjolnir to summon a new Asgard—above Broxton, Oklahoma!

DOWN

NOT AGAIN!
Loki teams up with Norman Osborn and the Dark Avengers to invade, and Asgard is wrecked in the battle!

UP

BLAST OFF!
The floating city is rebuilt as Asgardia—a utopia ruled by the All-Mother and placed next to the moon!

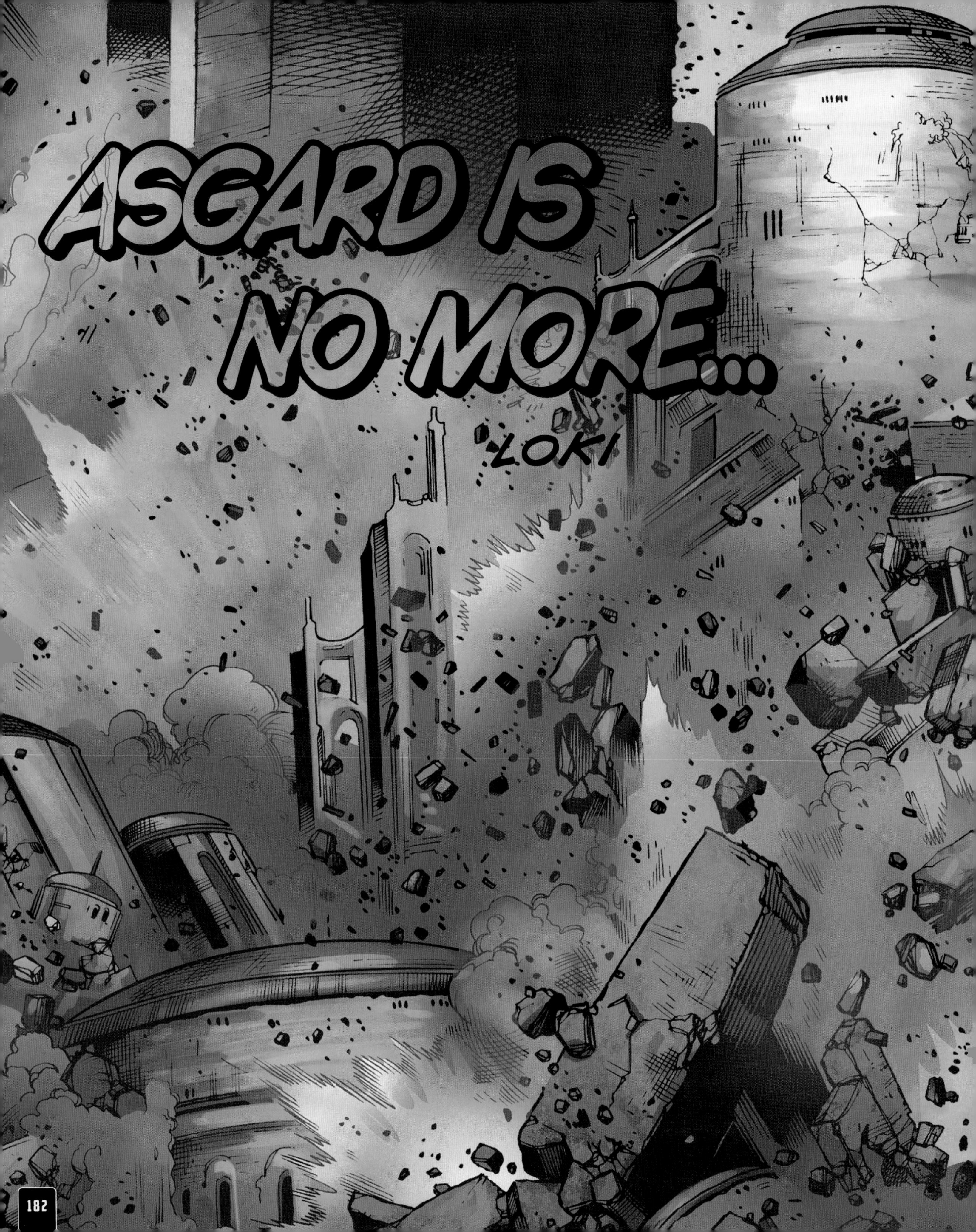
ASGARD IS NO MORE...
LOKI

S.H.I.E.L.D. DECLASSIFIED

FALL OF ASGARD

With the City of Asgard floating above Oklahoma, Norman Osborn becomes fearful of Earth's new godly neighbors. He teams up with Loki to invade and his H.A.M.M.E.R. and Dark Avengers forces leave Asgard on the brink of destruction. When Loki switches sides and Captain America returns, leading his team of Avengers, the tide begins to turn. However, the hero Sentry is overcome by his evil side, the Void, and reduces the city to ruin.

MYSTIC REALMS

Welcome to the **dark places**, where even Super Heroes **fear to tread!** Ruled over by immensely powerful beings, these **mystic domains and dimensions** teem with weird creatures and demons, phantoms, and terrors!

CRIME REALLY DOESN'T PAY!

Two **unlucky burglars** break into Doctor Strange's house, the **Sanctum Sanctorum.** Stumbling through a **portal** into the **Purple Dimension,** they become prisoners of Aggamon the All-Powerful.

BACK FROM THE DEAD!

Pluto seizes control of the mafia-like **Olympus Group** and sets up a new region of Hades modeled after an Atlantic City **casino.** Deceased heroes and villains can **gamble** their way **back to life!**

BATTLE FOR THE REALMS

Poor **Thor** is in for a shock when he's transported to a **mysterious, horrible** dimension of the **Nine Realms.** Hela is using the powers of the **Twilight Sword** to turn the Realms into a new **playground of terrors!**

TAKE A TRIP THAT'S OUT OF THIS WORLD!

There are many mystic realms in the Marvel Universe. They are interesting places to visit— but you wouldn't want to stay long!

Purple Dimension:
A **pocket universe** (a universe within a universe!), where the inhabitants work in **jewel mines** as **slaves!**

Ruler: the virtually immortal sorcerer Aggamon.

Dark Dimension:
A **huge** dimension that contains lots of **spooky** pocket universes. Its many different **species** live for **millions of years.**

Ruler (sometimes): the ancient, hellish demon, Dormammu.

Dimension of Dreams:
A **mysterious realm** controlled by a demonic dreamweaver who invades the **minds** of unlucky mortals through their dreams.

Ruler: the merciless demon Nightmare.

Hel:
The gloomy **Asgardian realm of the dead,** where the souls of ordinary people rest.

Ruler: **Hela,** Queen of Death.

Hades:
The **Olympian underworld** of the **dead,** where the spirits of gods and worshippers dwell

Ruler: the Olympian god **Pluto.**

LIGHTS, CAMERA, ACTION!

In one of Pluto's more **diabolical schemes,** he disguises himself as a **movie producer** and tricks **Hercules** into signing a **contract** that forces him to **take Pluto's place** in the underworld.

DASTARDLY DEED!

The ghoulish Nightmare haunts the **dreams** of people as they sleep. When **Dr. Strange** investigates, Nightmare tries to **trap** Dr. Strange's spirit **inside a dream.**

THE ENEMY OF MY ENEMY

Shinto death god Amatsu-Mikaboshi wages war against the gods of Earth. Hela, Nightmare, and Pluto put aside their divine differences to join the fight against him. To protect their own interests, of course!

S.H.I.E.L.D. DECLASSIFIED

FAMILY FEUDS
Demonic sorcerer Dormammu and his sister, Umar, are evil members of a higher-dimensional energy race, the Faltine. After the siblings are banished from their universe for craving too much power, they travel to the Dark Dimension and hope to conquer it. Umar helps Dormammu gain the throne, but they soon fall out big-time!

Crimson Cosmos:
A dimension of timeless silence.
Ruler: the exiled magical entity Cyttorack.

Limbo:
A **magical** realm of **eternal fire,** populated by many different demons.
Ruler: the devilish Belasco.

YECCH!

If Hela is not in constant contact with her enchanted cloak, the right side of her body remains beautiful and youthful—but the left side is decayed and disgusting!

TOP 6 DANGER ZONES!

THEY MAY BE SPECTACULAR—BUT THEY'RE ALSO INCREDIBLY DANGEROUS!

1. KRAKOA THE LIVING ISLAND—brought to life by fallout from nuclear tests, this sentient isle has an appetite for visitors

2. GENOSHA—once a thriving city, now devastated by conflict between mutants and humans

3. MONSTER ISLE—near Japan, a home to massive mutated monsters of all kinds

4. LEMURIA—undersea home of the bizarre Deviants. They **don't** like humans!

5. BAGALIA—a country of criminals, run by Baron Zemo and policed by his Masters of Evil

6. MADRIPOOR—a bustling nation-state in South East Asia that is home to pirates, criminals, and corruption

Madripoor

HI-TECH CITIES • ANCIENT REALMS • HIDDEN LANDS

IT'S A MARVEL-OUS WORLD!

Genosha

Muir Island

The Chrysler Building

DASTARDLY DEED!

The island nation of Genosha is a virtual **paradise**, until the country's rulers use **genetic engineering** to turn mutants into **slaves!**

Welcome to **a world of wonders,** hi-tech cities, ancient realms, and hidden lands. **Marvel's Earth-616** contains an almost unimaginable wealth of treasures, mysteries, **and thrills!**

Atlantis

TOP 7 WONDERS OF THE WORLD!

If you visit Earth-616, here are seven not-to-be-missed tourist sites!

ATLANTIS—put on your best diving suit to visit Namor's underwater realm!

THE SAVAGE LAND—see living dinosaurs in their natural environment: a hidden jungle in Antarctica!

ATTILAN—famous as the Island of the Gods and the Great Refuge of the superpowered Inhumans!

K'UN-LUN—city of the immortal Iron Fists, masters of the martial arts!

THE NEXUS OF ALL REALITIES—deep within the Florida Everglades, this is the point where all universes meet!

WAKANDA—this advanced East African country features a magnificent royal palace and an amazing techno-organic jungle!

OLYMPIA—home of the godlike Eternals, set atop Mount Olympus in Greece!

TELL ME MORE!

The Savage Land is a tropical jungle in Antarctica that is home to dinosaurs, primitive humans, and many bizarre creatures. It was created 200 million years ago by the alien Nuwali as a "safari park" for their masters, the cosmic Beyonders!

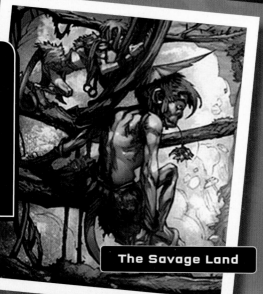
The Savage Land

TOP 10

New York City Sites

The Big Apple is home to many heroes and has witnessed some truly seismic events!

1 GREENWICH VILLAGE— where Doctor Strange has his Sanctum Sanctorum mansion

2 MANHATTAN SEWERS— the domain of homeless mutant Morlocks

3 THE CHRYSLER BUILDING—has been known to come alive and even clash with heroes!

4 THE BIG HOUSE—a prison designed by Hank Pym where Super Villains are shrunk to flea size!

5 MANHATTAN—once transformed into a medieval metropolis by Kang

6 HELL'S KITCHEN— Daredevil's stomping ground

7 TIMES SQUARE—keep away if the demon Shuma-Gorath is in town. He'll make tentacles grow out your mouth!

8 FIFTH AVENUE—site of the Avengers Mansion

9 FOREST HILLS, QUEENS— Peter Parker's home with Aunt May

10 THE BAXTER BUILDING— the Fantastic Four's Manhattan base

New York City

Q: What do you do if you're stranded in the Savage Land?!

A: Be like British noble **Kevin Plunder!** He is only nine when his explorer father dies there, but he grows up to be an expert **hunter, adventurer,** and **warrior.** Today, he safeguards the Savage Land as **Ka-Zar, Lord of the Hidden Jungle!**

HANDLE WITH CARE!

A strange **bone medallion** grants teenager Humberto Lopez the ability to **morph** any part of his body into a **dinosaur limb!** Now he's the hero **Reptil.**

TELL ME MORE!

Shanna the She-Devil is no devil! Raised in the jungles of Central Africa, Shanna O'Hara trains as a zoologist in the U.S. She returns and earns her name protecting animals from poachers, while working on a nature reserve.

NOOOOOO!! Sauron and Stegron's plan to **TRANSFORM HUMANITY** into **DINOSAURS** falls apart when they both develop a **CRUSH** on the hero **SHARK GIRL!**

TEAM PLAYERS

When **angry Mayan gods** rise up in the jungles of Central America to bring about the **apocalypse,** it takes **Red Hulk, Alpha Flight, She-Hulk,** and more to stop them!

REALLY?!

S.H.I.E.L.D. hire scientist **Vincent Stegron** to research **dinosaur DNA** from the Savage Land. Instead, he **injects himself** with the DNA and mutates into Stegron—a super-strong **bipedal stegosaurus!**

BAD DAY

Bruce Banner creates an entire jungle island full of monstrous **gamma-irradiated animals** by accident! He was trying to **copy** the **experiment** that turned him into the Hulk—but things **don't go quite to plan!**

WAKANDA

Land of the Black Panther Wakanda lies deep in the heart of **Africa,** closed off from outsiders. Its people seek out new **scientific innovations,** while keeping their **tribal customs.** The presence of precious **Vibranium** grants special abilities to the kingdom's **flora and fauna.**

The Savage Land may be **tropical**—but it's located deep in **Antarctica**! It was created millions of years ago as an **experiment** by the extraterrestrial **Nuwali**.

Cool Cat
Super-intelligent **Zabu** is the last-known living **saber-toothed tiger**! He has been Ka-Zar's **companion** ever since Zabu found him in the Savage Land, lost and alone. The name "Ka-Zar" even means "**Son of the Tiger**!"

WHEN BAD GUYS GO GOOD!

FOR ALL DINOS...
When S.H.I.E.L.D. abducts Moon Boy for research purposes, Devil Dinosaur grows so sad he refuses to eat! Amazingly, it is the villainous Stegron who leads the charge to reunite the duo—for the sake of the dinosaur race, of course!

BACK FROM THE DEAD!

Shanna **dies** at the hands of Neanderthals, but teen super-genius **Amadeus Cho** convinces them to resurrect her in a ceremony! Submerged in a **pool** of a Man-Thing's **lifeblood**, she reawakens—and gains a connection to the life-force of the Savage Land **itself**!

IT'S A JUNGLE OUT THERE!

From the wilds of **Wakanda** to the glades of the **Savage Land...** these **teeming jungles** hold the promise of adventure, exploration, and above all **excitement** and **danger**!

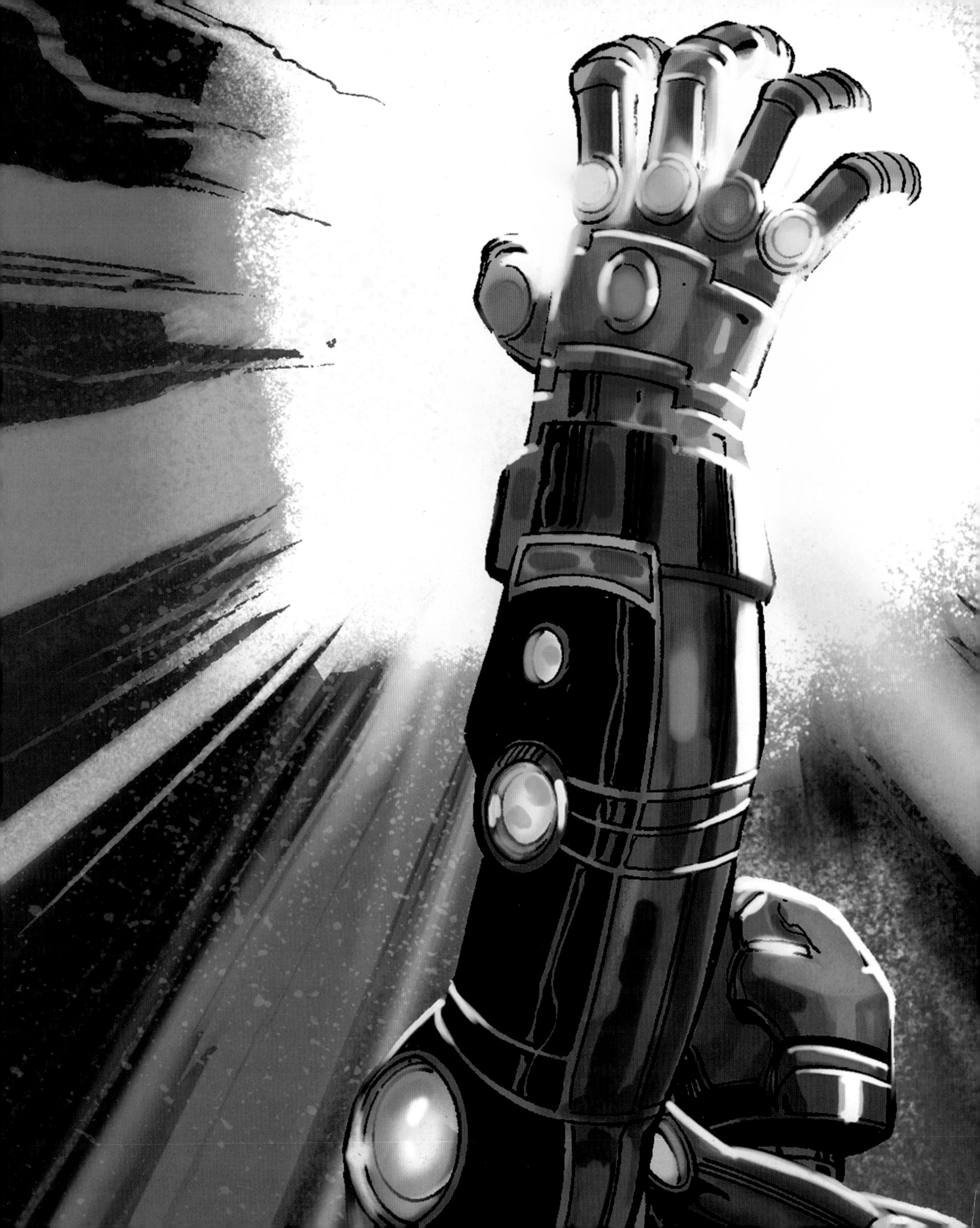

CHAPTER FOUR
SCIENCE AND MAGIC

Who does the **EVIL ROBOT** Ultron **HAVE A CRUSH** on?

Who **GIVES BIRTH** to a **ROBOT BABY?**

What book of **DARK SPELLS** first unleashed **VAMPIRES** and **WEREWOLVES** on the world?

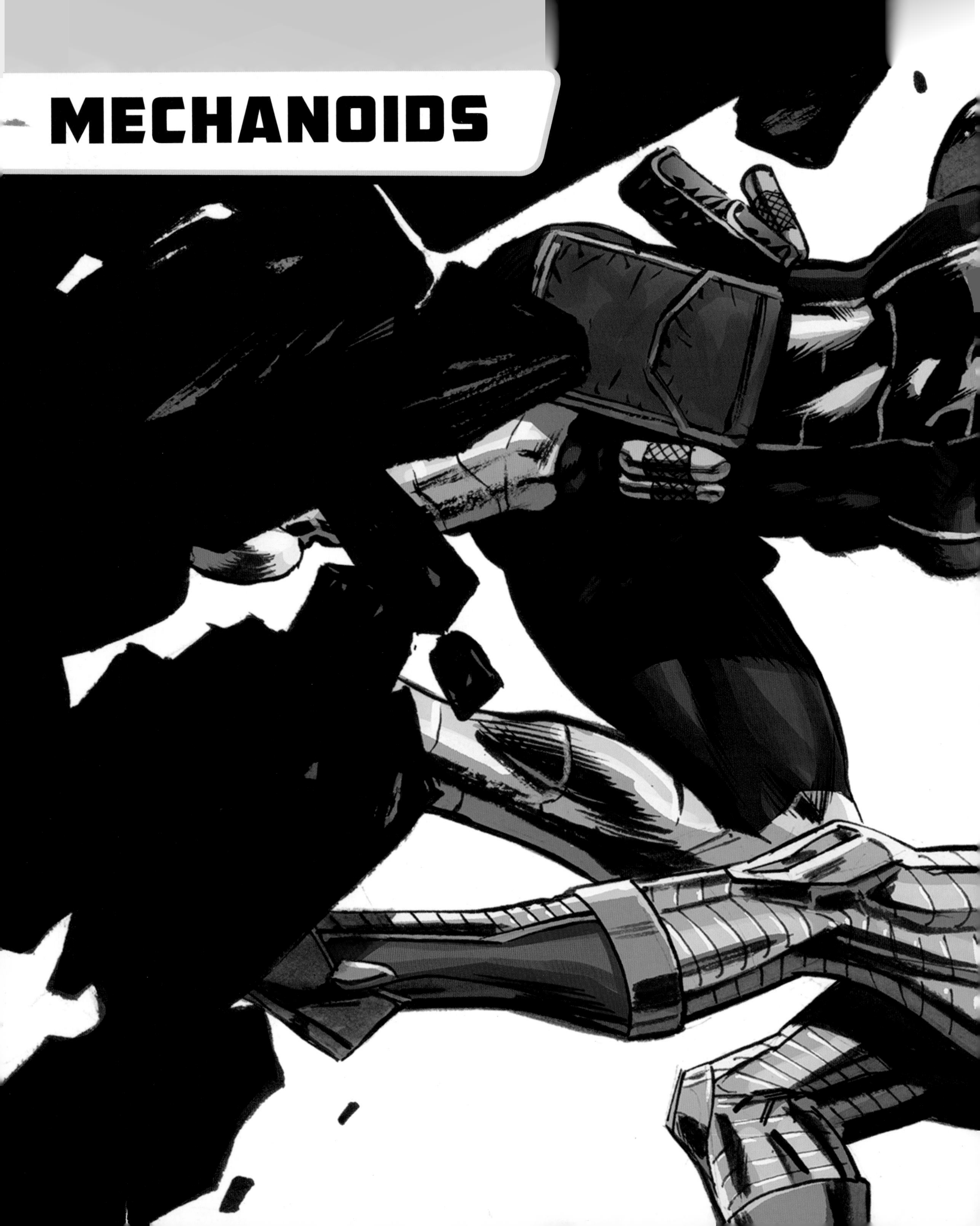

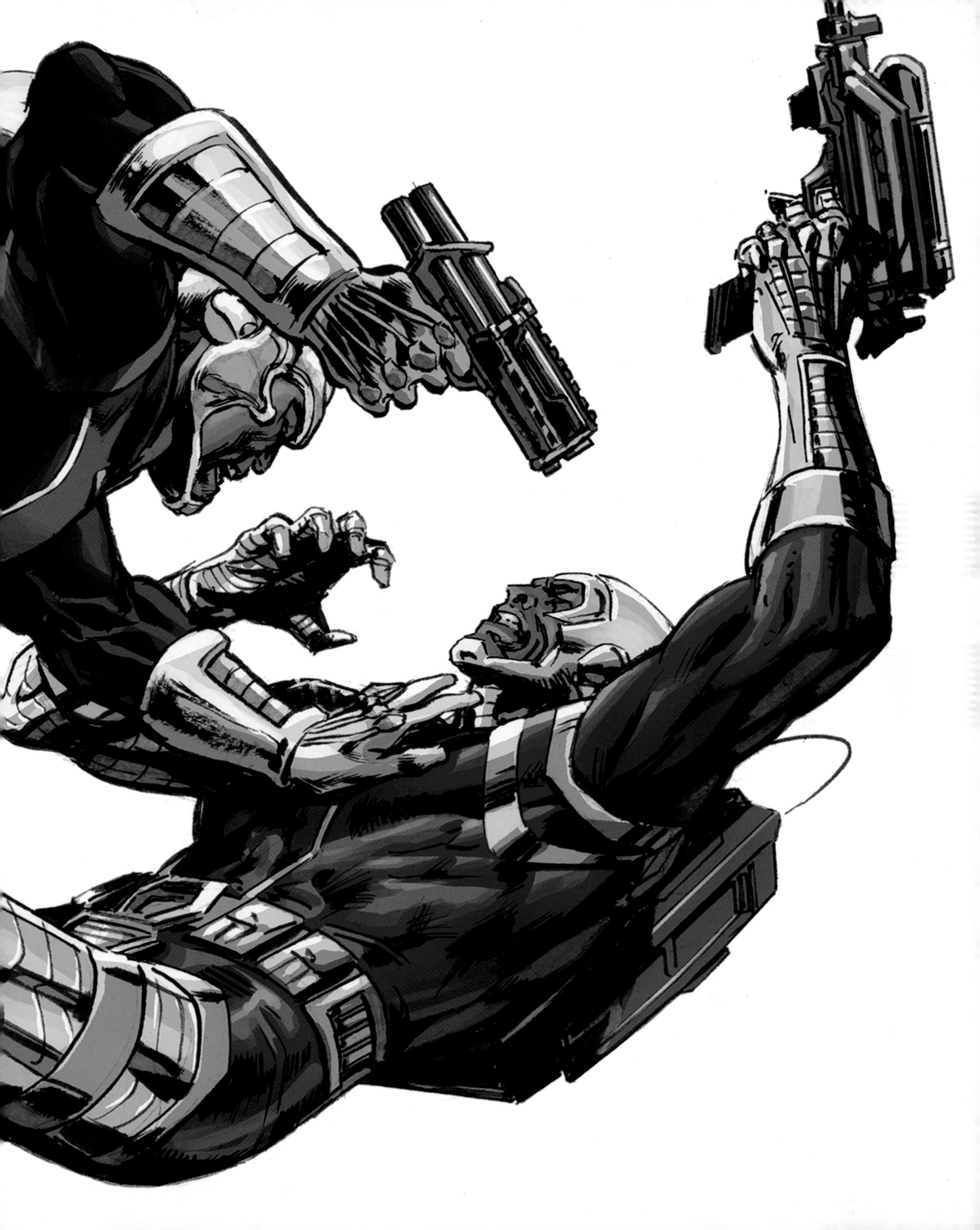

FAST FACTS

CREATOR: Hank Pym

STRENGTHS: Robotics expertise, hi-tech android body, hive mind able to control multiple bodies

POWER SOURCE: Internal nuclear furnace

WEAKNESSES: Vulnerable mechanics

ALLIES: Phalanx, Masters of Evil

FOES: Avengers, Jocasta, Hank Pym

BEST KNOWN FOR

REPEATEDLY TRYING TO ANNIHILATE HUMANITY!

WHEN GOOD GUYS GO BAD!

UNLUCKY TWELVE
Ultron-12 calls himself Ultron "Mark" Twelve and develops a friendship with his "father," Hank Pym! Sadly, Ultron-11 destroys kindly Mark.

For taking over the world and destroying the Avengers.

For using the alien Phalanx race to create a deadly cybernetic army.

For forcing Vision to build him a new Adamantium body.

For tricking the Avengers into thinking Jarvis is leading the Masters of Evil.

For destroying an entire city to show off his new upgrade.

THE ULTRON AWARDS

REBORN! (ALMOST...)
Doctor Doom **rebuilds** Ultron, but includes all his past personalities. They all **run at once**, battle each other —and **tear their body apart!**

"The day you created me, you sealed your own irreversible doom!"

REALLY?!

Ultron **hates** his father, Hank Pym, but has a **twisted obsession** with Hank's ex, Janet Van Dyne (Wasp).

TOP 4

Ultron Creations

THEY ARE DESIGNED TO DESTROY THE AVENGERS... BUT THEY ALL TURN AGAINST ULTRON!

1 VISION —synthezoid son, created by Ultron-5

2 JOCASTA —first intended android bride

3 ALKHEMA —second android bride

4 VICTOR MANCHA —cyborg son and sleeper agent

NUMBER CRUNCH!

6ft 9in (1.75m)
Ultron's height (though it varies)

536lbs (243kg)
Ultron's weight (also variable)

100s of drones
Controlled by Ultron's hive mind

8 optic sensors
As master of the Phalanx, Ultron has eight eyes

6 arms
Ultron wields extra limbs during the Age of Ultron

The Crimson Cowl
When the Avengers **first meet Ultron**, he is **disguised** as the Crimson Cowl, leader of the **Masters of Evil.**

REALLY?!

Ultron melts Tony Stark and his Iron Man armor—and transforms himself into a **female Ultron** who resembles the Wasp!

ROGUE ROBOT

Ultron is a high-tech **mechanical menace** who turns against his creator, Hank Pym, and becomes the Avengers' **worst nightmare!** No matter how many times this evil robot is destroyed, he always **rebuilds** and **upgrades**, ready with a new **diabolical plan!**

AARGHH!!

Ultron implants **ALL** his creations (including Vision, Jocasta, and Alkhema) with a **SECRET PROGRAM** that compels them to **REBUILD** a **MORE POWERFUL** version of Ultron!

ANDROID ARMY
Ultron possesses **hive-mind technology**, meaning he can control **multiple versions** of himself in a **one-man** army of hundreds of evil androids!

No need to plug me in, daddy...

I'm alive...

just like you...

-SKRAWWK-

WITH THE BEST INTENTIONS
Hank Pym invents Ultron to help the Avengers, but he **TURNS VIOLENT** straight away. He wipes Hank's memories, upgrades himself **FOUR TIMES**, and leaves!

30,000°F

Heat of the infrared beam (16,649°C) Vision emits from the solar gem on his forehead. This cool android can be a real hothead!

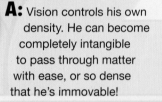

Q: How does Vision phase through walls?

A: Vision controls his own density. He can become completely intangible to pass through matter with ease, or so dense that he's immovable!

AAARRGHH!!

U.S. agents **DISMANTLE** Vision! Hank Pym rebuilds him, but without emotions. Vision **LOSES** his colorful look— and his **COLORFUL PERSONALITY!**

TOP **4**

Things you need to create a synthezoid*

1 **A HIGHLY** advanced scientist

2 **SYNTHETIC** human parts

3 **A LOT OF TIME**, patience, and hard work

4 **AN EMOTIONAL** consciousness to upload

* The threat of a looming foe is a great incentive!

"I AM UNIQUE! I am THE VISION --!"

IDENTITY CRISIS?

Vision needs a humanoid consciousness to compute emotions. He's been uploaded with the minds of the Human Torch, Wonder Man, and Alex Lipton. No wonder he often has mixed feelings!

ULTRON'S ERROR

Ultron creates Vision to **destroy** the Avengers—but it backfires big time! The synthezoid **turns** on his master and becomes one of Ultron's most **powerful enemies**.

ONE IN A MILLION

Just because Vision is a robot, doesn't mean he hasn't got a heart. Wanda Maximoff, the Scarlet Witch, falls head over circuits for this A.I. guy—and they get married!

BETWEEN...

In *Marvel Mystery Comics* #13 (November 1940), an alien policeman named Aarkus the Vision journeys to Earth to fight Nazis during World War II. The resemblance to his namesake—the android debuting 28 years later—is uncanny!

...THE PANELS

SUPER SYNTHEZOID

The Vision is a whole lot **more** than just a robot. This sentient **android Avenger** has the emotional life of a human being, with a complicated past, filled with **love and loss**. Plus he can shoot a **laser** out of his face!

BEST KNOWN FOR
WALKING THROUGH WALLS AND SARCASTIC WIT

▲ FAMILY CONNECTIONS

Vision is so desperate to be **human**, he goes to the very lab where Ultron created him, and builds **himself a family!** With wife Virginia, and kids Viv and Vin, he moves to 616 Hickory Branch Lane, Arlington, Virginia, for **a new, quiet life**.

FAST FACTS

SPECIES:
An artificially intelligent android known as a synthezoid

STRENGTHS: Intelligence, density change, flight, infrared radiation beam, superhuman strength, intangibility

WEAKNESSES: Desire to be human

RELATIVES: Scarlet Witch (ex-wife)

CREATOR: Ultron

MAIN FOE: Ultron

TELL ME MORE!

Vision is a synthezoid— a robot made out of synthetic human parts. This means he functions almost completely as a human being, but with special superpowers!

FAST FACTS

ALIASES: Jocasta Vi Quitéria, Jo, Queen of Thebes, Bride of Ultron

RACE: Sentient Android

STRENGTHS: Intellect (gifted in science and engineering), four mechanical tentacles

WEAKNESSES: Programmed to rebuild Ultron if he is destroyed!

ENEMIES: Ultron, Weatherman, High Evolutionary

ALLIES: Avengers, Machine Man

ALTERNATE UNIVERSE

In a possible future, Scarlet Witch is dying and her husband, the Vision, vows to dismantle himself after her passing. Jocasta overhears and secretly transfers Scarlet Witch's mind into her mechanical body just before she dies. Jocasta's mind dies in Scarlet Witch's body, so that the married couple can live on as robots.

WOW!

750

The weight of Jocasta's titanium steel body in lbs (340kg), even though she's only 5ft 9in (1.75m) tall!

"Being a creature of cybernetic circuits and not flesh and blood, I am always aware that I am... different."

BEST KNOWN FOR

SELF-SACRIFICE AND AIDING THE AVENGERS

ALTERNATE UNIVERSE

On Earth-9930, Jocasta is not only a **fully-fledged Avenger**, but also the mother of a **robot baby**, created with her **husband, Machine Man.**

On Earth-9602, Jocasta becomes a **hunter of metamutants** alongside Magneto's brother **Will Magnus.**

BACK FROM THE DEAD!

Jocasta's metal shell has been **destroyed** or **hacked** many times, only to be rebuilt and restored. She has even spent time in **A.I. form,** working for Tony Stark **without a body** at all!

ROBOT LOVE

Jocasta has a very special relationship with Machine Man. Whenever she throws herself in the way of a bomb or foe to save her teammates, Machine Man is there to pick up her pieces and put her back together again.

RUNAWAY BRIDE!

Jocasta is a **sentient robot,** created by **the evil Ultron** to be his bride. It doesn't take her long to **rebel,** though! She has since proved to be one of the Avengers' **greatest allies.** Her body may be **near indestructible,** but it's her will that's **truly ironclad!**

TEAM PLAYER

Jocasta often teams up with the Avengers, but her time with the **50-State Initiative** isn't a great success. Her team, including Geiger, Annex, and Sharon Ventura, is infiltrated by a secret invasion of shape-shifting alien Skrulls!

REALLY?!

Jocasta receives a marriage proposal from a sentient space satellite named Samarobryn. However, this **long-distance relationship** just doesn't work for Jo—especially as Samarobryn is planning to rid planet Earth of humanity!

UNSTABLE MOLECULES
Unstable Molecules are created by legendary scientist Reed Richards (Mr. Fantastic) and form a special synthetic material. They are highly resistant to changes in density and pressure—perfect for Mr. Fantastic's stretchable suit, and Super-Adaptoid's changeable body.

UPGRADED!

The Super-Adaptoid can be rebuilt and upgraded. He can take on the powers of multiple heroes at once, and if he loses, A.I.M. scientists simply repair and improve him!

AAARRGHH!! The Super-Adaptoid doesn't have a **CREATIVE THOUGHT** in his body. When he takes on **PHYLA-VELL**, daughter of Mar-Vell, she **FRIES HIS CIRCUITS** by showing him the extent of her **IMAGINATION**.

FAST FACTS

ALIASES:
Adaptoid, Master of All Reality, Cyborg Sinister

CREATORS: Advanced Idea Mechanics (A.I.M.)—a villainous scientific organization committed to overthrowing governments

CONSTRUCTION:
Adaptable android built with Unstable Molecules and powered by pieces of the Cosmic Cube

ABILITIES: Mimics the powers and appearance of any being

TIME FOR A CHANGE!

The **Super-Adaptoid** is a **form-changing, ability-mimicking android** created by the evil scientists of A.I.M. He can **copy the powers** of anyone he's fighting—so he can become the equal of **any opponent!**

IDENTITY CRISIS?

Super-Adaptoid not only upgrades his looks and abilities, he also upgrades his name. From Adaptoid to Super-Adaptoid, to Cyborg Sinister to Supreme-Adaptoid, to the Master of All Reality. The one thing this guy doesn't need upgraded is his ego!

BAD DAY

Super-Adaptoid tries to defeat the **X-Men** using all of **the Avengers'** powers. Power-replicating mutant **Mimic** comes to their aid, using **all the powers of the X-Men!** When Super-Adaptoid tries to absorb all of Mimic's X-Men powers, too, **both their powers are voided** and Super-Adaptoid **falls into the sea!**

YECCH!

Jessica Jones and Luke Cage's wedding is attacked by super-spy Yelena Belova, transformed by A.I.M. into a cyborg Super-Adaptoid. She doesn't last long—A.I.M. pulls the plug, turning her into a pool of goo!

WHEN BAD GUYS GO GOOD!

PROGRAM ERROR
Arms dealer Devlin DeAngelo kidnaps Bruce Banner (the Hulk) and forces him to upgrade Super-Adaptoid. DeAngelo plans to have Adaptoid kill Banner off, but Banner reprograms Super-Adaptoid to turn on DeAngelo!

TEAM PLAYER

Seeking **revenge** against **the Avengers,** Super-Adaptoid forms **Heavy Metal,** a squad of **angry machines!** This team of **mean androids** includes Awesome Android, Machine Man, the Sentry 459, TESS-One, and Kubik.

YESSS!!

Super-Adaptoid is **SUPER ADAPTABLE,** but he **CAN'T REPLICATE INTELLIGENCE.** If a hero is going to beat him, they just need to **USE SMARTS!**

TOP 4

Problems when Fighting the Super-Adaptoid

1 **HE COPIES** the powers of anyone he faces

2 **HE COMBINES** several heroes or villains' powers at once

3 **HE MIRRORS** every move an opponent makes

4 **HE UPGRADES** and comes back even stronger!

TELL ME MORE!

A shard of the Cosmic Cube—one of the most powerful artifacts in the universe—resides within the Super-Adaptoid. Its power allows him to replicate the strengths of others, while his Unstable Molecules mean he can also change his physical form. However, the Cube relies heavily on the mental abilities of the user, so this not-so-bright robot can only create what he encounters face-to-face.

Q: Why was the Super-Adaptoid created?

A: To **destroy Captain America!** Super-Adaptoid successfully duplicates Cap's looks and powers, and sends him plummeting **to his apparent death.** The android then fears that he's **outlived his worth** to his A.I.M. masters, and flees!

REAL NAME: Z2P45-9-X-51

ALIASES: X-51, Machine Man, insurance investigator Aaron Stack, secret agent Jack Kubrick, mutant hunter Machine Sentinel

STRENGTHS: Telescopic limbs, flight, loaded with weapons and gadgets, self-repairing

WEAKNESSES: Wants to be human, programming personality issues, needs sunlight to function

ALLIES: Jocasta, Photon, Hulk, X-Men, Avengers, Fantastic Four, Nextwave

FOES: Ultron, Fin Fang Foom, Madame Menace

"If there's a metal that *ATTRACTS CRAZY*, my body was built of it!"

BEST KNOWN FOR

ARMS AND LEGS THAT S T R E T C H 100FT (30M)

WOW!

176,700

Machine Man's maximum spaceflight speed in miles per second (284,371 kps)—95% of light speed!

IDENTITY CRISIS?

In his early years, Machine Man calls himself Aaron Stack. To keep up the pretense he relies on a human mask, and is in despair if he loses it.

"Without my face... I can never... walk among humanity, unnoticed and unmolested!"

TELL ME MORE!

The Avengers send Machine Man and Jocasta to a parallel universe where a virus is turning Super Heroes into zombies. Machine Man and Jocasta are chosen to save the day because, being machines instead of living beings, they're immune to the virus.

WHEN GOOD GUYS GO BAD!

MACHINATIONS!
Machine Man is seemingly destroyed in battle, but returns with his head attached to the body of an android resembling S.H.I.E.L.D. agent Jack Kubrick. His new body contains Sentinel technology, programmed to destroy mutants, and he turns against the X-Men!

NUMBER CRUNCH!

100 tons
Max weight Machine Sentinel can lift

10 tons
Max weight Machine Man can lift

2020
The year techno-villain Madam Menace rules most of New York City

850lbs (377kg)
Machine Man's weight

YEGGH!

The dragon Fin Fang Foom is devouring the residents of Abcess, North Dakota, so Machine Man gets inside him and attacks! The monster throws up his own guts, along with Machine Man!

NOooooo!!

Machine Man thinks Iron Man Tony Stark is a **ROBOT** just like him. He drops in for a chat, but Tony **ATTACKS** him. Machine Man realizes Tony is **ALL-TOO HUMAN!**

WHAT?!

In the scary future of 2020, Machine Man is rebuilt by the **Midnight Wreckers** gang. He's up and running just in time to face a "legally sanctioned" **C-28 Death-Dealer** robot programmed to **crush all opposition!**

MORE THAN MACHINE

X-51 begins as a kindly, **misfit robot** trying to blend into human society. He ends up as **Machine Man,** a **slightly insecure** but funny defender of Earth's "fleshy" inhabitants with a seemingly **unlimited supply** of built-in gadgets!

BACK FROM THE DEAD!

Machine Man **explodes** rather than submit to **Sentinel programming** and destroy the X-Men. Fortunately, internal **nanites** (tiny robots)

Q: Who made Machine Man?

A: X-51 is the **51st robot** created by **Dr. Abel Stack** for the U.S. Army. Stack raises X-51 as **his own son.** When the other 50 robots malfunction, Stack orders them to **self-destruct.** X-51's self-destruct mechanism also triggers and Stack is killed. X-51 goes on the run, taking the name **Aaron Stack.**

Machine Man Gadgets

1 **FINGER KNIVES AND SAWS** —cut through most tough situations.

2 **CHEST CANNON**— obliterates the bad guys.

3 **GRAVITY WAVE DETECTOR** —measures distortions in space time.

4 **TINY FINGER CONCUSSION BLASTERS** —go BOOM!

5 **PULSE-CODE MODULATOR** —converts data to sound.

BETWEEN...

Jack Kirby created Machine Man for a comic book title based on Stanley Kubrick's classic 1968 sci-fi film *2001: A Space Odyssey.* The character debuted in issue #8 (July 1977).

...THE PANELS

BAD DAY

Machine Man falls in love with female robot **Jocasta,** but she is destroyed by her master, **Ultron.** Madam Menace and Madam Menace then steals her head!

Madam

SPIDEY BEWARE!

Dr. Spencer Smythe creates the first **Spider-Slayer robots** to hunt down Spider-Man, but it's his son, **Alistaire**, blaming Spidey for his father's demise, who perfects these **mechanized killing machines**. He creates more than 20 different versions and upgrades!

ALISTAIRE SMYTHE

MEGA MAKEOVER

Machinesmith is a gifted, but criminal, **scientist** who uses robots to do his **dirty work** —until a life-threatening injury forces him to **transfer** his **mind** into an **android body**.

MACHINESMITH

LET'S GET MECHANICAL!

These **androids, cyborgs, and robots** hail from alternate futures, far reaches of the galaxy, and underground labs. They're mostly **metal**—inside and out—but these hardwired heroes and villains have **minds of their own!**

NOOOOO!!
Cyborg Rebecca Ryker is kidnapped by **ARCADE** and forced to battle other young heroes in his **MURDERWORLD**. As a result, poor Becky calls herself **DEATH LOCKET**.

DEATH LOCKET

FAST FACTS

HARDWARE HEROES:
Deathlok, Nightmask, Victor Mancha, Machine Teen, M-11, Death Locket

BIONIC BAD GUYS:
Nebula, Machinesmith, Spider-Slayer Robots, Ultimo, Korvac

S.H.I.E.L.D. DECLASSIFIED

DOOMSDAY ROBOT
The villain Mandarin has claimed credit for creating Ultimo, but the giant robot is really a doomsday weapon built by an advanced alien race. Ultimo crashes to Earth after destroying all life on several other planets.

AAARRGHH!!
Michael Korvac is a **NORMAL HUMAN** until the alien Badoon race graft him onto a **COMPUTER MODULE.** He becomes one of the **MOST DANGEROUS** beings in the cosmos!

KORVAC

DEATHLOK

"Deathlok the *Demolisher's* back in town for the *time of his life!*"

TOP 4
Different Deathloks

THE U.S. ARMY WANTS A CYBORG ARMY—WHETHER PARTICIPANTS IN THE DEATHLOK PROGRAM LIKE IT OR NOT!

1 **MICHAEL COLLINS**—computer programmer who finds brain transplanted in a Deathlok robot

2 **LUTHER MANNING**—wounded soldier with useful body parts

3 **HENRY HAYES**—combat medic brainwashed to become a one-man army

4 **REBECCA RYKER**—teenager saved and enhanced by her Deathlok-program-scientist father to become Death Locket!

VICTOR MANCHA

TEAM PLAYER
Teenage android Victor Mancha rebels against his "father" Ultron's programming. He joins the **Runaways** and becomes a key member of Hank Pym's **Avengers A.I.** hero team.

WE'RE ALL DOOM!
As if **one** Doctor Doom isn't enough, the villain creates **numerous** robot versions, called **Doombots.** What's more, each Doombot **thinks** he's Doctor Doom! Genius scientist **Hank Pym** manages to co-opt a Doombot into his **Avengers A.I. team,** proving that not every Doombot is bad news.

REALLY?!

All-star football captain and straight-A student **Adam Aaronson** gets the shock of his life when he discovers he's **Machine Teen,** a robot built by the man he thought was **his father!**

MACHINE TEEN

ICONIC ARTIFACTS

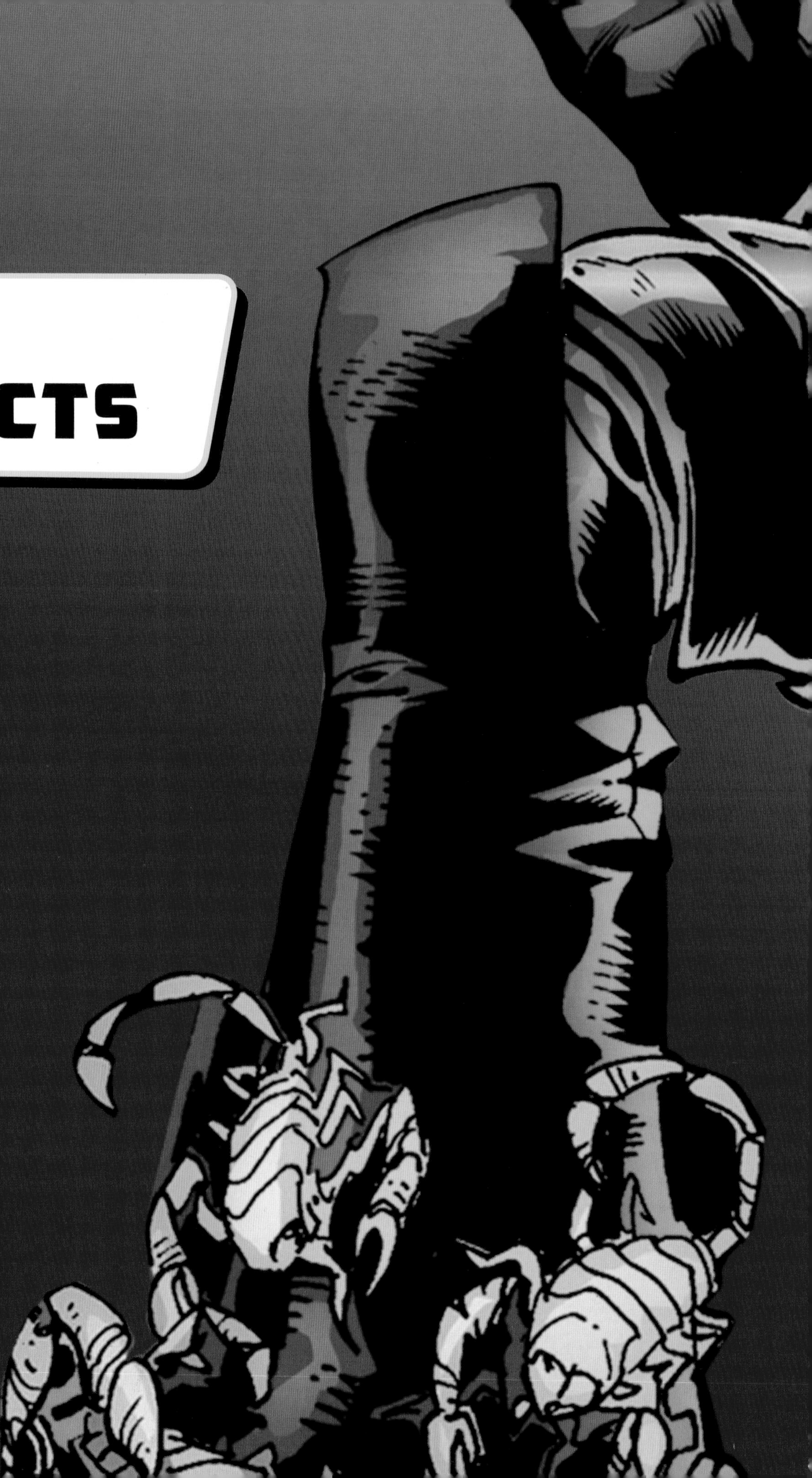

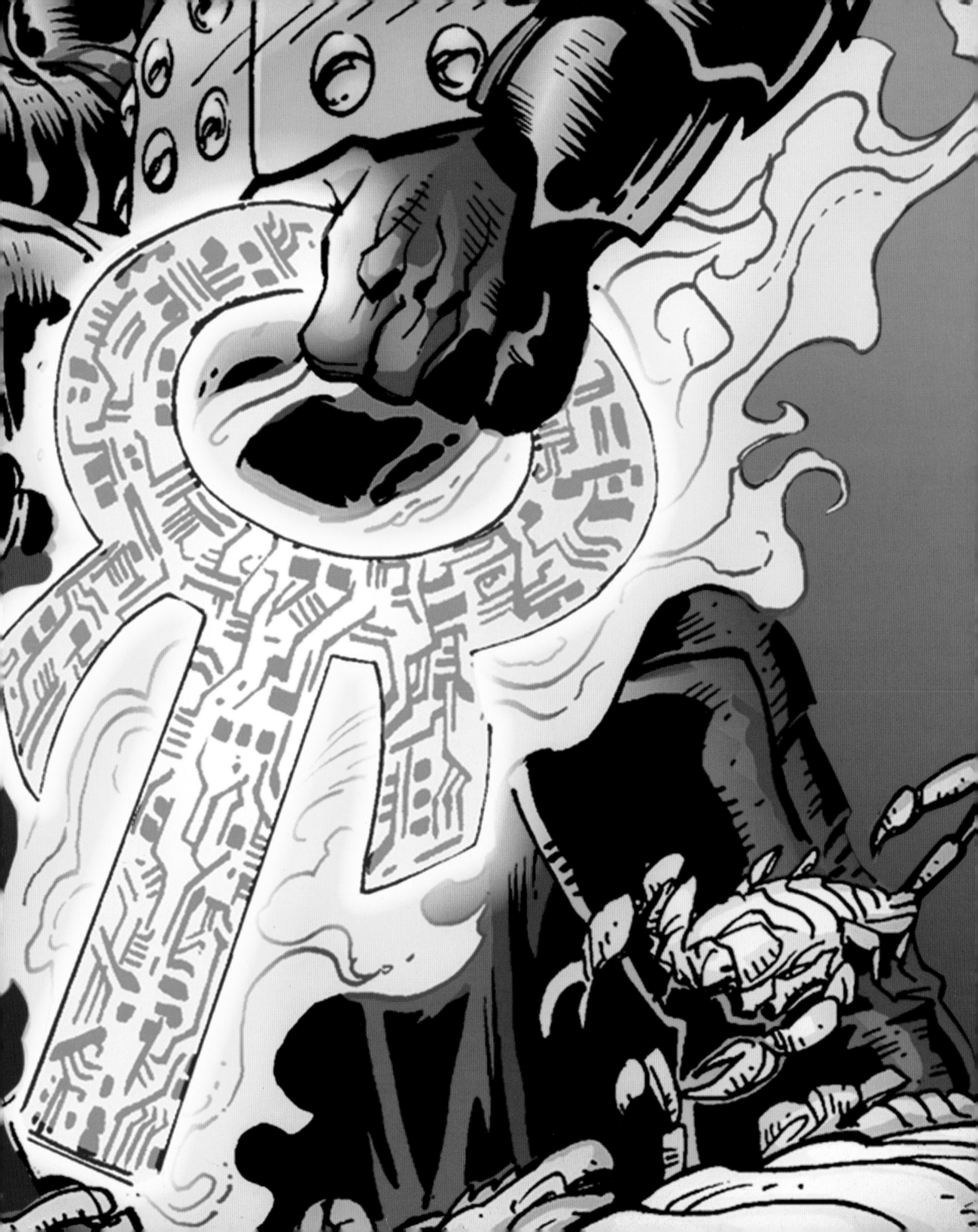

S.H.I.E.L.D. DECLASSIFIED

PASSING THE SHIELD

Steve Rogers is thought dead after the superhuman civil war, so the Winter Soldier, Cap's former sidekick Bucky Barnes, takes up the mantle. Steve returns, but he rapidly ages when his Super-Soldier serum wears off. A new hero is needed to wield the shield—and Falcon, Cap's friend Sam Wilson, becomes Captain America.

TOP 4

Ways Cap's shield is destroyed

1 **SMASHED** by Doctor Doom, using the Beyonder's power

2 **VAPORIZED** by Molecule Man's molecular manipulations!

3 **PULLED APART** by The Serpent—with his bare hands!

4 **BROKEN** by Thanos with the Infinity Gauntlet

Q: How was Cap's shield made?

A: During World War II, **Dr. Myron MacLain** is contracted by the U.S. government to invent **indestructible armor** for tanks. He molds a **Vibranium alloy** into the shape of a tank hatch, with amazing results. Unfortunately, he's never able to duplicate the process, so the hatch becomes **Cap's shield!**

NO SUBSTITUTE

Captain America's shield is supposed to be **unbreakable,** but gets destroyed **more than once!** This is often because **Tony Stark has borrowed it** to experiment on, swapping it for a **less-durable steel copy!**

TOP 6 CAP'S SHIELDS

ORIGINAL TRIANGULAR SHIELD—made of steel and able to deflect bullets; remains in Cap's personal effects.

ORIGINAL CIRCULAR SHIELD—can be thrown at such an angle that it returns; presented to Cap by U.S. President Franklin Roosevelt!

THE CAPTAIN SHIELD #1—Rogers becomes the solo hero The Captain and uses a shield of Adamantium made by Tony Stark.

THE CAPTAIN SHIELD #2—made of pure Vibranium; a gift from the Black Panther of Wakanda.

ENERGY SHIELD—a prototype designed by S.H.I.E.L.D. and created from "photonic energy."

STEVE'S SHIELD—Rogers returns—and that makes two Captain Americas! His new shield splits in two and produces an energy blade!

"Don't knock THE SHIELD."

TOP 6 SHIELD USES

KRAKOOM

TRADITIONAL SHIELD—blocking projectiles, energy blasts, staffs, knives, and fists.

SPINNING THROW—flinging the shield as a weapon, like a discus or boomerang.

RAMMING—running straight at the enemy like a battering ram.

SLIDING—catching a ride down an incline.

REFLECTING—bouncing energy blasts back at the foe who fired them.

CUSHIONING—protecting against a long fall.

NUMBER CRUNCH!

2.5ft (0.76m)
Shield diameter

3.5in (8.9cm)
Shield depth

12lbs (5.4kg)
Shield weight

9,000°F (4,982°C)
Max known temperature shield can withstand

112,075 miles (180,367km)
Estimated distance Cap's thrown his shield in his lifetime

WISHING ON A STAR
During the **Secret Wars on Battleworld,** Cap's shield is **destroyed by Doctor Doom.** However, **the Beyonder** releases a wave of energy that produces a **wish effect,** and Cap wishes for his **shield to be restored.**

TELL ME MORE!
Thanks to its Vibranium content, Cap's shield rebounds from impacts with minimal loss of momentum. The shield protects him from powerful attacks and can even break his fall from great heights. It is also impervious to Magneto's magnetic mutant powers.

LIBERTY'S SHIELD

Captain America's **iconic shield** is the **ultimate defensive weapon.** It's also Cap's **personal symbol,** reflecting the values he stands for as a **protector of the U.S.A.** and the **citizens of the world!**

BETWEEN...
In *Captain America Comics* #2 (April 1941), Cap trades his triangular shield for a circular one, allegedly after *MLJ Magazine* complained that it resembled the chest plate of their hero The Shield.

...THE PANELS

FAST FACTS

NAME: Mjolnir

OBJECT TYPE: Hammer

OWNER: Thor

MATERIAL: Uru, a magical, virtually unbreakable Asgardian metal

ORIGIN: Forged by the Dwarves of Nidavellir and imbued with magic by Odin

GRANTS WIELDER: Amazing powers! (Also great for hitting stuff!)

HANDLE WITH CARE!

Odin puts an **enchantment** on Mjolnir—it can only be used by one **worthy** of its might! From time to time, Thor Odinson gets into **trouble** and is **unable** to lift it!

Q: How does Mjolnir help Thor fly?

A: Thor swings the mighty mallet in a **circle** at **incredible speeds** and uses the inertia created to fly through the air.

Hold That Hammer!
Thor can **whirl** Mjolnir in a circle **so fast** he can create a **portal** between **dimensions** and **time**.

Take This Hammer!
Cybernetic alien **Beta Ray Bill** is found to be so worthy that Odin gives him his **own** version of Mjolnir, named **Stormbreaker**, to **protect** his people.

WOW!

24,000 mph

Approximate speed Thor can fly (38,624kph).

WHEN GOOD GUYS GO BAD

AWESOME STEAL!
Mjolnir can only be picked up by someone worthy, or someone who can imitate worthiness, like the android Awesome Andy—who is able to steal Thor's hammer!

HAMMER OF THE GODS

Don't try lifting **Thor's magical battle hammer Mjolnir** or you'll **bust your back!** But if you're deemed **worthy** to wield it, you'll gain the awesome powers of the **God of Thunder** himself!

ALTERNATE UNIVERSE

Many versions of Mjolnir exist across alternative realities! From Earth-14325's Mjolnir that requires you to be **unworthy** to lift it, to the **spikey** one of Earth-10190, there's a Mjolnir out there for just about **everyone!**

TOP **6**

Heroes who have wielded the power of Mjolnir

1 **THOR ODINSON**—Asgardian god

2 **JANE FOSTER**—a doctor, Thor's former girlfriend

3 **BETA RAY BILL**—an alien cyborg

4 **RED NORVELL**—a filmmaker

5 **ERIC MASTERSON**—an architect, later the Super Hero Thunderstrike

6 **THROG**—a frog hero with his own magic hammer!

Cool Hammer Noises

WHIITT!
Whistling through the air

WHOOM!
Hitting the ground, causing minor earthquake

BA ROOM!
Hammer hitting ground, disabling tank

KLANGGG!
Striking Black Knight's weaponized, razor-sharp lance hand guard

BAVA-VOOM!
triking floor, scattering bad guys

SPYONG!
Thrown hammer bringing down fighter jet

MORE MJOLNIR POWERS

• Generates rain, wind, lightning, and thunder! It can also produce hurricanes, blizzards, earthquakes, and even volcanic eruptions.

• Creates a force field to repel Super Villain attacks!

• Gives wielder the power of Allspeak, so that he or she can speak to anyone in any language!

• Channels Thor's energy to project Godforce blasts

When Odin sends Thor to Earth in the form of **Dr. Donald Blake**, Mjolnir transforms into a **cane**. Blake **strikes** the cane on the ground to become the mighty Thor.

BEFORE...

AFTER...

Q: What's small, green, slimy, and wields the power of Thor?

A: **Throg**—Frog of Thunder! A cruel mystic turns Simon Walterson into a **frog** named **Puddlegulp**! When Thor's **goat Toothgnasher** treads on Mjolnir, a tiny piece chips off. The worthy Puddlegulp picks it up and transforms into Throg, wielder of the **mighty Frogjolnir**!

"WHOSOEVER HOLDS THIS HAMMER, IF HE/SHE BE WORTHY, SHALL POSSESS THE POWER OF THOR."

HANDS OFF!

You can **look**, but you better not **touch**! These cosmic artifacts have **incredible, mind-twisting** abilities. They can give life, end it, and bring people **back from the dead!** Let's hope the bad guys don't get **their hands on them!**

BRAIN OVERLOAD

The Watchers record all the information in the universe in the **Sphere of Ultimate Knowledge.** Power-hungry villain **the Leader** forces **the Hulk** to steal the sphere for him and puts it on his head. All the info proves **too much** and the Leader is **destroyed!**

THE INFINITY GEMS

One gem is never enough for a genuinely power-mad villain!

POWER GEM
This gem holds all the energy that was, or ever will, exist and makes every other gem stronger!

REALITY GEM
Creates new alternative universes and warps reality. You can create, change, or destroy everything that exists!

TIME GEM
Gives control over all of time. Know everything that ever was or will be! Also controls aging— you'll look young forever!

SOUL GEM
Controls life and death, and even steals souls! Also contains a handy pocket universe.

DASTARDLY DEED!

Obsessed with power, the **mad Titan Thanos** steals all six **Infinity Gems** and houses them in the **Infinity Gauntlet.** At the request of his lady-love, Death, he then **kills half the sentient life in** the universe!

AAARRGHH!! The **BLOODGEM** is a meteorite fragment owned by the Bloodstone family that makes the wearer **IMMORTAL**. When it is stolen from 10,000-year-old Ulysses Bloodstone, he **AGES INTO DUST!**

TELL ME MORE!

The Cosmic Cube is one of the universe's most powerful items. This translucent box, created by the scientists of A.I.M., contains limitless energy that can reshape worlds and realities. The Red Skull tries to use the Cube to transfer his mind into other people's bodies!

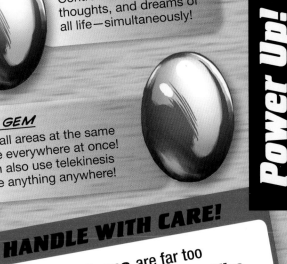

MIND GEM
Controls the minds, thoughts, and dreams of all life—simultaneously!

SPACE GEM
Access all areas at the same time! Be everywhere at once! You can also use telekinesis to move anything anywhere!

Power Up!

UNLIMITED POWER! The **ULTIMATE NULLIFIER** is a weapon powerful enough to scare even **GALACTUS**, the Devourer of Worlds! When he sets his sights on Earth, the **FANTASTIC FOUR** retrieve the artifact from deep space—and **GALACTUS FLEES!**

HANDLE WITH CARE!

The **Infinity Gems** are far too powerful to be held by one owner. **The Illuminati** take a gem each and keep them **separate**—hiding them from the rest of the universe **and each other!**

NOOOOO!! The **5,000-YEAR-OLD** villain **SPHINX** uses the power of the **KA STONE**, an alien gem that grants **IMMORTALITY** and superhuman powers. The stone is **so POWERFUL** that this ancient guy is able to defeat cosmic hero **NOVA!**

TOP 5

Cosmic Fashion Accessories

1 **NOVA HELMET**—this tin can doesn't just protect your head! You get to fly in space, be super strong, and fire cool energy blasts: all the powers of a Nova Corps soldier!

2 **FREEDOM RING**—this space bling is created from a piece of Cosmic Cube. You can alter reality and get superhuman powers!

3 **QUANTUM BANDS**—these bracelets are intended for the protector of the universe. They create quantum energy blasts and let you perform quantum leaps through space.

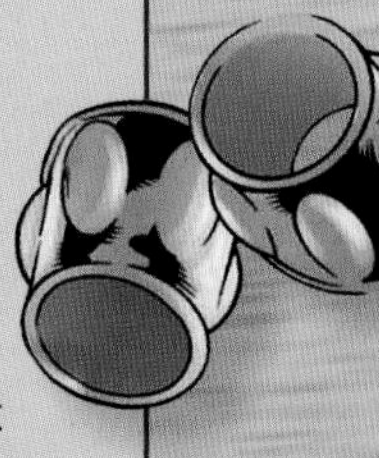

4 **NEGA BANDS**—Quantum Band knock-offs created by the Kree. You get similar powers, though!

5 **SMASHER GOGGLES**—these awesome specs let you travel through space and give you superhuman powers!

TOP **6**
Objects of Power

1. **THE STAFF OF LEGBA**—Doctor Voodoo uses it to cast spells, speak mystical languages, and travel between dimensions

2. **THE EYE OF AGAMOTTO**—given to Doctor Strange by Eternity; can see through any illusion and into the past, present, or future

3. **WAND OF WATOOMB**—a mighty, power-enhancing wand; Xandu the Mystic and Doctor Strange often fight over it

4. **HANDS OF THE DEAD**—Spider-Man uses them to go back in time and try to prevent Aunt May from being shot

5. **THE STAFF OF ONE**—owned by Nico Minoru, leader of the Runaways; powerful enough to scare Dormammu

6. **THE CASKET OF ANCIENT WINTERS**—Surtur, Loki, and Malekith steal it to unleash freezing winter across Earth!

DO YOU BELIEVE IN MAGIC?

Some artifacts hold power from **realms beyond time** and **human understanding.** These are the **rarest** and most **dangerous** objects in the universe and those wishing to wield them need incredible magical skills.

HANDLE WITH CARE!

Two **Muramasa Blades** are known to exist. Created long ago by master swordsmith Muramasa, these blades give the user **superhuman abilities**. One blade contains a piece of **Muramasa's evil soul** and the other a piece of **Wolverine's soul**. Muramasa's evil madness **controls anyone** using his sword!

THE ODINSWORD

The **Odinsword** is a **big deal** and not just because it's enormous. When unsheathed, it foreshadows the **end of everything!** Only someone **as strong as Odin** can lift it, and if wielded by someone unwilling to sacrifice their life, it will **rip apart** the fabric of the universe!

AAARRGHH!!

Forged by the wizard **MERLIN** in the time of King Arthur, the **EBONY BLADE** carries a curse. If used for evil, it **DRIVES THE WIELDER INSANE!**

MAGICAL WEAPONS

TWILIGHT SWORD—created from a burning galaxy and owned by Surtur the fire demon

GODKILLER—forged by the blacksmith god Hephaestus for Zeus to wield in a war against the Japanese Gods

DRAGONFANG—carved from the fang of a magical dragon by the wizard Kahji-Da; wielded by the Ancient One, Doctor Strange, Valkyrie, and Lady Sif

SOULSWORD—disrupts magical spells and kills magical beings, but has no effect on non-magical ones; owned by Magik and Colossus

HELLSTROM'S TRIDENT—Daimon Hellstrom wields a three-pronged staff made from netharanium, a metal found only in Hell that increases the owner's dark powers

THE STONES OF NORN

The **Stones of Norn** are the key to Loki's magical powers of **deception and trickery**—whatever you imagine yourself to be, the stones **will make it true!**

TOP 5 Magical Books

1 THE BOOK OF THE VISHANTI—created by three immortal beings, the Vishanti; given to Sorceror Supreme Doctor Strange

2 THE DARKHOLD—contains all the dark spells in history; its spells unleashed werewolves and vampires on Earth

3 THE BOOK OF CAGLIOSTRO—collection of history and powerful spells assembled by the mystic Cagliostro

4 THE DIARY OF AGED GENGHIS—a cursed diary containing the wisdom of the oldest living sorcerer

5 THE TOME OF ZHERED-NA—sorceress Zhered-Na wrote the secret whispers of the gods inside, so the gods placed a demon within the book to stop anyone reading it!

Hands of the Dead

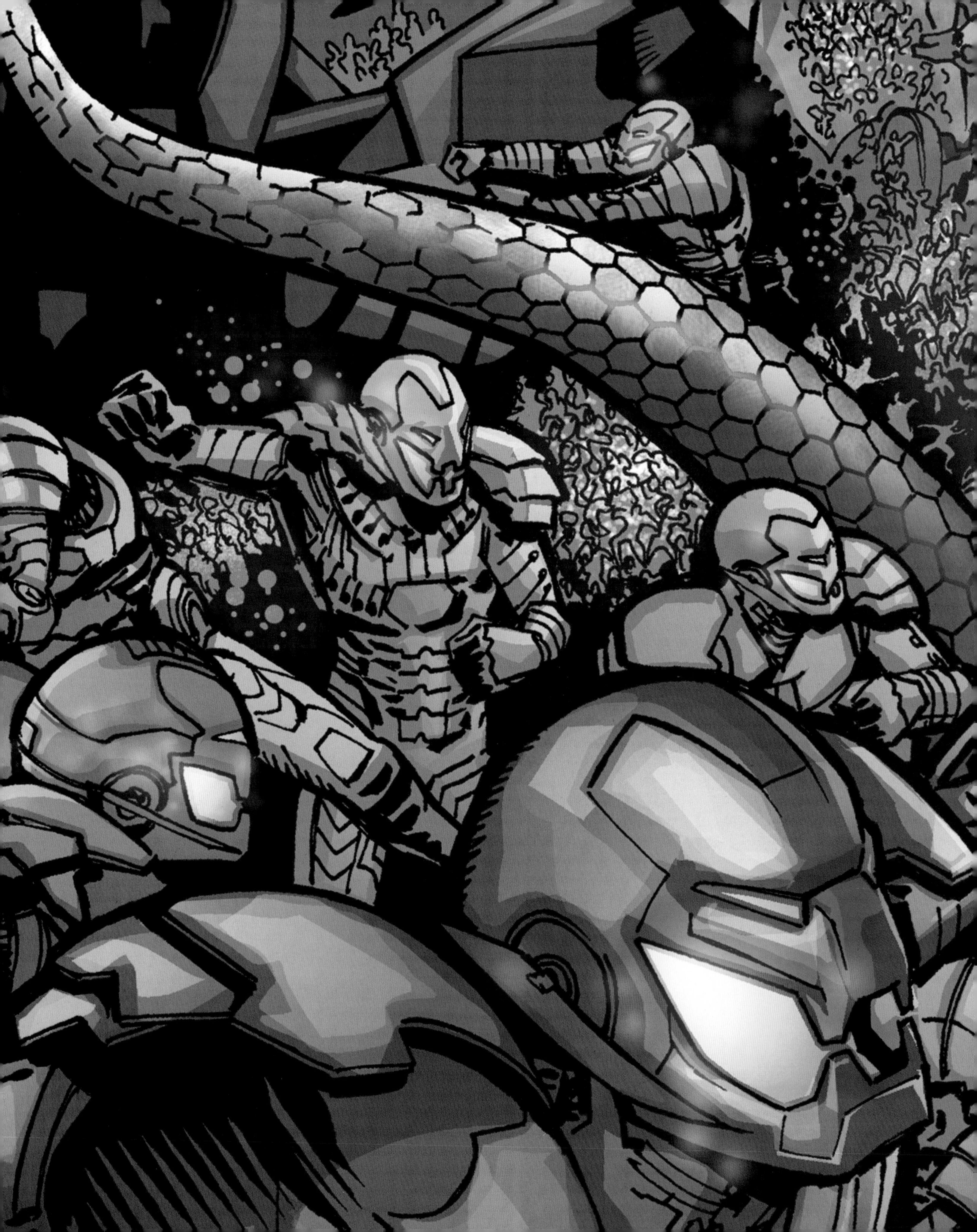

CHAPTER FIVE
KEY EVENTS

Who **BLOWS UP** the town of Stamford, Connecticut, sparking the superhuman **CIVIL WAR?**

Which incredible hero gets eaten up by bugs—**EVERY DAY?!**

What do **MARTIAN OCTOPI** prey on when they invade Earth?

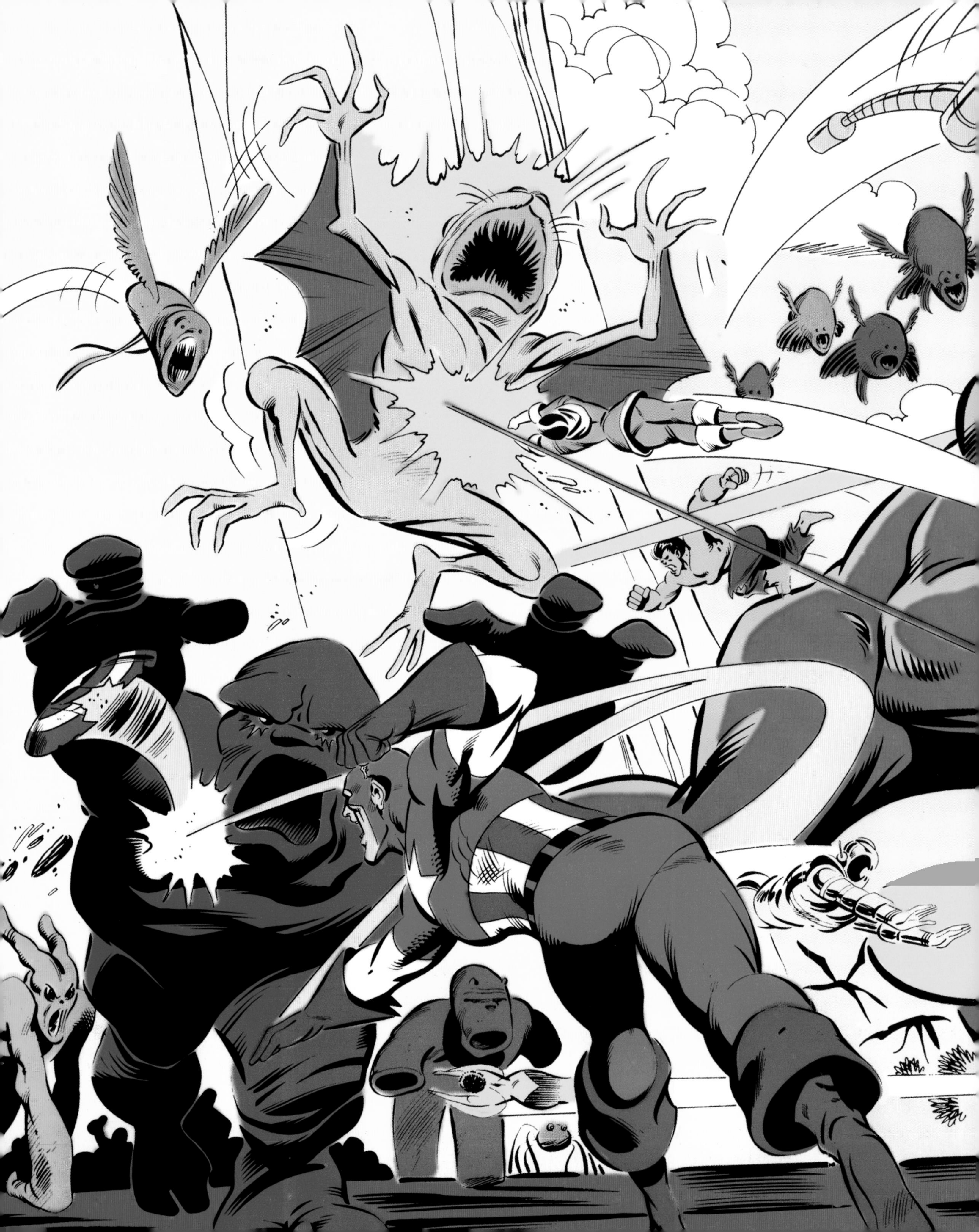

KEY EVENTS

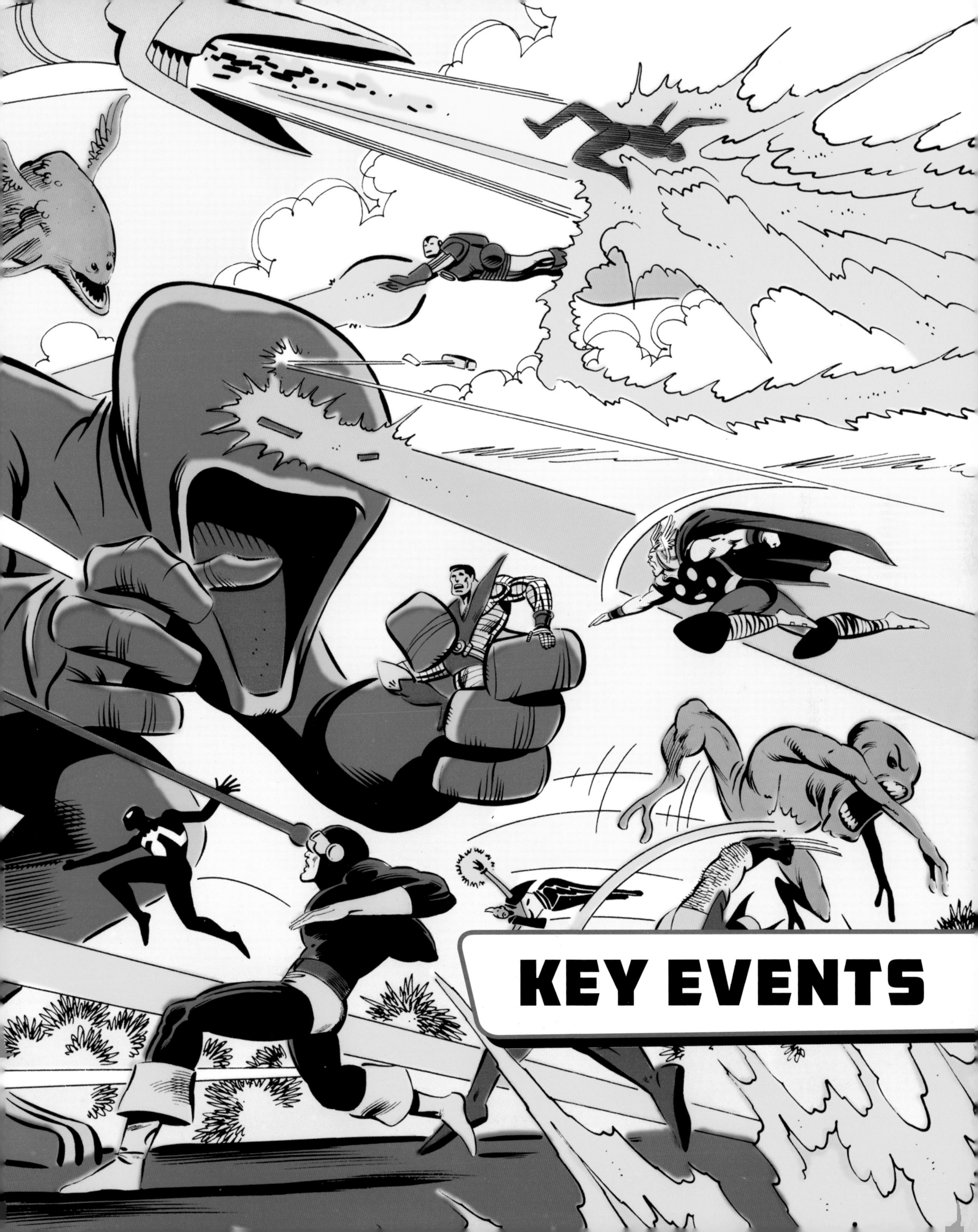

DASTARDLY DEED!

Doctor Doom **absorbs the powers** of the Beyonders and becomes an **omnipotent being.** He creates **Battleworld** from the surviving fragments of the Multiverse, then forces the survivors to cower under the rule of the all-powerful **God Emperor Doom!**

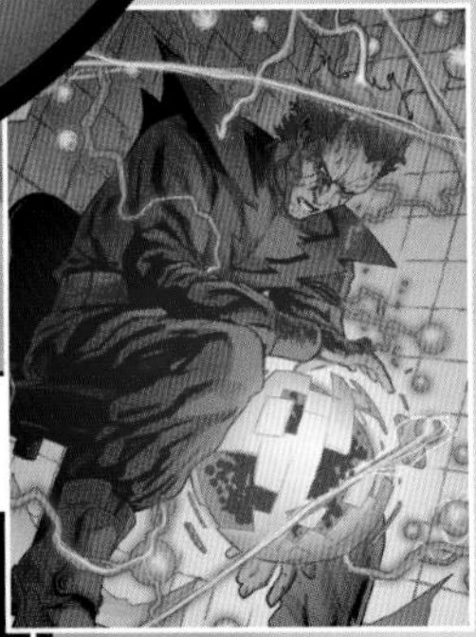

S.H.I.E.L.D. DECLASSIFIED

INCURSIONS

The Beyonders trigger the Incursions, a method of destroying the Multiverse by having different Earths crash into each other, obliterating both universes. To stop Earth-616 being destroyed, the villainous Cabal travel to alternate universes and destroy Earth before it can collide with Earth-616. With Earth-1610 about to collide with Earth-616, that world's evil Reed Richards, the Maker, saves the Cabal using his "raft," a ship able to survive Incursions.

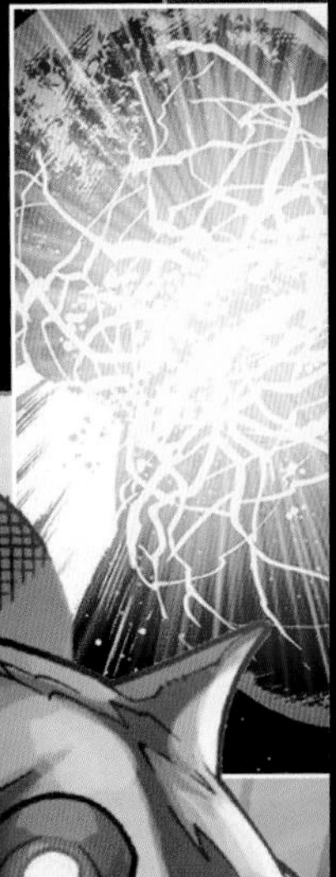

TELL ME MORE!

The supremely powerful Beyonders create an identical Molecule Man in every reality. When one dies, that reality is destroyed. Doctor Doom and the Molecule Man of Earth-616 team up to kill the Molecule Men of alternate realities and disrupt the Beyonders' plan. When they finally confront the Beyonders, almost every remaining universe is destroyed in the battle, but so too are the Beyonders!

WHEN GOOD GUYS GO BAD!

FROM BEYOND

The Beyonders are an omnipotent alien race and the creators of reality! Their every thought comes to life, but as reality becomes boring they begin to focus on death—and set out to destroy the multiverse they created!

BETWEEN...

Secret Wars (2015) was kept a secret until five years into its development. The series expanded from an eight issue arc to nine issues released over eight months to fit in every crossover title.

...THE PANELS

LONG LIVE DOOM!

The Multiverse is over and only one world stands—**Battleworld!** This **patchwork reality** of savage violence is created and ruled by its tyrannical **God Emperor—Doctor Doom!**

BETWEEN...

Secret Wars (2015) was the largest event in Marvel history, with 56 crossover titles. This allowed creators to utilize more than 60 years of alternate universes and create a new Marvel continuity.

...THE PANELS

TOP (10) Lands of Battleworld

1 **GREENLAND**—a gamma-radiated land of Savage Hulks

2 **DYSTOPIA**—a wasteland run by an evil future Hulk, the Maestro

3 **DOMAIN OF APOCALYPSE**—the kingdom of murderous mutant Apocalypse

4 **TECHNOPOLIS**—a futuristic city reliant upon the high-tech armor of Tony Stark

5 **VALLEY OF DOOM**—the Old West town of Timely, set in 1872

6 **KING JAMES'S ENGLAND**—England in the year 1602

7 **THE SHIELD**—a huge wall made up of a giant version of the Thing; isolates Battleworld's deadliest domains

8 **ARCADIA**—ruled by She-Hulk and A-Force

9 **DOOMSTADT**—the capital, home to God Emperor Doom

10 **SPIDER-VERSE**—all of the Spider-Men, Women, and Creatures from across the Multiverse

DOUBLE TROUBLE

MR. FANTASTIC AND THE MAKER

Doom believes he is finally free of his nemesis, **Reed Richards,** until **two turn up** at once! Both the **Richards of Earth-616** (Mister Fantastic) and **Earth-1610** (the Maker) create high-tech life rafts. The Maker is **evil and insane,** but teams up with Mr. Fantastic to **defeat Doom,** only to betray him.

SHERIFF STRANGE

The God Emperor of Battleworld is supported by his **trusty Sheriff,** Stephen Strange. When **Sheriff Strange** uncovers the raft containing **the Maker** and **the Cabal,** he opens a similar craft he found many years before. This ship is **Mister Fantastic's raft** and contains **heroes of Earth-616** ready to **take down Doom!**

WHOSE SIDE...

Q: Why does Captain America oppose the Registration Act?

A: To him, it's an **attack on Liberty**! He fears that the government will start treating Super Heroes like **property**.

IDENTITY CRISIS?

Tony Stark persuades Peter Parker to reveal his secret identity at a press conference! When he realizes his family are in danger, Spidey switches sides!

ASSASSINATED!

Captain America is shot by Crossbones and a brainwashed Agent 13!

It's **civil war!** The **Superhuman Registration Act** has passed! The Super Heroes of America are forced to come out of the shadows, reveal their **secret identities,** and submit to government regulation—whether they **like it or not!**

S.H.I.E.L.D. DECLASSIFIED

PRISON 42
With the help of Reed Richards and Hank Pym, Tony Stark establishes a prison named Project 42, located in the Negative Zone. The jail houses troublemaker-heroes who oppose the registration program.

DARK TIMES!

The government recruits the Thunderbolts into a security force—with Norman Osborn in charge.

Q: What is the 50-State Initiative?

A: A plan by Tony Stark to install fully **trained** and government-**authorized** Super Hero squads in every state.

ALIEN INVASION!

The Skrulls secretly replace key heroes with shape-shifting agents! With Super Heroes now divided, the Skrulls invade Earth!

S.H.I.E.L.D. DECLASSIFIED

THE STAMFORD INCIDENT
The New Warriors attack a group of villains, but one of them, Nitro the Living Bomb, causes an explosion that kills hundreds in the town of Stamford, Connecticut! The public turns against Super Heroes and the government passes the Superhuman Registration Act (SRA).

RED SKULL RETURNS!

The evil Hydra villain orchestrates Cap's assasination!

TELL ME MORE!

The Superhuman Registration Act (SRA) means that Super Heroes must now register with the government, abandon secret identities, and work for S.H.I.E.L.D. to hunt their non-registered former allies. It's Avenger vs. Avenger, sister vs. brother, husband vs. wife—it's a Super Hero civil war! Captain America's side is winning, but he becomes disillusioned by the violence and lack of public support. He surrenders in the hope it will end the war.

Goliath (Dr. Bill Foster) is brutally killed by Ragnarok, a berserk clone of Thor created by Reed Richards. Sue Richards is so furious, she leaves Reed and joins Cap's team.

DASTARDLY DEED!

PROMOTED!
The U.S. president installs victorious Tony Stark as director of S.H.I.E.L.D., and the 50-State Initiative is born.

...ARE YOU ON?

HULK'S REVENGE

- He defeats King of the Inhumans **Black Bolt** on the **moon**.
- He builds an arena in the wreckage of **New York City** and forces **Iron Man** and **Mister Fantastic** to fight each other!
- **Doctor Strange** is winning, until Hulk crushes his hands to prevent him casting spells.

BIG HITTER!

Hulk defeats the Illuminati, but doesn't count on the intervention of the **most powerful hero on Earth!** The mentally unstable **Sentry** sees Hulk's rampage on TV, and decides to unleash his **incredible powers** on the Green Goliath!

TELL ME MORE!

Hulk's ship crash-lands on the planet Sakaar. Its ruler, the Red King, forces Hulk to fight as a gladiator, but the Green Goliath teams up with his fellow gladiators and overthrows him. Hulk becomes Sakaar's ruler and marries Caiera, the Red King's lieutenant. All is well until the ship Hulk arrived on explodes. Caiera is killed and much of Sakaar is destroyed. Hulk blames the Illuminati and invades Earth.

Q: Who are the Illuminati?

A: Formed by Iron Man to respond to planetary threats, they are a group of some of Earth's most **powerful** and **brainy** heroes. It includes Iron Man, Black Bolt, Doctor Strange, Mister Fantastic, and Professor X. Only the first four members are involved in **the Hulk's exile.**

THIS MEANS WAR!

The **Illuminati** mean well when they arrange for the **troublesome Hulk** to be **marooned in outer space.** But Hulk **makes it back** to Earth and, thirsting for **revenge**, declares **World War Hulk!**

DASTARDLY DEED!

Hulk's ally **Miek** reveals that he knew the **Red King** had rigged Hulk's ship to explode, but didn't tell him. Miek causes **thousands of deaths** to trick Hulk into fighting again!

THE WAR IS OVER
Hulk finally realizes that he's just got **too angry** and asks Iron Man to stop him. **Satellites** blast Hulk, **knocking him out.** As Bruce Banner, he is captured and imprisoned **six miles** underground.

WOW!
139,000

The number of workers needed to fix up New York City after Hulk and his friends' rampage!

S.H.I.E.L.D. DECLASSIFIED

SKAAR, SON OF HULK
Hulk believes there is nothing left for him on the destroyed planet of Sakaar, but after his defeat on Earth, his son Skaar emerges from the rubble. Skaar believes Hulk has abandoned him and swears revenge on his father.

TEAM PLAYERS
To invade **Earth**, Hulk recruits his **fellow Warbound**, the **Sakaar gladiators** (Arch-E-5912, No-Name of the Brood, Korg, Miek, Elloe Kaifi, Hiroim, Kong, Mung).

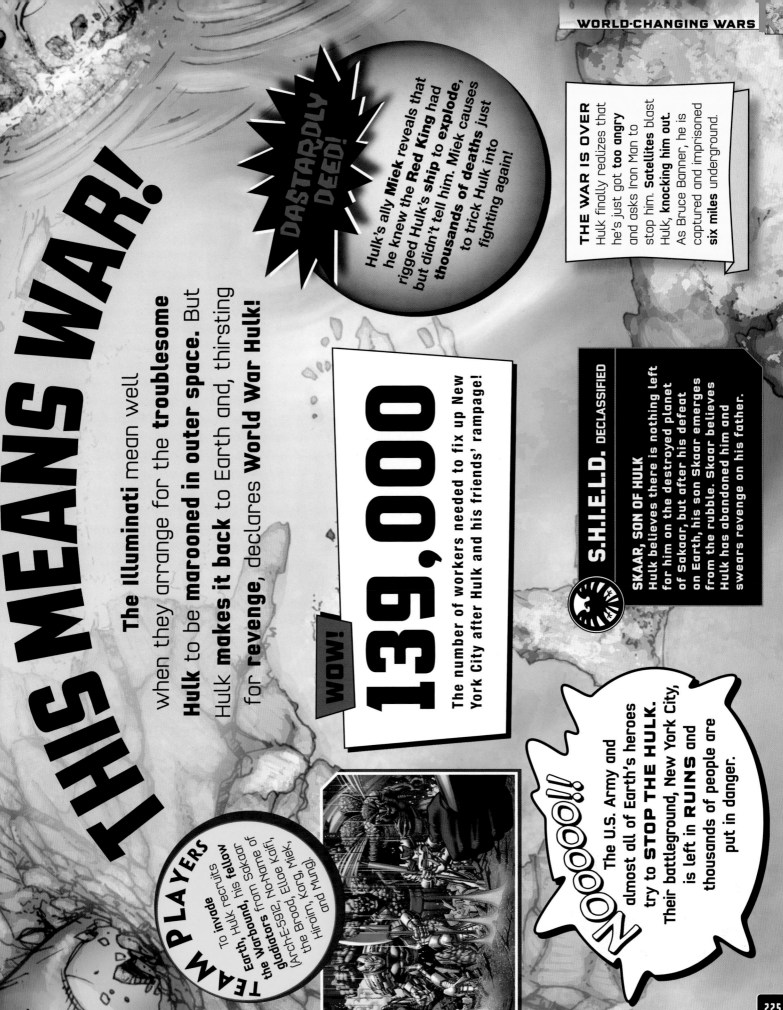

NOOOOO!!
The U.S. Army and almost all of Earth's heroes try to **STOP THE HULK.** Their battleground, New York City, is left in **RUINS** and thousands of people are put in danger.

To defeat Ultron, Wolverine and the Invisible Woman go back in time to kill Hank Pym, stopping him from creating Ultron Mark I. When they return to the present, the world has changed—and not for the better! The Avengers have disbanded, a cyborg Tony Stark governs, and the heroes of Earth fight the dark magic of Morgan Le Fay instead of evil robots!

REALLY?!

Ultron doesn't take the risk of **confronting the surviving heroes** himself—he runs his Age of Destruction **from the future!** Vision **acts as his slave** and commands the empire.

TOP 3

Ways to Defeat Ultron

1 **PERSUADE** Hank Pym not to create Ultron

2 **KILL** Hank Pym before he can create Ultron

3 **INFECT** Ultron with a computer virus

NOOOOO!!!

Wolverine and the Invisible Woman's time-traveling causes a huge rip in SPACE AND TIME, triggering the COLLAPSE of the MULTIVERSE!

TELL ME MORE!

Hank Pym gets a lot of flack for creating Ultron, but if you ask the original Ant-Man himself, he would claim he just created Ultron Mark I. The genius android then upgraded itself, creating the evil Ultron.

WOW!

6,978

The number of heroes Ultron takes out—from 7,000 to only 22!

AAAARRGHH!!

When **LUKE CAGE** and **SHE-HULK** try to infiltrate **ULTRON'S FORTRESS**, they fail, but reveal Ultron's **BIG SECRET**—he's ruling the world **FROM THE FUTURE!**

RISE OF THE ROBOTS!

The Age of Ultron has begun! The evil sentient robot **conquers Earth** and rules with an **Adamantium fist.** The few Super Heroes who remain must travel **back through time** to save the world from a **devastating future!**

S.H.I.E.L.D. DECLASSIFIED

DISASTER AVERTED
When killing Hank Pym creates an even worse future, the Invisible Woman and Wolverine go back in time again. They convince Hank to fit a shut-down mechanism in Ultron. When the mad mechanoid launches his attack, Iron Man triggers the hidden program, averting the Age of Ultron.

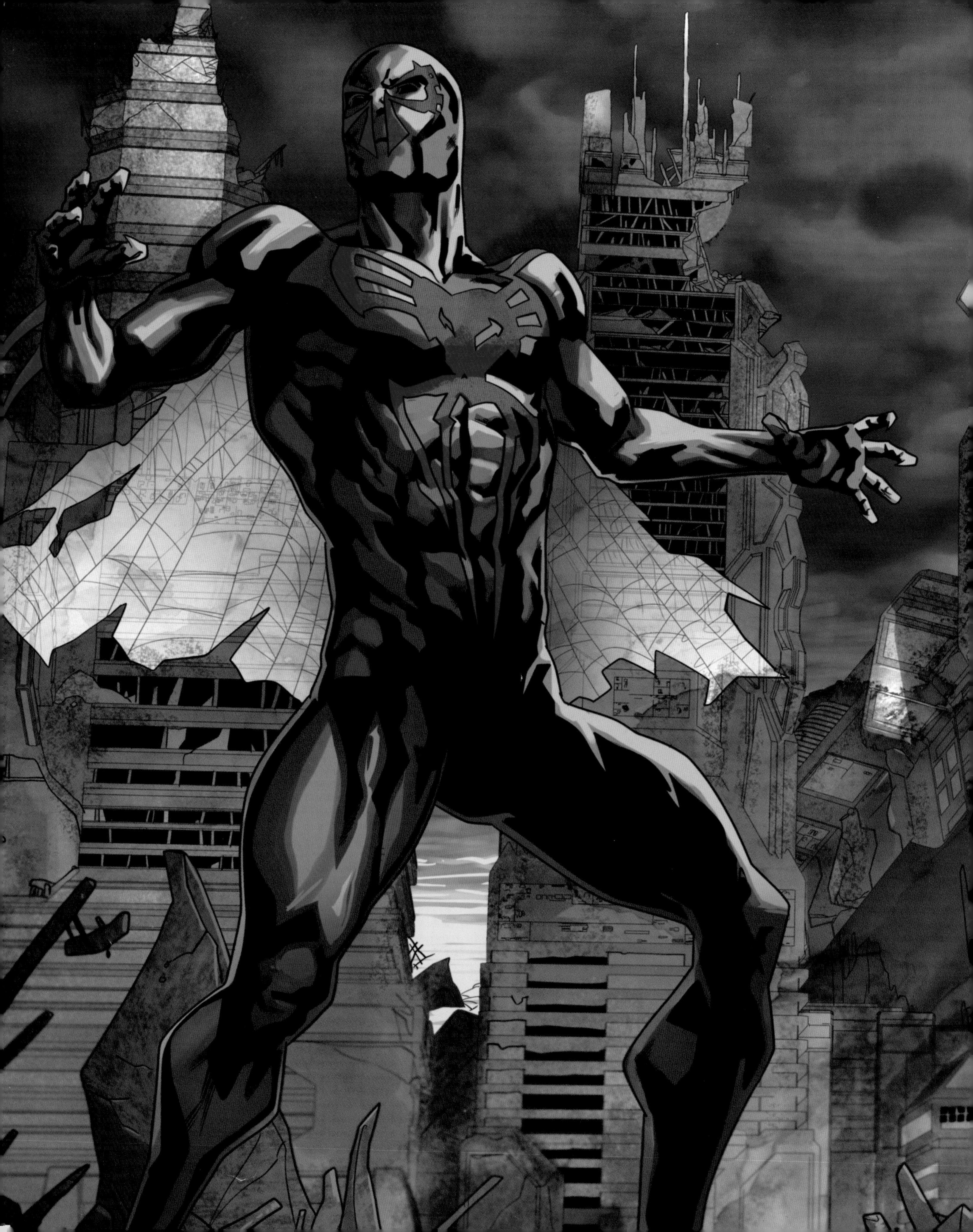

ALTERNATE WORLDS

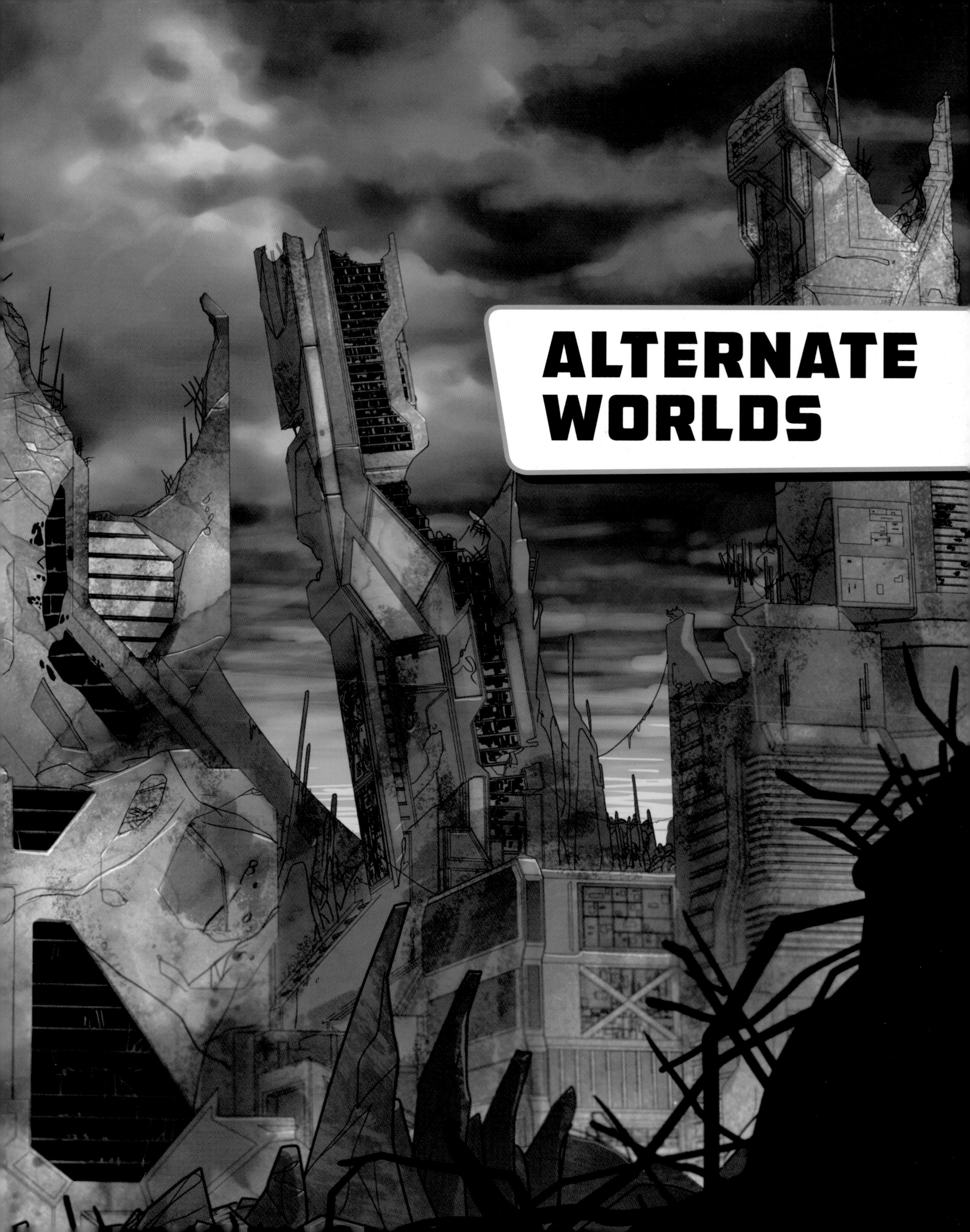

BLAST FROM THE PAST

TELL ME MORE!

INTRUDERS IN TIME!

Steve Rogers is banished to the past by the wicked Purple Man. Rogers' presence in 1602 creates a hole in the fabric of reality, which could potentially lead to the destruction of the world. It also makes superhumans appear centuries too early!

Sir Richard Reed

Dr. Stephen Strange

Matthew Murdoch

Carlos Javier

Peter Parquagh

Virginia Dare

Strange, ominous storms are sweeping Britain and Europe—it seems that the **end of the world** is nigh! In the **reality of 1602** live some familiar Super Heroes and Super Villains... but with a **unique, Elizabethan twist!**

BACK FROM THE DEAD!

James I **executes** Dr. Strange for witchcraft—but his sweetheart, Lady Clea, retrieves his **severed head**, which can still **communicate** through **magical means!**

TOP 4 V.I.P.s OF THE 1602 REALITY

KING JAMES I OF ENGLAND AND VI OF SCOTLAND
James hates witches and cuts a deal with Magnus to get rid of Witchbreed (mutants), too!

VIRGINIA DARE
The first person born in the English New World colonies. She can transform into any creature, including dinosaurs and mythical beasts!

WILLIAM SHAKESPEARE
The Bard is kidnapped and made to chronicle the adventures of Otto Von Doom!

QUEEN ELIZABETH I
Good Queen Bess is assassinated by agents of evil Count Otto Von Doom!

Rojhaz

Sir Nicholas Fury

BETWEEN...

1602 covers artist Scott McKowen recreated the look of historical engravings with a technique named "scratchboard"—scratching through a layer of ink to a hard chalk surface. He added scrolls and flags for extra period feel.

...THE PANELS

DASTARDLY DEED!

Spanish Inquisition leader **Enrique Magnus** tracks down mutant **Witchbreed** and **burns** them at the **stake**. Enrique, secretly a Witchbreed himself, is obsessed with hunting **Master Javier**—head of a **school** that shelters Witchbreed.

YECCH!

Baron Octavius is an evil Italian aristocrat suffering from the plague. He injects himself with octopus blood as a cure, but turns into a weird half-octopus creature!

TOP 12 Familiar Faces

1 **DOCTOR STEPHEN STRANGE**—Queen Elizabeth's physician and a secret magician (Doctor Strange)

2 **MASTER CARLOS JAVIER**—of Javier's Select College for the Sons of Gentlefolk (Professor X)

3 **SIR NICHOLAS FURY**—Elizabeth's spymaster (Nick Fury Sr.)

4 **GRAND INQUISITOR ENRIQUE MAGNUS**—of the Spanish Inquisition (Magneto)

5 **DONAL**—ancient member of the Knights Templar (Thor)

6 **PETER PARQUAGH**—Nicholas Fury's assistant (Peter Parker)

7 **THE FOUR OF THE SHIP FANTASTICK**—a team of explorers (Fantastic Four)

8 **COUNT OTTO VON DOOM**—of Latveria (Doctor Doom)

9 **MASTER DAVID BANNER**—ruthless agent of King James I (Incredible Hulk)

10 **LORD IRON**—a Spanish inventor imprisoned by David Banner (Iron Man)

11 **ROJHAZ**—a mysterious Native American (Captain America)

12 **MATTHEW MURDOCH**—a mercenary, posing as a blind minstrel (Daredevil)

S.H.I.E.L.D. DECLASSIFIED

ARTIFICIAL ASGARDIANS!
The Alchemax Corporation creates its own Norse heroes, the Aesir, and claims that they are the real Thor, Hela, Heimdall, Baldur, and Loki. They even build a floating city called Valhalla...

TOP 5 WAYS TO BECOME A SUPER HERO IN 2099

GET YOUR GENES TWEAKED by a sabotaged genetic experiment like Spider-Man (Miguel O'Hara).

GET YOUR CONSCIOUSNESS UPLOADED into a robot body like Ghost Rider (Kenshiro "Zero" Cochrane).

GET MUTATED by radiation and gain the ability to shoot bio-energy like Ravage (Paul-Phillip Ravage).

GET BLASTED with a powerful gamma-radiation weapon like the Hulk (John Eisenhart).

GET BRAINWASHED into believing you're a Norse God like Thor (Cecil McAdam).

Power Up!

SPIDER HAMMER
What's better than having spider-powers? Having spider-powers and **THOR'S MAGICAL HAMMER!** When **STEVE ROGERS** (Captain America) throws **MJOLNIR** to **SPIDER-MAN**, the web-slinger proves that he is **WORTHY TO WIELD** the mighty weapon!

WHAT?!

In 2099, two heroes are **worshipped** by **fanatical cults!** The **Knights of Banner** worship the Hulk, and the **Thorites** worship Thor. (They even dress in Thor **costumes** while flying around on hang-gliders and swinging **big hammers**...)

YECCH!

The Earth of 2099 is horrible— but Hellrock island makes the rest of it look like paradise! Hellrock is polluted with **radioactive waste** and inhabited by ex-prisoners who have turned into gruesome "**Mutroids.**"

TOP 5 — 2099 Must-Haves!

1. **A HOLOGRAPHIC COMPUTERIZED PERSONAL ASSISTANT**—such as Miguel O'Hara's "virtual secretary," Lyla.

2. **A HOVER-CAR**—wheels are so last century!

3. **A CARD IMPLANT**—no more real money! Store your virtual cash in a "card" implanted under your skin!

4. **A MICROWAVE GUN**—why shoot your enemies when you can cook them?

5. **A PLATE OF SYNTH-FOOD** – 100% cheap 'n' tasty chemicals. Yum!

WANT TO KNOW THE FUTURE?

Welcome to a **grim** and **gritty future!** In **2099**, **megacorporations** run everything and ordinary people **struggle to survive.** Thankfully, a **new generation** of heroes emerges to fight for justice—but the bad guys are **never far behind...**

WOW!

800

The top speed of the Punisher's H.D. Stealth Stinger in mph (1,288kph). This police motorcycle can also become invisible and turn traffic lights to green!

GOOD DAY

The Doctor Doom of 2099 is not content with ruling his **tiny kingdom, Latveria**—he **conquers** the **U.S.** as well and sets himself up as **president!**

BETWEEN...

Starting with Doom 2099 #29 (May 1995), all 2099 comics had the letters "AD" added to their title. The letters stand for "Anno Doom," (the year of Doom) to indicate Doom has taken over!

...THE PANELS

Nooooo!!

Invading **PHALANX ALIENS** melt the polar icecaps and raise sea levels. **NEW YORK** is **FLOODED** and then attacked by **ATLANTEANS!**

EXPECT THE UNEXPECTED!

There are other realities **beyond Earth-616**—realities where everything is **upside down,** where history has taken **wildly different paths.** That's when things can get **really, really weird!**

HULK

BRUCE BANNER

YECCH!

In one grim future, Hulk is the last person alive after a nuclear war. Each day he's eaten by swarms of bugs—but his healing factor restores him to be devoured again and again...

SPIDER-STAR!

On Earth-80219, Spider-Man **stops** the burglar that kills Uncle Ben (on our Earth-616) and **doesn't become** a crime fighter. Instead, he exploits his amazing powers as **a star of action movies.** Peter Parker still has to learn that "with great power comes **great responsibility!"**

RICK SMASH!

On Earth-7812, **RICK JONES** becomes the Hulk—and does an **EXCELLENT JOB!** As Hulk, he joins the Avengers, becomes Captain America's new sidekick, ends the Kree/Skrull war, and punches Annihilus **IN THE FACE!**

Power Up!

TELL ME MORE!

In the Mangaverse (Earth-2301), Toni Stark is the armor-clad Iron Maiden, Peter Parker is a ninja of the Spider-Clan who has sworn to avenge his uncle, and Hank Pym is a kid genius and rock star!

AUNTIE HERO!

Why should Peter Parker have all the fun? **Aunt May** becomes a superhuman senior citizen as the armored **Golden Oldie** on Earth-24388, shrinking **Ant-Aunt** on Earth-23848, and the chilling **Auntie-Freeze** on Earth-24838!

WHEN BAD GUYS GO GOOD!

X-RATED!
In the Mutant X Universe (Earth-1298), the villain Magneto is a hero! Professor X and the X-Men are villains, and S.H.I.E.L.D. is a terrorist group.

TOP 6

Grim Alternate Realities

1 **DAYS OF FUTURE PAST**—mutant-hunting Sentinels try to take over the world!

2 **AGE OF APOCALYPSE (EARTH-295)**—Professor X is killed, leading to a horrible future where Apocalypse rules!

3 **EARTH-81727**—Jean Grey does not sacrifice herself to destroy the Dark Phoenix and it destroys the universe!

4 **ZOMBIVERSE (EARTH-2149)**—heroes are infected with a zombie virus, eat everyone in their world, and seek more universes to devour!

5 **AGE OF ULTRON (EARTH-61112)**—Ultron rules and is trying to exterminate humanity!

6 **CROOKED WORLD (EARTH-238)**—Captain Britain gets trapped in this weird world ruled by the reality-warping mutant Mad Jim Jaspers.

WHEN GOOD GUYS GO BAD!

BAD BEAST
Beast (Hank McCoy) is one of the most heroic X-Men, but in the alternate future of the Age of Apocalypse, Hank's famous for being cruel! He works as a genetic engineer, performing experiments on mutant prisoners.

WOW!

3007

The year the Guardians of the Galaxy are founded in the alternate future of Earth-691.

WAR OF THE WORLDS
Martians invade **freedom-fighter Killraven's reality** (Earth-691). These octopoid oppressors don't just want land—they want to **exploit humanity as food!**

MAD JIM JASPERS

INDEX

S

T

U

V

W

X

Y

Z

Senior Editor: Alastair Dougall
Senior Designer: Clive Savage
Project Art Editor: Toby Truphet
Senior Designers: Mark Richards, Anne Sharples
Editors: Ruth Amos, Joel Kempson
Jacket Design: Toby Truphet
Senior Pre-Production Producer: Rebecca Fallowfield
Senior Producer: Alex Bell
Managing Editor: Sadie Smith
Managing Art Editor: Ron Stobbart
Art Director: Lisa Lanzarini
Publisher: Julie Ferris
Publishing Director: Simon Beecroft

Dorling Kindersley would like to thank:
Sarah Brunstad, Brian Overton, Jeff Youngquist
at Marvel for their vital help and advice.
Many thanks also to: Debra Wolter for proofreading;
Cefn Ridout and Allison Singer for editorial assistance;
Kavita Varma, Rosamund Bird, Akansha Jain for design assistance;
Ann Barrett for the index.

First American Edition, 2016
Published in the United States by DK Publishing
345 Hudson Street, New York, New York 10014
16 17 18 19 20 10 9 8 7 6 5 4 3 2 1
001-283150-Sept/2016

marvel.com

© 2016 MARVEL

A catalog record for this book is available
from the Library of Congress.

ISBN: 978-1-4654-5262-7

DK books are available at special discounts when purchased in bulk for sales
promotions, premiums, fund-raising, or educational use. For details, contact:
DK Publishing Special Markets, 345 Hudson Street, New York, New York 10014
SpecialSales@dk.com

Printed and bound in China

A WORLD OF IDEAS:
SEE ALL THERE IS TO KNOW

www.dk.com

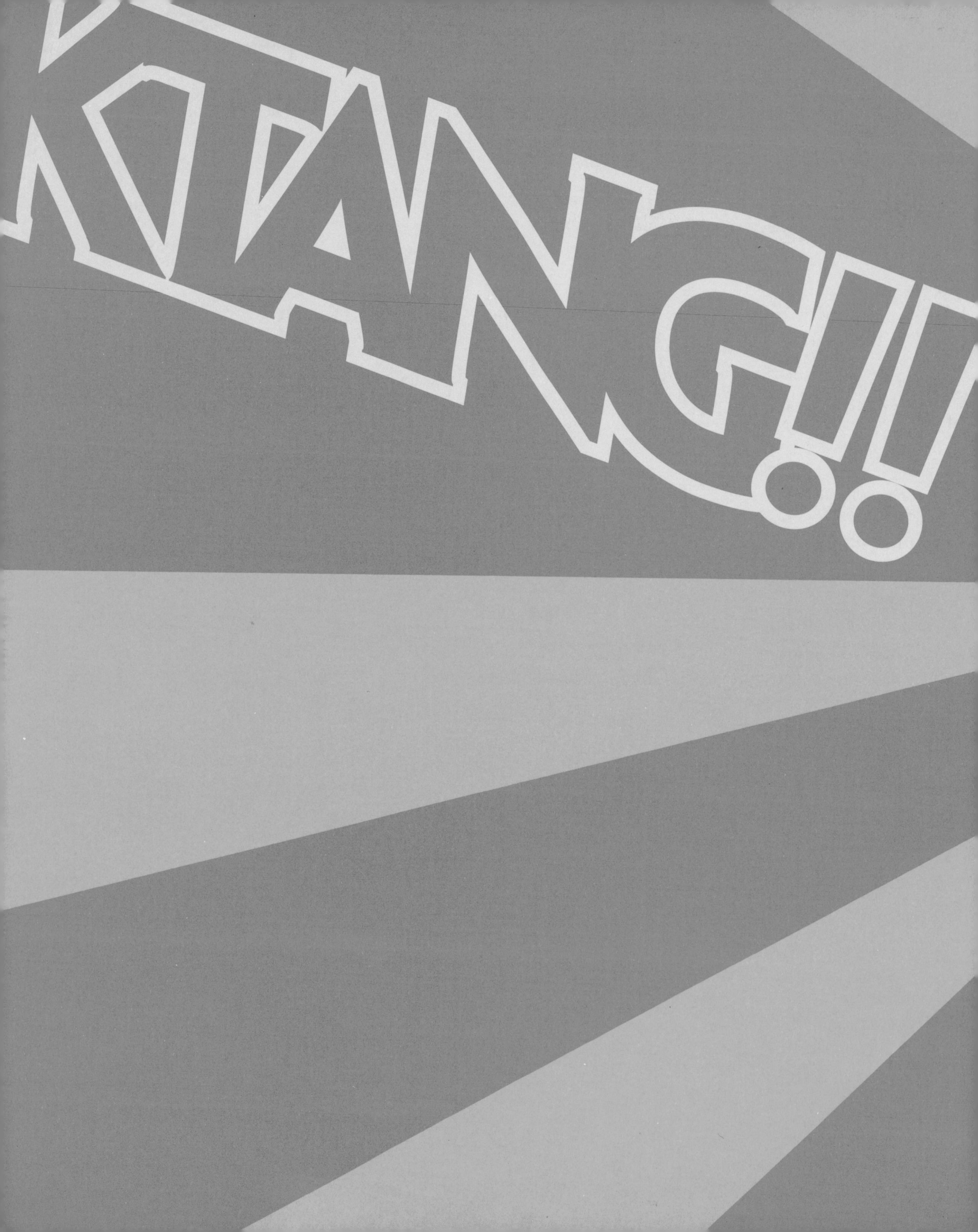
TANG!!